THE FEMININE SUBJECT IN CHILDREN'S LITERATURE

CHRISTINE WILKIE-STIBBS

Routledge
Taylor & Francis Group

NEW YORK AND LONDON

Published in 2002 by
Routledge
29 West 35th Street
New York, NY 10001
www.routledge-ny.com

Published in Great Britain by
Routledge
11 New Fetter Lane
London EC4P 4EE
www.routledge.co.uk

Children's Literature and Cutlure Vol. 22

Routledge is an imprint of the Taylor & Francis Group.
Printed in the United States of America on acid-free paper.

Library of Congress Cataloging-in-Publication Data.

Wilkie-Stibbs, Christine, 1948–
    The feminine subject in children's literature / Christine Wilkie-Stibbs.
        p. cm.— (Children's literature and criticism ; 22)
    Includes bibliographical references and index.
    ISBN 0-415-92996-2 (alk. paper)
        1. Children's literature—History and criticism. 2. Feminist literary criticism. I. Title.
    II. Series

PN1009.A1 W52 2002
809'.89282—dc21

                                                                                2002024915

Contents

Series Editor's Foreword   ix

Foreword   xi

Chapter 1: Theoretical Introduction: *The feminine* **in Children's Literature**   **1**

Lacan and the Subject   4
The Speaking Subject: "other" and "Other"   12
The Psycho-Dynamics of Text/Reader Relations   14
Literary Transference   16
The Textual Unconscious   20
The feminine Fantastic   23
Summary   27
Notes to Chapter 1   29

Chapter 2: Writing the Subject in Children's Literature: *l'écriture féminine*   **37**

Theoretical Introduction to the Chapter   37
Summary   43
The Tricksters   44
    The feminine in Metafictional Mode   44
    Desire in Writing   48
    The feminine Fantastic   50
    The feminine Carnivalesque   52
    The Incest Taboo   53
    The Gaze   55
    The feminine Intertextual Space   57

The Elemental *féminine*   60
l'écriture féminine   62
The Other Side of Silence   63
     Language, Madness and *The feminine*   65
     Fictional Selves/Self as Fiction   68
     The-Name-of-The-Father   70
     The feminine and Abjection   71
     l'écriture féminine   73
Notes to Chapter 2   74

Chapter 3: Reading the Mother in Children's Literature:
le parler femme   **81**

Theoretical Introduction to the Chapter   81
Summary   91
Pictures in the Dark   93
     Abjection and Return   94
     Women's Time   97
     Semiotizing the Symbolic   98
     Body Language   98
The Tricksters and *The Other Side of Silence*   99
     Monstrous Mothers   99
     The Maternal *feminine*   104
Dangerous Spaces   106
     Speaking the Body   106
The Changeover   107
     The Looking Glass from the Other Side   107
     The feminine Imaginary and the Witch   109
     Discourse of *le parler femme*   111
Notes to Chapter 3   113

Chapter 4: *The feminine* Postmodern Subject in
Children's Literature   **119**

Theoretical Introduction to the Chapter   119
Summary   125
Memory   127
     The feminine Postmodern Landscapes   127
Wolf   133
     Fragmented Subjectivity   133
     Cultural Nostalgia   134
     The Hyperreal   135
Notes for Chapter 4   137

Chapter 5: *The feminine* **Textual Unconscious in**
Children's Literature **141**

Theoretical Introduction to the Chapter   141
Summary   149
Memory   150
    Metaphor, Metonymy, and Memory   150
    Sexual Subjectivity   153
    Fictional Time and Memory   156
Wolf   157
    Dreaming the Wolf   157
    From Other to (M)other   161
    Imaginary Pleasure/Symbolic Law   163
Dangerous Spaces   164
    Dual Ontology   164
    The *Vel* of Alienation   166
    Revenant   168
Notes to Chapter 5   170

Conclusion   **175**

Une lecture féminine   175
Notes to Conclusion   177

Bibliography   **179**

Index   **193**

Series Editor's Foreword

Dedicated to furthering original research in children's literature and culture, the Children's Literature and Culture series includes monographs on individual authors and illustrators, historical examinations of different periods, literary analyses of genres, and comparative studies on literature and the mass media. The series is international in scope and is intended to encourage innovative research in children's literature with a focus on interdisciplinary methodology.

Children's literature and culture are understood in the broadest sense of the term children to encompass the period of childhood up through adolescence. Owing to the fact that the notion of childhood has changed so much since the origination of children's literature, this Routledge series is particularly concerned with transformations in children's culture and how they have affected the representation and socialization of children. While the emphasis of the series is on children's literature, all types of studies that deal with children's radio, film, television, and art are included in an endeavor to grasp the aesthetics and values of children's culture. Not only have there been momentous changes in children's culture in the last fifty years, but there have been radical shifts in the scholarship that deals with these changes. In this regard, the goal of the Children's Literature and Culture series is to enhance research in this field and, at the same time, point to new directions that bring together the best scholarly work throughout the world.

Jack Zipes

Foreword

The concept of *the feminine*[1] derives from the French school of feminist criticism, especially the work of Hélène Cixous, Luce Irigaray and Julia Kristeva, and has been appropriated here as an aesthetics of the body expressed through speech and writing. Within a certain body of children's fiction, *the feminine* functions as a consciously corporeal use of language that manifests itself in the physical, psychical, material and textual landscapes. This book takes a selection of focus texts from the works of Margaret Mahy and Gillian Cross as paradigms of texts of *the feminine*, to show how they attempt to "speak the body" because they are inscribed in the conscious and unconscious of language.

This book arises from a perception that the criticism of children's literature has not yet developed a fully articulated critical discourse through which to engage with *the feminine* in children's texts. Its intention, therefore, is to explore and expose some of the gaps and silences of critical discourse to produce new paradigms of textual engagement and to widen the discursive field. It will be of interest to the large international audience of academics and teachers with a research and teaching interest in the field of children's literature studies, and to the significant international body of students engaging in children's literature studies at graduate and undergraduate levels. It builds on the important contributions of other feminist approaches to children's literature, such as the work of Roberta Seelinger Trites, Lynne Vallone, Lissa Paul, Kimberley Reynolds, and Shirley Foster and Judy Simons.[2] But it is different in that it is not only a meta-critical work of children's literature criticism, but also rigorously interrogates actual children's literature texts through a particular strain of French feminist and psychoanalytical thought; as such it situates the texts dynamically in the literary exchange in a process analogous to Transference in

psychoanalysis, to achieve a fully realized feminine poetics of literary identity
through acts of reading.

The present study draws on the work of the French critics, Cixous, Irigaray,
and Kristeva, as well as Jacques Lacan's psychoanalytic work on subject formation, because each of these critics and theorists has inscribed the human subject in
language (albeit through their own distinctive approaches). It is argued here that
the various inscriptions in language discussed through these theoretical positions
is axiomatic to an understanding of *the feminine* in the especially *literary* subjectivity that is embedded in the act of textual engagement. Language is fundamentally present in the dynamics of literary exchange, in a process proposed as
analogous to Transference in psychoanalysis. *The feminine* in children's literature
is explored through such sections as "Writing the Subject: *l'écriture féminine*,"
"Reading the Mother, *le parler femme, the feminine* Postmodern Subject," "*The
feminine* Textual Unconscious." Themes like metaphor, metonymy and memory,
dreaming, transformation and return are all illustrated by reference to the focus
texts. These, and the many chapter subheadings throughout the book, are the basis
of the *the feminine* poetics in children's literature.

These new readings in *the feminine* show how literary identities are
inscribed at many levels in the literary exchange, and that the literary subject of
children's literature includes, but is not always or exclusively the child of, generic
definition. They show how readings in *the feminine* are not gendered exclusively
as either male or female, and that texts of *the feminine* do not always relate exclusively to the fictional works written, and/or read, by women, even though it is the
case that the focus texts featured here happen to be both written and read by
women.

The book therefore identifies the unique forms of literary identity or, "subjectivity," which readings in *the feminine* may produce. Literary subjectivity is
positioned in the discursive space where reading subjects and literary texts converge, interplay, and are implicated in the signifying systems of language. The
book, therefore, draws upon a wide critical field, from psychoanalytic criticism,
which includes Freud as well as Lacan, the three variants of French feminist criticism mentioned, and textual criticism more generally. This is especially so where
psychoanalytical criticism and textual criticism meet in the textuality of *the feminine* postmodernism which is pursued in chapter 4. The model of readership
adopted is founded on the premise that there is a reading subject whose faculties
of language (at whatever age or developmental stage) permit entry into a shared
discursive space in which there is *a* reading. There is, then, in this model of readership, an acknowledgedly individualist and private reading, but, simultaneously,
the reading is plural by the fact of the literary subject's position in the intertextual
space where, as Roland Barthes has said, "all readings are plural."[3]

The emphasis, then, is on *reading* and, indeed, *rereading* in *the feminine*,
which theoretically speaking is available to readings across the spectrum of liter-

ature. However, it is the case that the manifest and latent characteristics of particular children's fictions are more readily and effectively predisposed than others to the kinds of textual engagements that operate in *the feminine* definition. The book focuses on just seven paradigm works of children's fiction: Margaret Mahy's *The Changeover*, *The Tricksters*, *Memory*, *Dangerous Spaces*, *The Other Side of Silence*, and Gillian Cross's *Pictures in the Dark*, and *Wolf*.[4] As paradigm texts, these seem to provide sufficient scope for the exploration of *the feminine* through this particular combination of critical perspectives, to liberate new readings that have ramifications and implications for a wider body of children's fictions which reside either wittingly or unwittingly in *the feminine*.

In terms of generic characteristics and plot structures, these paradigm novels share many similarities that are not necessarily suggested here as being in any way generically definitive but which, nevertheless, seem to suggest themselves as symptomatic of cases of *the feminine* in children's literature. For example, all the texts feature a central, focalizing character, either female or male, who, though central to the narrative, is always positioned at the margins of their particular social milieu. S/he is, in some way, either physically and/or mentally displaced from "home" into another elsewhere that may be a magical, or a "real," and/or a surreal place which becomes their transformational space: in *The Tricksters*, the central character Harry is holidaying at the family's summer residence known as Carnival's Hide; in *The Other Side of Silence*, Hero insinuates herself into the house and world of Miss Credence at Credence House; in *The Changeover*, Laura's initiation into witchery takes place in the Carlisle House of Janua Caeli; in *Pictures in the Dark*, Peter is banished from his family home to the garden shed and from thence to the river in his manifestation as an otter; in *Memory*, Jonny Dark takes up temporary residence at Tap House in the house of old Sophie; in *Wolf*, Cassy is ejected from her home with Nan into her mother, Goldie's, squat; and in *Dangerous Spaces*, Anthea comes to terms with the death of her parents in the out-of-time space of Viridian. Each narrative features a magical, surreal, or supernatural character, or characters, who are the agents of transformation: it is the Carnival brothers as trickster-figures in *The Tricksters*; the mysterious witch-like Miss Credence in *The Other Side of Silence*; the equally witchy Carlisle sisters of *The Changeover*; in *Pictures in the Dark* it is the surreal otter; in *Memory* it is the aphasic Sophie; in *Wolf* it is the elusive and ephemeral wolf of Cassy's dreams; and it is the ghostly and mythical Griff of *Dangerous Spaces*. All the narratives are framed in familial structures in which the family, whether present or absent, is in all cases somehow dysfunctional: either through being split, as in *Wolf* and *The Changeover*; or because the parents are violent, inadequate or domineering, as in *The Other Side of Silence*, *Wolf* and *Pictures in the Dark*; or the parents are either absent or dead, as in *Dangerous Spaces* and *Memory*; or the parents are duplicitous and treacherous, as in *The Tricksters*.

In these paradigmatic texts of *the feminine* there is a constant slippage and blurring of the logic and boundaries between fantasy and "reality," past and present, and a continuous interplay between psychic and everyday life, and between fantastic and realistic modes of narrative. There is a recurrent narrative patterning of separation, integration, and return which is classically mythopoeic and intrinsically linked to the great mother myths. These narratives, therefore, favor circularity, fluidity, mutability, intertextuality, and specularity through doubling and metafictional modes, which render them resistant to readings in the mode of an either/or binary logic, in hierarchical structures, or as linear temporality.

These kinds of narrative characteristics clearly manifest themselves in a vast range of children's fictions for which readers of this book will be able to supply their own personal anthologies, the point being that these generic markers of *the feminine* are not located in the handful of texts featured here, but are infinitely transferable across a spectrum of other texts that are now opened up to different readings by their newfound inscription in *the feminine* textuality.

Chapter 1, "Introduction: Reading *the feminine* in Children's Literature," introduces the theoretical context and purpose of the book, and explains why a poetics of *the feminine* in children's literature is desirable and necessary. It introduces the overarching theoretical positions, such as Lacan's work on subject formation, and the significance of the idea of literary Transference for the recovery of *the feminine* as a textual unconscious. It proposes that Cixous's idea of "*l'écriture féminine*," Irigaray's "*le parler femme*," and Kristeva's "Semiotic" may act as agents of *the feminine* Imaginary in the act of reading, which concepts are later developed and exemplified through the book. Thereafter, each chapter is preceded by a more detailed interpretation and critique of the theoretical approach(es) it adopts, followed by a reading of the focus text(s) in that mode as an exemplification of it.

Chapter 2, "Writing the Subject in Children's Literature: *l'écriture féminine*," defines and explains Cixous's idea of *l'écriture féminine* and focuses on two texts (Mahy's *The Tricksters* and *The Other Side of Silence*) that epitomize a generic strain in children's fiction, figuring a central female character on the cusp of adolescence who, in the course of the narrative, realizes self-definition through a process of subjective transformation. It describes this process in terms of a recovery of *the feminine* Imaginary, achieved, in these cases, through the characters' connecting with their own *bodies* in and through the agency of their own writing which simultaneously mirrors, and is mirrored in, the experience of the reading subject in the act of reading the text. The particular transformational events described are, therefore, as much a textual as a readerly phenomenon, and are explained as a manifestation of the *corporeality of writing and reading* that Cixous has appropriated to *the feminine* in her idea of *l'écriture féminine*. The chapter demonstrates how both these fictions bear the qualities of discursive fluidity and open structure that Cixous and Irigaray have identified as *the feminine* in their respective definitions of writing and speech, and how in this mode the identity of the reading subject, therefore, de facto is inscribed both as and in *the feminine* at many narrative levels in these kinds of fictions.

Chapter 3, "Reading the Mother in Children's Fiction: *le parler femme*," theorizes the ambiguous mother figure, and the mother/child dyad, ubiquitously present but seldom theorized in children's literature. They are present in the familial metaphors, and in instances of maternal absences, silence and exclusion from signification that Gilles Deleuze and Félix Guattari described as the "imperialism of Oedipus," and Irigaray described as the "blind spot of the old dream of symmetry." It discusses *Pictures in the Dark* as a narrative of "The Mother Tongue," embracing Kristeva's conception of the "Thetic," inscribing the language of the maternal body in terms of connectedness and fluidity. It explores how the specter, and the spectrum, of the "phallic mother" is present, and is conflated, in the mother figures which feature in Mahy's *The Other Side of Silence*, and *The Tricksters*, as both patriarchy's pre-castrated and, therefore, desiring—and also fetishized—mother, and positions them against Cixous's and Irigaray's critiques of the idea of the "phallic mother." Mahy's *The Changeover* is explored in terms of the struggle for female liberation from an all-consuming male tyranny in the character of Carmody Braque, and is explained in terms of Irigaray's "speculum." Laura's "changeover" is compared with Irigaray's subversion of the Lacanian Mirror in the story of *Alice*, who transited from one state and place to arrive at an alternative language at "the other side of the looking glass," to achieve a condition of psychic and corporeal redefinition and logic, expressed in *The Changeover* as changed mother/daughter relations, and related here to Irigaray's place and space of *le parler femme*.

Chapter 4, "*The feminine* Postmodern Subject of Children's Literature," focuses on *Memory* and *Wolf* and shows how *the feminine* is indexed in the fragmented subjectivities which motivate the plots of these two novels. It discusses how the psychical, material, and textual landscapes are related in "classic" postmodern discourses of fragmentation, dissolution, and marginality in which subjectivities are gendered both male and female. They are dispersed across a kaleidoscope of refracted surfaces that confound premodernist conceptions of interiority, depth, and transcendental individualism. However, and paradoxically, these narratives also simultaneously sustain the paradoxical notions of a single center of focus and agency, and notions of "reality" and "truth," and the chapter argues that it is these uniquely paradoxical features that inscribe these children's fictions in the explicitly *feminine* postmodern definition as it is described here, and that these focus texts are paradigmatic of a substantial body of children's literature in which complex narrative structures and experimental forms that are the mark of "classical" postmodern narratives are encoded in seemingly straightforwardly realist modes.

Chapter 5, "*The feminine* Textual Unconscious in Children's Literature," draws on Lacan's and Freud's work on dreaming and memory in relation to language, and appropriates them to *Wolf*, *Memory*, and *Dangerous Spaces*, which are defined here as "dream texts." The chapter shows how the recovery of *the feminine* textual unconscious is achieved through a series of metaphoric substitutions and metonymic images, and how the process of literary Transference described in chapter 1 can best be exemplified through readings of these dream texts because they share the same theoretical characteristics as dreaming and memory. The chapter also argues that the distinguishing characteristics of dreaming and memory—fluidity, mobility, a locus in the unconscious and an indifference to the symbolic laws of logic—have much in common with the characteristics of *the feminine* Imaginary as described by Irigaray, and also is the locus of *the feminine* textual unconscious. The place called Viridian in Mahy's *Dangerous Spaces* is positioned as an example of a feminine circular narrative of return, and as an occluded dream-space in which the central character moves from death through mourning to the reconstitution of subjectivity in *the feminine*.

The conclusion suggests further children's fictions, which, in their particularities of discursive and manifest contents, reside either knowingly or unknowingly in *the feminine*. The book concludes that the theoretical positions uncovered, especially the idea of a recovery of *the feminine* Imaginary through literary Transference in the act of reading, have implications for the way we as adults read children's literature, and how we teach children's literature to children and adults alike, because it extends the range of textual engagements and the critical discourses through which we as academics, teachers, researchers—and all of us readers—engage with a certain body of children's literature of which these focus texts are paradigms. Therefore, the book's identification of a poetics of reading *the feminine* in children's fiction widens the parameters of the dialectic of readerly engagement through which literary subjectivity has been historically and traditionally inscribed in children's literature. It proposes that these kinds of readings are available equally to the historical and implied reader who, as the reader-in-the-text, assumes a literary identity that transcends the limitations of age, gender, and/or experience. In this sense the book concludes that the reading subjects of these kinds of fictions, whether they are gendered male or female, could be quite properly described as *une lecteur féminine*.

NOTES TO FOREWORD

1. The term *the feminine* is translated into English from French feminist criticism's "*le féminin*." In the context of this book it bears the same theoretical meanings as were first intended by the French usage (see chapter 1 "Theoretical Introduction") which is quite distinct from the connotations of the word "feminine" in the popular English usage.
2. Roberta Seelinger Trites, *Waking Sleeping Beauty: Feminist Voices in Children's Novels* (Iowa City: University of Iowa Press, 1997); Lynne Vallone, *Disciplines of*

Virtue: Girls' Culture in the Eighteenth and Nineteenth Centuries (New Haven, Conn: Yale University Press, 1995); Lissa Paul *Reading Otherways* (South Wood-chester, Glos.: Thimble Press 1998); Kimberley Reynolds, *Girls Only Gender and Popular Fiction in Britain, 1880–1910* (Hemel Hempstead: Harvester Wheatsheaf 1990); Shirley Foster and Judy Simons, *What Katy Read: Feminist Re-Readings of "Classic" Stories for Girls* (London: Macmillan, 1995).

3. Roland Barthes, *S/Z*, trans. R. Miller (London: Jonathan Cape, 1976), 16.

4. All references to the focus texts are taken from the following editions: Gillian Cross, *Wolf* (London: Penguin Books, 1990); *Pictures in the Dark* (Oxford: Oxford University Press, 1996); Margaret Mahy, *Memory* (London: Penguin Books, 1987), *The Changeover* (London: Magnet 1985); *The Other Side of Silence* (London: Hamish Hamilton, 1995); *The Tricksters* (London: Penguin Books, 1986); *Dangerous Spaces* (London: Penguin Books, 1991).

1

Theoretical Introduction: *The feminine* in Children's Literature

The feminine is an exploration of an alternative aesthetics for children's literature that gives voice to some latent silences and apparent absences in a body of children's literature texts, and in the critical discourses about children's literature that have been otherwise unexpressed, unwritten, and therefore unread. *The feminine* derives from the French school of feminist criticism, especially the works of Hélène Cixous, Luce Irigaray, and Julia Kristeva, and is used here with a very specific meaning, both nominally and adjectively, of an aesthetics of corporeality in speech and writing,[1] appropriated in this case to the writing and reading of children's literature. The entire project, then, serves to extend and widen the critical language and parameters of literary engagement in a body of children's literature texts by reading them in *the feminine*, and the focus texts introduced in the foreword have been selected to act as paradigms.

The French school of feminist criticism is preferred[2] because, even while acknowledging the discrete and unequivocally distinct premises from which Cixous, Irigaray, and Kristeva operate, they are especially relevant in the way each has embraced a sustainable aesthetics of the inscription of human subjectivity in *language* and the body as an alternative signifying system which is, it is argued, axiomatic to the idea of the especially *literary* subjectivity and the idea of both the historical and textualized subject of, and in, children's literature that are considered equally here.[3] Cixous's idea of *"l'écriture féminine,"* Irigaray's idea of the *"le parler femme,"* Kristeva's interest in the linguistic relations between what she has called the "Semiotic Chora," and the "Symbolic" of the Lacanian definition, which are engaged through the chapters of this book, all share an idea of the possibility of a language that is spoken characteristically in *the feminine*.[4]

1

In Cixous's understanding, *the feminine* is not reducible to biological or sexual definition, neither does it preclude sexual difference. It includes women but does not exclude men.[5] It is, rather, as Cixous believes, potentially the province of both sexes,[6] but by connecting in new ways with their own bodies, women are potentially the subversive agents of what these three critics, in their different theorizations of the subject, have collectively regarded as the masculinist economy of language in the Lacanian appropriation of the "Symbolic Order" to spoken and written discourses. The critical perspectives equally adopted here then are not reducible to biological or sexual definition: to men's and boys' versus women's and girls' versions of writing and/or reading and/or characterization, because *the feminine* is being proposed not only as an aesthetics of the literary subject but also as a mode of literary engagement that is not gender specific nor gender determined. The fact that the focus texts are written by women does not imply that the idea of *the feminine* in literary subjectivity excludes literary works written by men. *The feminine* is about a distinctive contribution to language, and about the way that it both creates and sustains alternative forms of narratives and narratological relations in children's literature in, on the one hand, particular combinations of narrative devices and plot structures and, on the other hand, between text and reading subject, and at the meeting point between them both. The critical perspectives circulating round the idea of *the feminine*, therefore, make a distinctive contribution to an understanding of textual relations in these focus texts and others like them which straddle generic boundaries but nevertheless, as will be shown through the chapters of this book, share in the aesthetic of *the feminine*.

However, despite Cixous's declaration of the non-biological specificity of *the feminine*, the way that these three feminist critics have theorized mother/child relations, especially their attempts to restate maternal psychic and physical relations with girl children and to redress the balance of what they have perceived to be women's de facto exclusion from language in the Lacanian definition—in which she has been defined only in terms of "lack," or "absence," or "the same" all that is repressed and disavowed[7]—make a focus on women and girls an inevitable consideration here. The women, as mothers—"good," "bad," and indifferent—as daughters, as wives and lovers in familial and non-familial relations, as widows and witches, and the girls as daughters, lovers and sisters, whom we see in Mahy's *The Tricksters, The Changeover, The Other Side of Silence*, and *Memory*, and in Cross's *Wolf*, are symptomatic in their singular importance to a strain of children's literature, but their narrative roles and function have been relatively untheorized in the discourses of children's literature criticism.[8] Women and girls are an inevitable consideration here, but not exclusively so. *The feminine* in children's literature also embraces the narrative role and function of men and boys as fathers, husbands, brothers, sons, friends, and lovers, such as feature in *Memory, The Tricksters*, and *Pictures in the Dark*. In addition to gender considerations, *the feminine* also encompasses particular patternings of plot structures, and the coming together of narrative devices in unique and distinctive combinations, all of which bear upon our modes of textual engagement.

Within these definitions a psychoanalytic model of reading analogous to the psychoanalytic process of Transference is assumed and is described in more detail below in the section "The Psycho-Dynamics of Text/Reader Relations." But, briefly, in these terms, the reading subject is positioned as analyst in relation to the literary text. In the process of what is described here as literary Transference, the act of reading is an act of *interpretation*, and is a dynamic, dialogic, and dialectical process becoming, by turn, counter-Transference as the textual structures interplay with conscious and unconscious systems in the reading subject, and inscribe the act of reading as a process of recovery of the "textual unconscious." The term "textual unconscious" derives from Jacques Derrida's work on deconstruction,[9] and is conceptually similar to Fredric Jameson's idea of the "political unconscious,"[10] but here it describes how, as James Mellard has said, "A literary text is created as a textual unconscious and mirrors the human unconsciousness which, for Lacan, is an unconscious texture if not precisely a text."[11] Some of the elements and processes of what is named here as literary Transference are comparable with reader-response criticism; but literary Transference extends the premises of reader-response criticism because it conceptualizes a hermeneutical notion of the "text as psyche," "the psyche as text," and "the reading subject as text," which is the site on which an especially *literary* subjectivity is inscribed in a dynamic exchange during the act of reading. It is questionable whether Transference in analysis is entirely analogous to the literary exchange, but the principle of dialectical unconscious relations in the process is sustainable, and the idea of literary Transference as described and defined here, would seem to be crucial to the especially *literary* subjectivity of *the feminine* which is defined and described in more detail below and developed through this book. There is also a methodological problem because the idea of literary Transference, in common with reader-response theory itself, describes a theoretical *process*, in this case, of conscious and unconscious engagement between literary text and the reading subject, not a *method* of reading. It is, therefore, the case that *a* reading of a literary text, such as feature in this book, is itself an act of literary Transference. So, instead of endlessly repeating the detailed workings of the process, it is the case that the readings of the focus texts in this book imply all of the theoretical positioning and textual exchanges that are exemplified here and extended in chapter 4.

Irigaray, Cixous, and Kristeva are positioned here as the three major critical voices: their critical oeuvre is extensive. They have been variously charged with "essentialism," "positivism," "empiricism," "negativism," and of being "apolitical," and "ahistorical," each point of which has been argued and counter-argued across the factions and spectrum of feminist criticism.[12] But, it seems, none of these critics has supplied a substantial or comprehensive alternative that is not

somehow embedded in an understanding of the human subject residing in conscious and unconscious contents; neither, post-Lacan, has the critical establishment ignored the significance of the role of language in subject formation.[13] While
often critiquing and criticizing what feminist criticism has labeled the "phallocentric" (and Derrida has termed the "phal*logo*centric") assumptions upon which
Lacan's work is founded, these three French critics nevertheless have each appropriated a Lacanian topology to their conceptions of subject formation, even if only
for the purpose of deconstructing it, and even while attempting to distance themselves from his name.[14] It is, therefore, against a background and in the context of
the Lacanian conception of the subject that these critical voices are being positioned here. And to know what they were reacting against, as well as to understand
the status (or non-status) of Lacan in this branch of feminist psychoanalytical criticism, what follows is an outline of some of the key concepts and terminologies in
Lacanian thought that have made their distinctive contribution to an understanding
of subject formation. The vast work of Lacan, sustained over a wide field of psychoanalysis and a long career, often means that poststructuralist commentaries on
Lacan's work on subject formation use the same terminologies and formulas with
different interpretations, or with different emphases which nuance their meanings
in shades and colors that can be confusing or misleading.[15] This is not surprising
given that Lacan himself at different stages of his developing work used the same
terminologies to connote different meanings.[16] Many commentaries and commen-
tators are openly critical of Lacanian models, especially those from a feminist perspective, which includes the work of Cixous, Irigaray, and Kristeva.[17] The
theoretical framework outlined in this chapter and developed throughout the book
is, therefore, necessarily a selection from various critical fields (though not uncritically). Selection implies omission which, in its turn, implies that there is always
an alternative position to be adopted, and an alternative version to be written.
Acknowledgedly, this is the inevitability of treading critical minefields of such
extensive and widely written about areas as psychoanalytic, feminist, and postmodernist criticism. Readers who are already familiar with the work of Lacan,
may wish to go straight to "The Psycho-Dynamics of Text/Reader Relations,"
and/or "*the feminine* Fantastic in Literature" (below), or straight on to chapter 2.

LACAN AND THE SUBJECT

Lacan's version of subject formation is described in his model Schema L,[18] of the
formation of consciousness and unconsciousness[19] in which he defines such terminologies as: primary and secondary narcissism, splitting, alienation, desire as it
exists in dialectical relations to "lack" and the "Law," the tropes of metaphor and
metonymy, the parent/child triangle in relation to the "other" of the Imaginary
phase of subject formation in Lacanian epistemology, the great "Other" of the
secondary unconscious symbolized in language and the "Law," and the symptoms

of hysteria, psychosis, and neurosis. Lacan also, and quite controversially for feminist criticism, proposed the idea of the phallus as the "universal signifier" and prescribed its distinctive role in sexuality.

Lacan distinctively repositioned the subject, semiotically, in *language* (in a way that Freud, whose work Lacan built on, did not), by making distinctions between what he called the subject of speech (who speaks: "*énonciation*") and the subject of language (who is spoken: "*énoncé*"). James Mellard has pointed out that whereas Freud was attempting to go *through* language to something else (actual persons, events or happenings, etc.), Lacan conceived the subject as constituted *in* and *by* language.[20] While the work of Freud and Lacan are inextricably linked by the very fact that Lacan built on the work of Freud, and both theorists have their part to play in this book, Lacan is particularly important because the especially *literary* subjectivity in focus is grounded in language as a semiotic system, and because from this we have an understanding of the *textualization* of the subject. Lacan's work can, therefore, be readily appropriated to *literary* criticism and literature, to explain and explore the textual nature of the reading subject, the writer, the written text, constructions of character, their dialectical relations to each other, and their status in narrative. It is also tangential to an understanding of the literary subject of *children's* literature for its attempts to explain and situate primary relations between the developing child, the world and its initiation in language. However, the aim has not been to make the chapters which follow a dogged application of every detail of Lacanian thought, just as it has not been an intention to appropriate every aspect of the work of the three French feminist critics, but, rather, to offer a wide contextual framework against which to read the idea of a *feminine* literary subject.

The subject in Lacanian theory is constituted in three cognitive registers that he has named the "Imaginary," the "Symbolic," and the "Real;" and two temporal moments known as: the "Mirror Phase" and the "Oedipus Complex." In order to assume full subjectivity in Lacan's schematic thesis of subject formation, the child must eventually insert itself into the Symbolic Order, which is language. The genesis of the subject therefore is proposed on the basis of successful movement across this series of temporal transformations and registers: from the Imaginary to the Symbolic, and from the pre-Mirror to the Mirror Phase and the Oedipus Complex. In the pre-Mirror, prelinguistic Imaginary time (which has proved to be especially interesting to the critical thinking of Cixous, Irigaray and Kristeva), the child experiences its own body as a series of unconnected, disassembled parts and is in a state of boundarilessness. This prespecular moment is the time of the fragmented body and union with the primordial mother which Kristeva subsequently renamed the "Semiotic." The moment of the mirror, in the Mirror Phase, takes place when the child first recognizes itself as a fiction, or fantasy, of wholeness. About this gestalt of bodily unity, which, as if seen through a mirror, is an image or "*imago*," Lacan says:

> I am led, therefore, to regard the function of the mirror-stage as a particular case of the function of the *imago*, which is to establish a relation between the organism and its reality—or, as they say, between the *Innenwel* and the *Umwelt*.[21]

The child is both perceived, and perceiving; and at this stage its perceptual apparatus is focused on the image but also includes "what is heard, touched and willed by the child."[22] At the moment of its first recognition of itself as whole, the child experiences a simultaneous split by recognizing its own separateness from its mother's body. The child now perceives the mother as "other" than itself. It is important to note here, as Ellie Ragland-Sullivan has pointed out, that the relationship between the child and the mother is meant to express the idea that the human subject first becomes aware of itself by identification with a person (object), *usually* the mother, or "(m)other."

The moment of the Mirror is, then, the first of several paradoxical experiences for the developing subject because it is an experience of unity in separation: the child's narcissistic self-gazing at its own image effected by the mother's presence, and its blissful contemplation of its unitary body in a metaphorical and, sometimes, a literal, mirror is coincidentally interrupted by the stark intrusion of objectification.[23] This phase of the Imaginary is also the stage of primary narcissism, the mirror being a key metaphor of narcissism.

The bonds of dependence that exist between mother and child in the Imaginary are the desire of love, expressed in Lacan's double genitive "desire of the mother," meaning the desire of the child for the mother's desire, and hers for the child, soon to be ruptured by the intrusion of the father. The fiction of wholeness in the mirror which has precipitated the child's entry into the register of the Imaginary is a "fiction" because the experience of wholeness is relatively short-lived in the overall scheme of subject formation.

However, the Imaginary and its attendant traits are another paradox because, on the one hand, they must recede to allow the child's entry into the next projected register of subjectivity, the Symbolic Order, and, on the other hand, they must persist as traces to provide the necessary dialectical tensions between the two products of entry into the Symbolic: consciousness and its antithesis, the *unconscious*. With the birth of the conscious and unconscious comes also the birth of the ego (or, *moi*) which is the *consequence* of the birth of the unconscious at the subject's entry into the language, but is not the *subject* of the unconscious. According to Ragland-Sullivan, the unconscious, "occupies a subject-like space in consciousness and refers to those unconscious aspects of being that delineate a sense of 'self',"[24] or what Lacan has called the *ideal ego*. In this sense, then, the unconscious, as well as acting as a repository for all that is repressed from consciousness, is also permanently present in consciousness; meanwhile, the ego, as a property of the unconscious, permanently intrudes in the subject of consciousness.

This drama is played out against the register of the Real which has proved to be one of the most elusive and most contradicted areas of Lacanian thought. For Lacan the Real is the given field (what *is*), synonymous with an idea of Truth, and is unsymbolizable in language:

> Truth shies away from language. The history of humanity is punctuated by valuable discoveries in what Lacan calls the "conjectural sciences," but, although these "anchoring points" point in the direction of truth, they always miss the important point, namely the impossible, the Truth, the Real.[25]

Lacan has likened the Real to a Möbius strip in which the Real is the single strip of paper, and each plane of the single twist in the strip represents the continual interplay of the Imaginary and the Symbolic.[26] These two planes represent the splitting of the conscious and unconscious subject across the field of the Real and are the site of illusion as the Imaginary and the Symbolic vie for the recognition of the symbol from the position of their own peculiar and irreconcilable status in language.

Elizabeth Wright has most clearly described the Real as:

> The given field of brute existence over which the Imaginary and Symbolic range in their rival attempts to control: one can say that it is that to which all reference and action have relevance but which can only be handled through signifying practices.[27]

In his translation of Lacan's work on language, Anthony Wilden refers to the coexistence of the Symbolic, the Imaginary and the Real: "They interact in the subject—the Real is not synonymous with external reality, but rather with what is real for the subject."[28] James Mellard has proposed his own alternative algorithm: "R/r," to represent an idea founded in philosophical realism that the Real is available to apprehension by the subject he calls the "Symbolic Real," which has priority over Lacan's idea of the Real.[29] The unsymbolizable "Primal Real" is now relegated to a lower case status in Mellard's construction. This is useful, not least because it gives the critic an anchoring point for discussing the symbolized Real, via objects that the subject apprehends through the signs and symbols of language: "A symbolized Real that veils—or is cut off from—a primordial unsymbolized and unsymbolizable real."[30] However, Mellard's definition of the Real suffers in that it also could be understood as the place of ideology. In contrast, Ellie Ragland-Sullivan, quoting Lacan's Seminar on Joyce, says: "Language produces a Real which does not have any *corresponding* reality."[31]

Like so much of Lacanian epistemology, the concept of the Real is fraught with difficulties and contradictions, but we should take from it that the Real is inseparable from the orders of the Symbolic and the Imaginary: in the words of Serge Leclaire, "The experience of the Real presupposes the simultaneous exercise of two correlative functions, the imaginary function and the symbolic function."[32] Terry Eagleton in a review article has described the Real as a classically post-structural paradox:

> What makes something impossible is also what makes it possible . . . As Zizek sees it, the Real for Lacan is almost the opposite of reality, reality being for Lacan just a low-grade place of fantasy in which we shelter from the terrors of the Real. . . . The Real is what cannot be included within any of our symbolic systems, but whose very absence skews them out of shape, as a kind of vortex around which they are bent out of true. It is the factor which ensures that as human subjects we never quite add up, which throws us subtly out of kilter so that we can never be identical with ourselves . . . The whole point of the Real is to give language the slip, block it from the inside, bend the signifier out of true.[33]

On entry into the Symbolic Order of language, as the child must to become what Lacan described as a "normative subject," the child suffers a necessary alienation, that is, it represses its Mirror-phase identity and Imaginary experiences with the mother as a precondition to entry into the Symbolic Order that will usher in prohibition and the Law. According to Lacan, therefore, the condition of subjectivity is a condition of alienation and loss, and this is one of the areas of subject formation in classical psychoanalysis that has been much criticized and much debated in the works of Cixous, Irigaray, and Kristeva (see below). The subject experiences alienation first by the split induced in recognizing its separateness from the mother, and later on entry into the Symbolic; it is split by the need to repress its desires for what Lacan described as "primordial objects of desire," those properties of its Imaginary identity which characterized its pre-specular and specular relations: the breast, excrement and the urinary flow, the mother, the phallus as symbolized object, and, in Lacan, the voice and the gaze.[34] The subject's desires for these lost objects continue to impose themselves as traces in the conscious subject and are sublimated into transitional objects (*"objet petit a,"* or, the objects of the "other" [*"autre"*]), or persons (*"ego ideals"*) in the material world.[35]

Here we might note that the *ideal ego*, which characterizes the subject's Imaginary identity and constitutes the ego, is displaced (but does not disappear) into *ego ideals* in the Symbolic as the subject seeks confirmation of its identity through the agency of social others. In this Lacanian theorization, the binaries of loss in continuous and, unsatisfiable, dialectical tension with desire are *the* energizing force, and the *condition* of subjectivity; and the alienation thus induced by the division of the subject into conscious and unconscious contents is its defining characteristic.

The drive toward satisfaction of insatiable Imaginary desires upon the subject's accession to the order of language (the Symbolic Order) shifts, like language itself, from signifier to signifier without resolution of meaning, and we might want to consider this as Lacan's semiotic version of Freud's idea of the death drive: the final resolution of desire being death. Conversely, the pull towards recovery of primary narcissism, or the child's failure to sever its Imaginary relations in its refusal of the Symbolic, results in psychosis.[36] But before the child can move from the Mirror Phase to the Symbolic Order, it must pass through another transitional moment—and another area of controversy in feminist critiques of classical psychoanalysis considered in more detail below—the "Oedipus Complex."

The struggle toward subjectivity takes place in a triangular relationship between the child, the mother, and the father and is known as the Oedipus Complex. At the center of Lacan's theorization of the Oedipus Complex is the controversial "phallus" which, as Lacan famously insisted, is not synonymous with the penis, as it was in Freudian theory. Rather, it is a universal, "transcendental signifier" of difference. In what feminist criticism has described as the "phallocentrism" of Lacan's theory of the phallus, the male and female child identify themselves as sexual subjects in relation to their perceived possession, or lack of possession, of the phallus as signifier. Lacan later referred to the phallus as the "paternal metaphor" and used the term to indicate the father's non-literal status in the process of subject formation. Jacqueline Rose used four definitions of Lacan's term *metaphor* in her feminist translation: first, as the metaphorical substitution of the father for the mother; second, as the status of paternity itself that can only ever logically be *inferred*; third, as the place and function of the father that is not reducible to the presence or absence of an *actual* father; and, finally, as a signifier to separate the father's function from the "idealized father" of the Imaginary which must be circumvented in the child's negotiation of the Oedipus Complex.[37] This is important because, for Lacan, the phallus is the single most important defining characteristic of subjectivity. It defines the subject first, by the child's success or failure to negotiate it in transition from the Imaginary to the Symbolic (and in this sense the phallus constitutes what Lacan conceives as the "bar" between the conscious and unconscious subject); and, second, because of its presence is a marker of sexual difference. The role and function of the symbolic status of the phallus as the key signifier of the Symbolic Order of language, and the corollary of women being thereby excluded from language and defined only in terms of absence, or lack, are also central to feminist criticism generally, and to the three French critics featured here in particular.

The "Law-(or Name-)of-the-Father" that grows out of the paternal metaphor is, for Lacan, the defining characteristic of language; language therefore is a rule-governed system which initiates the subject into regulations, laws, and prohibitions. To successfully negotiate "normative" subjectivity, the child must sever its primary identification with the mother as "other" in the Imaginary and align itself with the rule of Law, by permitting the intervention of the father as signifier and agency of the Symbolic. It is clear, then, that Lacan would have us believe that his ideas of "phallus" and "father" and "Name-of-the-Father" relate, not to any biological or sociological referent, and not always and everywhere to a real father, but to the *paternal function* in the Oedipal triangle. In addition, the phallus, in these terms, relates to prohibition and the Law that imposes the experience of loss on the child subject, and in relation to which the child assumes its sexual identity. Most crucially, by defining the phallus as a Symbolic function, Lacan inscribes language as a masculine function; this is the basis of a great deal of the feminist criticism of the work of Lacan. Both women and children have been positioned as "Other" in classical psychoanalytic conceptions of the subject.[38] Both, therefore, are marginalized groups who have suffered double alienation, first by their necessary entry into language via what has been described by Lacan as the Oedipal process, and second, their alienation from the signifying practices of a language which has failed adequately to locate them psychoanalytically and historically as speaking subjects, or to understand their ontological experiences.

It is not difficult from all this to perceive how such masculinist axioms as these (founded in the anthropological work of Claude Lévi-Strauss), have been challenged by feminist thought; how interesting arguments have been built up in feminist criticism around the relations of girl children and boy children to their mother/father, as well as feminist challenges to a notion of gendered identity determined by the possession, or not, of the fundamentally male phallus.[39] These arguments are pursued in more detail in subsequent chapters, but the points to note here are these: that sexual difference in the Lacanian subject is seemingly undifferentiated until the moment of the Oedipus Complex and the recognition of the phallus, which precipitates the subject's entry into the language; and, more importantly as far as feminist criticism is concerned, that the subject is undifferentially *masculine* to this point; that sexuality itself becomes a signifier because it is founded in the signifier of the phallus; that sexual identity is determined not by biology but by cultural axioms, and is rooted in the order of language. Therefore sexual identity is designated Symbolic and is *defined* by difference (possession or non-possession of the phallus).[40] Also, from this we can deduce that in Lacanian epistemology there is a determining psychic reality distinct from the body. This suspicion is confirmed by Lacan when he says:

> There is nothing in the unconscious which accords with the body. The unconscious is discordant. The unconscious is that which, by speaking, determines the subject as being.[41]

The child of the Lacanian model is fully positioned in the Symbolic and, by so placing it, Lacan brought to bear upon the subject the full weight of semiotics in its diachronic and synchronic aspects, as well as in the unstable, bifurcated relations between the signifier (now dominant) and signified. He based his model of subjectivity on a structural model of Saussurian linguistics that identified the unstable relation between the signifier (word) and the signified (concept) in Saussure's well documented formula s/S. By the simple act of inverting Saussure's formula s/S to the algorithm S/s Lacan overturned the priority status Saussure accorded to the concept (signified) in subordination to the word (signifier).[42] In the Lacanian algorithm the word assumes priority status over the concept, not only by inversion, but also by being designated in the upper case. In justification of his action Lacan said:

> For it is still not enough to say that the concept is the thing itself, as any child can demonstrate against the pedant. It is the world of words that creates the world of things.[43]

The word does not merely represent the concept, it "enters" it, and there is, in Lacan's words, an "incessant sliding of the signified under the signifier."[44] For Lacan (as with Émile Benveniste, whose work on structural grammar Lacan also used),[45] the signifier and the signified are commutable; language is inherently metaphorical and in his model Lacan maintains that, in the metaphor, a new signifier replaces the previous signifier. The old signifier then "drops" to the level of the signified to create a new algorithm S1/S, and this is Lacan's metaphorical model for the kind of repression that happens when unwanted conscious signifiers or contents (thoughts, images, and memories) are displaced into other conscious signifiers as the old ones are repressed into the unconscious, as in dreams.

The algorithm S/s is connotative of the structuring of the conscious and unconscious, where the conscious subject (as signifier) is positioned *over the bar*, "/", in relation to the unconscious: the great Other as signified. As has already been pointed out, Lacan appropriated different meanings to the same terminologies; so the use of the term *Other* here is taken to mean the unconscious of the fully realized subject of the Symbolic. The S/s algorithm is also indicative of the structuring of the unconscious itself which gave rise to the famous, and much misinterpreted, Lacanian pronouncement that "the unconscious is structured *as* a language." The ineffectual-seeming *bar* between the signifier and signified is probably the most important component of the textualized subject because it shows, topographically, the gap of alienation that exists between the conscious and unconscious regions of human subjectivity, and relates to the idea of the textual unconscious.[46]

According to Lacan, it is in this gap between the conscious and unconscious that the human subject is constituted, "between signifier and signified, precisely the gap where language exists in the structure of the subject."[47] We can make sense of this definition of the subject if, for example, we consider it on the synchronic axis in relation to the play of meaning that exists between the unstable relations of signifier and signified, and the elusiveness of meaning in the chain of words along which the subject moves in a perpetual motion of loss and desire. Also, on the diachronic axis, the subject in, and of, language subsists in the gap that exists in the interplay of conscious and unconscious properties: between the Imaginary and the Symbolic. This idea of the "bar," as a signifier of loss in the lacuna of conscious and unconscious desire has implications for subjectivity in theories of fantasy and the fantastic and is pursued further in chapter 2.

Ragland-Sullivan points out that, for Lacan, the unconscious "is made of perception that negotiates unconscious desire and repression by substitution (*objet a*), one substitution being language itself and another being meaning."[48] Here we must include the tropes of metaphor and metonymy, identified by Roman Jacobson as the prime constituents of language.[49] Metaphor and metonymy are in fact sites of desire because the primal desires which are born of lack are condensed (repressed) on entry to the Symbolic; they bounce along the chain of signifiers in language (metonymy) in continual and endless, but ultimately unsatisfiable, pursuit of closure because in language meaning is always deferred. The concept of postponed closure as the engine of desire is significant for its appeal to reading literature pursued further in chapter 2. This metonymic act of sliding from one signifier to the next is also itself a metaphor for the elusive and allusive qualities of both the subject and meaning. Metaphor and metonymy function in the idea of the textualized subject as equivalent to the psychoanalytic phenomena of condensation and displacement where repression is a metaphor operating on the basis of combination, and displacement is metonymy operating on the basis of contiguity.[50] In this sense, the subject exists, like language, in a system of difference.[51]

THE SPEAKING SUBJECT: "other" AND "Other"

The child's accession to the Symbolic Order is not the whole story of Lacanian subject formation, because there is to be a further split precipitated in Lacan's distinction between language and speech: between the subject who is spoken (*énoncé*) and the subject who speaks (*énonciation*). Accession to language confers on the subject an ability to symbolize, but speech brings the ability of the subject to name itself as "I" in discourse: to name itself as the subject of the sentence, and to begin to *tell its own story*. These conditions prove to be irreconcilable, however, because the "I" who speaks is not synonymous with the "I" of the discourse, who is spoken. This idea of the split subject of language can be explained in terms of the distinction between *langue* and *parole* in which language preexists the individual utterance: where the concept of *langue* represents the subject who is spoken and *parole* represents the utterances of speaking subject. Lacan believed that the organization of language could only be understood in terms of the subject's relations to language and so he displaced Saussure's two terms with a single word "*lalangue*" to embrace the intrusion of unconscious processes of language (*langue*) in the subject's utterance (*parole*). Thus, the conscious and unconscious contents of language, the *moi* and the *je*, are always present in Lacan's psycholinguistic term "*lalangue*." In addition to these Lacanian divisions the pronominal signifiers "I" and "you" are further complicated when, as Benveniste points out, we recognize that they are not stable, but are endlessly interchangeable in discourse:

> The signifier 'you' addressed by one person to another immediately translates in the mind of the second person into 'I,' and 'here' and 'there' function in much the same way.[52]

The effects of these terminological elisions go well beyond the subject's own understanding and Lacan points out in this respect that:

> In order to liberate the subject's Word, we introduce him into the Language of his desire that is into the *primary Language* in which, beyond what he tells us of himself, he is already talking to us unbeknownst to him and in the symbols of the symptom in the first place.[53]

Lacan conjectured, therefore, that this subject who is spoken is included in his use of the term "Other." This is the great Other referred to above, often confused in commentaries with the asocial "other." The Other embraces the real and Symbolic father and all the prohibitions of the father's Law, and infers the subject's family history.

Jacqueline Rose has interpreted the Other as the subject's fantasized and persistent belief in a point of certainty, of knowledge, and of truth, to which the subject refers when addressing its demands outside itself.[54] The Other, then, is intersubjective, it is the place from where the subject speaks ("it speaks in the Other"),[55] but it is *not* synonymous with what the subject actually utters: "Otherness is always irreducibly outside the subject; it is fundamentally alien to him."[56] It is in this sense, and in conjunction with all that has preceded subject formation, that the subject of post–structuralism is decentered. The "I" who speaks is not the center of knowledge and meaning, but is, rather, subject *to* the social and psychic forces which are both outside itself and also are subjugated within it: these forces are, as Lacan says, "an elsewhere":

> The 'I' of the speaker that recedes from the statement in the very act of making it—the articulating 'I' as opposed to the articulated 'I'—the 'I' who slips behind the spoken word, or underneath the succession of signifiers. This is the 'I' who is subject to the *un*conscious signifiers.[57]

The subject which identifies itself as "I" in speech, like language itself, can only do so by recognizing its position in a system of difference: by recognizing and acknowledging the "not-I" the "you" (as other signifiers), about which Benveniste has spoken.[58] Identity, which is defined by difference in the poststructuralist subject, is illusory, elusive, multilevel, and diffuse. And the subject, in Lacanian post-structural thought, is, as already suggested, divided between a speaking "I" of consciousness which believes itself to be in charge and which *thinks*,[59] and an "I" of the Other (separated by the "bar"), located in the unconscious with all its material contents as outlined above. Together these two "I"'s comprise the dialectical agencies of the alienated, split, subject, and the decentered subject of postmodernist discourse that have a particular kind of resonance in children's literature and are pursued in more detail in chapter 4.

THE PSYCHO-DYNAMICS OF TEXT/READER RELATIONS

Although Lacanian models have been much debated and criticized, they nevertheless offer a dynamic and dialectical, *spatial,* model of subject formation. The subject thus oriented in the Symbolic Order is both split and decentered; and it is the subject's bifurcated, decentered, status on entry to the Symbolic, and the Lacanian focus on language, that offers rich potential as an exploration of literary subjectivity, especially when it is critiqued in the light of the particular branch of feminist criticism featured here and in relation to the *the feminine* subject of postmodernism in children's literature which is pursued in chapter 4.

What follows is an overview of some of the ways in which the psychoanalytic theories of Lacan have been appropriated to literary texts and reading subjects by, for example, Peter Brooks, Shoshana Felman, Jane Gallop, and others; and in Roland Barthes's work on textual *jouissance* and the discourses on *love*. These theorizations, in their turn, have been restated in the work of Cixous, Irigaray and Kristeva in their attempts to give voice to *the feminine* in writing and in speech that otherwise are silenced and negated in Lacanian-based psychoanalytic theories of literary subjectivity perceived as phallocentric.[60]

The especially literary subjectivity in focus here is concerned with the discursive space where reading subjects, and literary texts, converge in the signifying systems of language, and in the dialectics of the literary exchange. Therefore, it implies both psycho-social and literary intertexts where meanings (in the plural) are made in the name of literature. This is the site where an especially *literary identity* is inscribed in written, literary language, as distinct from speech, and in these senses the term literary subjectivity focuses on the idea of the subject *of* literature—relations between texts and reading subjects—as much as the subjects *in* literature—characters as textual constructs, their inscription in narrative structures, literary worlds, and how these strata of literary subjectivity interact with and relate to each other. The term *text* here includes authors, readers, and the words on the page, since each has a dialectical relation to language; in this sense each is a semiotic system, the coming together of which, in an act of reading, is the essence of an especially *literary* subjectivity and relates to any and all phases of literary development. A description of the literary exchange in this context is, then, that there is a reading subject whose faculties of language permit entry into a shared discursive space in which there is *a* reading which is not definitive. This is not to suggest that the relations between reading subjects and texts are unproblematic, or that the passage from text to reading subject and back is transparent. As with any discursive exchange there is interference from distortion, misreading, repression, and suppression, all of which imply transformations. Into these considerations we must throw the whole question of the gendered subject's relation to language which is being raised here. It is not possible, therefore, to generalize from the particular about literary subjectivity, or to suggest that subjectivity itself is singular and fixed. Literary subjectivity is constantly reactivated, is always in process, and is the site of multiple, contradictory, narrative, textual, linguistic, socio-cultural, and psychoanalytic codes being activated in the act of reading a single text by a reading subject. In this broadest sense of intertextuality, therefore, literary subjectivity is itself both intersubjective and intertextual. So, the readings of the children's literature texts featured here is only a contribution to the multiplicity of possible other readings of these texts, and to an understanding of literary subjectivity as it is being described and defined.

This spatial model of readership implies text/reader relations to the kind of semioticized, textualized literary subject that is in focus here. It includes the discursive "I"/"you," implying Benveniste's commutative relations between speaker and listener, which are here transposed in literature respectively to refer to the reading subject and the narrative voice. Benveniste has proposed that the signifiers "I" and "you" which the mass of writing (*discourse écrit*) reproduces, always imply a speaker, "I," and a listener, "you," that are endlessly reciprocal, and forever unstable in discursive situations.[61] The idea of commutability also involves what Kaya Silverman has described as the "suturing"[62] of the reading subject into the semiotic space of the words on the page (the language of literary texts, the agency of enunciation), and the reading subject's subjective relationship to the fictional worlds: characters, and their actions and interactions.

Any consideration of literary subjectivity, especially one which, like this one, positions the subject in post-structural, psychoanalytic models, must take into account the implications of a *textualized*, semiotic, version of the text/reader relationship and of the idea of Transference. In this sense the act of reading becomes a convergence of texts: the reading-subject as text, the literary text-as-text, and the intertexts in which they both participate and are produced. As Peter Brooks pointed out in the wake of Lacan:

> We constitute ourselves as human subjects in part through our fictions . . . the study of human fiction-making and the study of psychic process are convergent activities and superimposable forms of analysis.[63]

Brooks implies that through our fictions, and in our reading of fiction, we symbolize unconscious contents, an idea which Ellie Ragland-Sullivan picks up much more radically in her "The Magnetism between Reader and Text"[64] which is explored in more detail below.

Brian McHale's term "the text continuum"[65] is a useful metaphor through which to match the idea of the spatialized model of readership with texts, because it implies a spatial model of the fictional universe, and because the hierarchy of narrative levels within it is valuable for the question of *how* these literary texts interpolate the reading subject who operates in a network of codes and is itself already constituted by them.[66] He has proposed literature as a series of "zones," and as "a skeleton of layers," or "ontological strata," which he has aimed specifically at describing the postmodernist novel, but aspects of which can be appropriated more generally. "The text continuum" refers to the words on the page. This is the conceptual space of language itself that is actualized by the reading subject in the act of reading. McHale points out that words are effectively *spatialized* when we conceive the linguistic sign as being composed of a signifier and a signified, introducing an *internal* space within the sign:

> This space between the signifier and the signified may be wider or narrower; there may be slippages, displacements of one tier *vis-à-vis* the other. The gaps and slippages are what permit the free-play of the signifier, in effect annex linguistic space to the projected space of their fictional universes.[67]

LITERARY TRANSFERENCE

Literary Transference is at the center of this process. As has already been mentioned the idea of literary Transference is similar to a reader-response model of readership,[68] with a similar mix of limitations and insights, because it is premised on the idea that meaning is not in the text, or wholly contrived by the reader, but is a dialogic struggle between the two to activate textual possibilities. Like the reader-response model of readership, literary Transference is also hermeneutic, intersubjective, dialogic, and intertextual. But it is unlike the reader-response model because the latter relies implicitly on the idea of an "ideal" reader and a passive text,[69] even while proclaiming itself as a theory of reciprocity and indeterminacy. In the process of literary Transference, on the other hand, the semioticized notion of *language* is the sole agency of exchange between the literary text and the reading subject, now constituted as *je* and *moi* in the system of texts, the significant link between the two being not the text, or the reader/writer continuum, but the *act of reading* on which site a psychoanalytic interpretation of literary subjectivity is inscribed in a dialectical process that is akin to the process of Transference in analysis.[70] Elizabeth Wright has pointed out that the terms *reader* and *writer* become indistinguishable in this process because:

With the influence of Lacan's definition of the unconscious as structured as a language, the phenomena of transference in reading becomes all-pervasive, the structures of desire in language turning (in a sense affecting) reader and writer alike.[71]

Ellie Ragland-Sullivan has described how both text and reading subject become enmeshed in a mutual dialectics of self-definition: "The text constitutes the reading subject as the reading subject constitutes the text."[72]

In this Lacanian-based model of literary Transference, the literary exchange is not so much interested in *identification* as a mode of literary engagement as it is with *projection* of the subject's ego (*moi*) upon the text and, conversely, of the textual *ego* upon the subject which are in continual struggle with the dominance of the signifier and under the control of that other aspect of the conscious subject, the *je*: the "I" that is the speaking subject. Both the *moi* and the *je* are socially constructed and positioned in the conscious and unconscious of the subject. "The *je*," Ellie Ragland-Sullivan points out:

> Stabilizes the *moi* by anchoring its sliding identifications and spontaneous fusions through naming and labeling these responses. In this way the speaking *je* provides a sense of unity to the opaque yet potent force (of the *moi*) . . . We could, therefore, talk about the *moi* and the *je* of the text.[73]

Here, Ragland-Sullivan explicitly has made connection between the "text as psyche" and "the psyche as text": the text both speaks and has a disconcertingly present ego. She speaks about the text's operating "a magnetic pull on the reader,"[74] saying also that the subject's *moi* is a text, a fiction, a "composition of myths, fantasies and desires taken from others,"[75] which occupies a limited space in consciousness and is constituted (is in continual process of being constituted) by the Other and others (including the literary text) upon which it has relied from a very young age for value, identity, and recognition. In thus proposing an essentially textual ego, residing in both text and subject, Ragland-Sullivan can now propose the act of reading (and, presumably, the act of writing) as projections of both the text's and the subject's ego, upon which each is mutually reliant for the exchange of the recognition and value it requires.

> The ego is thus a partial or—in Lacan's terms—a fragmented text that, in the case of the author, "writes" itself and, in the case of the reader, "reads" itself *as if completed* in the text.[76]

Transference in the act of reading situates both texts and reading subjects as sites of desire in the Symbolic. However, we need to consider not only the discursive *voice* bound up with the speaking subject *je* and the narcissistic *moi*, but also manifestations of that other desiring presence in the subject that mediates the passage from the Imaginary to the Symbolic, which are the specular relations emanating from the Imaginary in the act of *looking*: the "gaze." The gaze, like the act of reading itself, is discursive, if not to say solipsistic, in that it involves not only *looking*, but also *being looked at* and, further, *looking at oneself being looked at*: "I see and at the same time 'I am *photo-graphed*.' "[77]

The gaze effectively textualizes the subject and is present in every act of seeing. So the gazing subject simultaneously is both subject and object, at once voyeur and exhibitionist seeking confirmation of its own imagined fantasies of itself in others, and in the Other. Its implications for the act of reading have to do with the "gazing position" between the reading subject *of* the text, the reading subject *in* the text, and narratorial points of view, "a mirror-maze of glances in which they and the reader become enclosed."[78]

In the act of reading the subject not only seeks confirmation of its own image in the text, but also sees itself being gazed at by the text. Roland Barthes has likened the act of reading to a lover seeking the reflection of its fictionalized self in the Other/the text; the continuum of discursive complexities which induce either states of pleasure, "bliss," or forms of fetishized love in "*jouissance.*" Conversely, the gaze of the *text* is like a luring lover: "The text is a fetish object, and *this fetish desires me.*"[79] In it, the one who is desired (the reading subject) finds (the illusion of) self-completion in the text as ideal object:

> You address yourself to me so that I may read you, but I am nothing to you except this address; in your eyes, I am the substitute for nothing, for no figure (hardly that of the mother): for you I am neither a body nor even an object (. . . I am not the one whose soul demands recognition), but merely a field, a vessel for expansion.[80]

And John Lechte has pointed out in the context of Kristeva's work on love[81] that:

> Love is fundamental to psychoanalysis in the transference . . . Love is a synthesis of ideal and affect. In other words the ideal object has to be sought (desired) with passion . . . Passion *in* language is what we are talking about.[82]

Lechte goes on to describe how Kristeva's idea of "metaphor as condensation," is more than a linguistic phenomenon: "It approximates to the nature of love by being the point at which ideal and affect come together in the language of artistic discourse."[83]

The gaze has been much discussed in feminist criticism, not least because the gaze has positioned women as the specularized Other.[84] Located in the scopic drive it is, of course, founded in the primary and secondary narcissism: the former belonging to the Mirror Phase and separation from the mother displaced by the formation of the ego and objects of secondary narcissism (ego ideals) in the Symbolic. As already indicated, it is premised on a notion of love (for oneself and for others and for the image of oneself through others). Now, as a repressed, unconscious drive that continuously tries to infiltrate the conscious, it is circumscribed by the Symbolic.

The tensions and contradictions existing in the scopic drive are, therefore, not so much between the *moi* (ego) and the speaking *je* (though these still are implicated), but between the gaze and the libidinal, pleasure-seeking "eye," as the organ of perception; as Lacan has pointed out, the eye and the gaze will always deceive each other. The act of looking always implies an absence and a presence as the gaze that was once fixated on the mother is now displaced, in the signifier, to objects (others) that always are out of reach and comes always from the Other: "This signifying process comes to affect all looking, every recognition, it is at once a finding and a failure to find."[85] As it is with subjective relations to voice in the act of reading, so too it is with the gaze. We can begin to appreciate the complexities of gaze and voice in narrative, and their implications for the reading subject (as is shown in chapter 2 in "*The feminine* in Metafictional Mode," and "The Gaze" in relation to *The Tricksters*), when we relate them to the interplay of several diegetic levels; when those acts of looking (and speaking) are embedded in reciprocal Transference between reading subject and text; when they are caught up in the tensions between the Imaginary and the Symbolic and the alienation induced by this movement between the two; and when extra-, inter-, and intra-diegetically, the voice and the gaze are not singular, or plural, but (as in *The Tricksters*) are multiple, and are dispersed across a range of viewing positions and "zones."[86]

This territory between the conscious and unconscious subject of reading and writing is another potent site of critical debate in feminist psychoanalytic criticism, especially in the work of Cixous and Irigaray who, in their writings, have repositioned and reimagined both the textual voice and landscape of written discourses that otherwise have been positioned as unexamined assumptions of Lacanian–based psychoanalytic criticism such as we see here in the work of Ragland-Sullivan. Meanwhile, for Ragland-Sullivan, whose work has contributed greatly to the idea of a textualized subject, the uneasy relations between the *moi* and the *je* together comprise the discursive narrative *voice*. Ragland-Sullivan has described the *je* as an "unreliable narrator" inasmuch as it obeys the letter of the Law by being the bearer of speech (the *port parole*). However, despite appearances, the *je* is not where the subject's identity lies. Similarly, we might say, the narrating "I" of the literary text is not the place of textual identity; in this sense, the narrating voice is, in fact, always an unreliable narrator.

Shoshana Felman has described Transference as the acting out of the reality of the unconscious: symptoms speak in words. Words, Lacan tells us, "are the only material of the unconscious. . . . Every word indicates the absence of what it stands for."[87] Felman raises the question whether, "all stories, all narratives, imply Transferential structure," if they contain, that is, what she describes as, "a love relation that both organizes and disguises, deciphers and enciphers them."[88] Transference (becoming by turn counter-Transference), is shared between the text (as Other), and the reading subject (as self-definition), and vice versa, in a recip- rocal relation that sees both (also by turn) as analyst and analysand, linked by acts of *interpretation* in the act of reading. In Transference, the reader as analyst is "the subject presumed to know," who identifies traces of the unconscious in the gaps, the silences, in the subject's discourse, and behind the words that he or she utters, which the analyst then interprets and returns to the subject:

> These moments of seeming silence within and around discursive events—those moments when language would appear to cease, and with it subjectivity—are not really silent at all. They are filled with the inaudible sounds of a second discourse, a discourse of which the subject remains oblivious. The subject inhabits one psychic space consciously, but another unconsciously.[89]

James Mellard claims that the human value of interpretation lies in this deeply Transferential relation between text and reading subject and, echoing Ragland- Sullivan, says:

> For what the reader has found in the text, the text has found in the reader as well. And what both reader and text find in each other are . . . the reconfigurations of the mirror stage and Oedipal triangulation, the endless recapitulations of the dialectics of Desire and Law in human subjectivity.[90]

These are the Transferential relations which inscribe literary subjectivity in the act of reading. Mellard has suggested it is this "deeper," more unconscious rela- tion, which makes our reading of literature,

> So vibrantly meaningful for us, and explains why we cannot always say why a work will touch us so powerfully. The power of affect is the one that comes from the unconscious, whether it lies in us or in the texts that seem to bring it up or from which we bring it up.[91]

THE TEXTUAL UNCONSCIOUS

These aporia between conscious and unconscious contents when related to the lit- erary exchange, and contained in the idea of "the text as psyche"/"psyche as text," are a latent or unseen discourse identified by Derrida as a *"textual* unconscious."[92]

> For Derrida, texts always contain their own undermining or subversion: these are irreducible textual elements—whether figures, literary devices, remarks, punctua- tion or other linguistic conventions. His object, like Lacan's, is thus a *textual uncon- scious*, a repressed materiality at work in all texts.[93]

The literary text is therefore conceived as embracing a textual unconscious and mirrors the human unconscious as an unconscious *texture* if not precisely a text. Jonathan Culler has firmly situated the textual unconscious in Transference by likening the text/reader exchange to: "What is at work in the analyst's Transferential relations. I want to call this provisionally a 'textual unconscious.' "[94] Culler does not consider the commutative relations between text and reading subject, but we must infer that what is true for the reading subject, as analyst, equally must be true of the reading subject as analysand, and conversely, of the text as analyst. Culler suggests, then, that the role of the reading subject is synonymous with the analyst and that the textual unconscious is present in moments of "self-referentiality in which the reading subject is caught up":

> When critics claim to be interpreting the story, standing outside it and telling us its true meaning, they are in fact caught up in it, playing an interpretative role that is already dramatized in the story. . . . In identifying this sort of transference as the key to a literary unconscious I am focusing on what seem to be moments of self-referentiality, when statements in the text ostensibly about something else prove to apply to its own condition and situation as text.[95]

Culler also suggests that the "literary unconscious" is an authorial unconscious inasmuch as it is an unconscious involved in the production of literature; and, he says, the notion is thus useful for raising questions about the relations between what gets into the work and what gets left out, and about the sorts of repression that may operate in the production of literature.[96]

So, the reading subject as author (that is, as creator and producer of the text) is implied in this idea of repression and literary production, and especially so in poststructuralist theory and in psychoanalytic criticism where the two have now become conflated in the textualized subject—both readers and writers are producers of texts. The question, then, also should be asked about what gets into the work and what is left out not only in writing but also in the process of *reading*; and because of what has here been established from Culler's notion of the textual unconscious, there must be, on the other side of the coin, a manifestation of a "readerly unconscious" produced by the text.

The language of literary discourse, as with language per se, operates by sliding between the Imaginary, as the identificatory register grounded in Desire, and the register of the Symbolic, grounded in cultural codes, conventions, and the Law (of the Father). In this process the signifier is dominant, and is repression. So too, the act of reading slides between, on the one hand, the words on the page as signifier and the Law, and, on the other, the subject's (and the text's) desire for the *signified* (literary content). The act of reading exists in the gap between the textual Imaginary and the Symbolic; it is between, in other words, the textual conscious and the textual unconscious that the—now alienated, split, and decentered—*literary* subject is constituted, "over the *bar*" in the act of reading.

Other versions of Lacanian-based psychoanalytic criticism have identified in the act of reading a constant reenactment (a repetition) of the Oedipal triangle that operates in a process of loss.[97] Literary texts are, therefore, proposed as sites of reciprocal desire, and reading is inscribed in a dialectics of absence and presence—a movement between Desire and the Law identified by Freud as the drives towards Eros and Thanatos. Lacan himself has likened the movement along the signifying chain in (futile) pursuit of meaning and closure to Freud's notion of the death drive, the ultimate closure of meaning occurring only at the point of death. The pull towards the Imaginary, on the other hand, is a move towards the Imaginary and fantasy equivalent to Freud's pleasure principle.[98] We could relate Freud's idea diachronically to the temporal movement of the reading subject *in* the text which is metaphor (and suppression—and, in Juliet Flower Macannell's definition, masculine)[99] and, synchronically, to the text's and the reading subject's temporal existence in the chain of signifiers activated by the subject's (and the text's) desire for impossible completion (closure), which is metonymy (and displacement—and, in Flower Macannell's definition, feminine). Desire, Peter Brooks tells us: "Is precisely the driving power, of plot certainly, since desire for Lacan is a metonymy, the forward movement of the signifying chain."[100]

Elizabeth Wright has described the pull between the Imaginary and the Symbolic in the act of reading as a process of "lure" and "capture:" "The double view of the text . . . consists in the letter (the text) being both lure (in it I will find my desire) and capture (in it my desire will be alienated, subject to another's desire)."[101] The act of reading, in these psychoanalytic descriptions, is, then, not just a two-way process; it is a three-way pull between the Imaginary Mother, the Symbolic Father, and the text. Wright has spoken in this regard about the literary text's "uncanny capacity to reveal the unsaid, this time to let the mother and the maternal speak."[102]

In such a psychoanalytic theory of literary Transference, therefore, the "gaps in the text" that were axiomatic to reader-response theory's notion of textual indeterminacy take on new significance inasmuch as these silences bear witness to acts of repression and are manifestations of unconscious contents that the reading subject/text as analyst/analysand, interprets. So, absence operates in the act of reading as part of the way in which meanings are made, in a constant juxtaposition of "the said" and "the unsaid" (or the unsayable) of the conscious and unconscious. Such indeterminacies mean that there can be no final text, as there can be no final subject, because new significances continually are being made as the story is retold, reread, and reworked during the act of Transference, and as repressed contents surface. It is in the spaces of these repressed contents, in these textual "gaps," "absences," and "silences" that Cixous, Irigaray, and Kristeva have attempted to write their alternative discourses of the subject.

THE FEMININE FANTASTIC

The seven children's literature texts in focus here all feature an element of fantasy or "otherworldliness" that, in the case of *The Tricksters*, *The Changeover*, *Wolf* and *Pictures in the Dark* is located in the respective novels' characterization, and is found in the psychic and/or material landscape in the cases of *Dangerous Spaces*, *The Other Side of Silence*, and *Memory*. These texts hesitate in a position of ontological uncertainty between primary characters or zones that are recognizably real and characters or zones that are supernatural, or dream, in short, that are unquestionably other. They subvert the unities of time and space and displace characters and readers across these fictional zones, thus blurring the boundaries between concepts of real and unreal, and eroding any pretension to notions of truth. Arguably, these are the generic characteristics of narratives which reside in *the feminine*. Other books which readily spring to mind that may be open to readings in *the feminine* are Natalie Babbitt's *Tuck Everlasting*, David Almond's *Skellig*, and Tim Bowler's *River Boy*,[103] all of which share with these focus texts elements of the "unreal" as a given in an otherwise "real" of either characterization and/or landscape or both and are raised again in the conclusion to this book.

Tzvetan Todorov uses the term "the fantastic" to describe narratives of "epistemological uncertainty," which hover between "the uncanny" and "the marvelous" in his taxonomy of fantasies.[104] McHale would have us read fantastic narratives not as epistemologically uncertain but as *ontologically* uncertain, but it would seem reasonable to suggest that both conditions happily could be sustained in a single narrative. To qualify as narratives of the "pure fantastic," the ambiguity produced by the text posed by the question of events or characters being natural or supernatural must be sustained to the end of the narrative by both reading subjects and characters. Most importantly it is the ambiguity about whether the event has a supernatural or natural explanation, and the hesitation induced in the reading subject and encoded in the text which sustains the work as a narrative of the fantastic. When the ambiguity is resolved by an explanation of its being either a natural or supernatural phenomenon, (which is not the case in any of the focus texts), it slips over into the realm of the "uncanny":

> If the supernatural events *eventually* receive a natural explanation, we are in the fantastic-uncanny; if the events are not supernatural but strange, horrific, incredible, we are in the uncanny (with the accent on the reader's fear, not on his hesitation).[105]

All of the focus texts qualify for the status of fantastic narratives within the range of the fantastic/uncanny. Framed in a seemingly realist mode, these texts undermine realist conventions from within their own discourses and structures. Rosemary Jackson has described fantasy literature (but she is arguably referring as well to the fantastic in literature) as existing in a parasitic or symbiotic relation to the real; it recombines and inverts the real but does not escape it.[106] And she has described the fantastic as the fiction of:

> All that is not said, all that is unsayable through realist forms. . . . It is a literature of desire, which seeks that which is perceived as absence and loss. The fantastic traces the unsaid and the unseen of culture: that which has been silenced, made invisible, covered over and made absent.[107]

Semiotically, texts of the fantastic open up the space between signified and signifier, across which multiple meanings and plural identities roam, a condition described by Todorov as the:

> Fragility of limits between matter and mind which engenders several other fundamental themes: multiplication of personality; collapse of the limits between subject and object; the transformation of time and space.[108]

The fantastic is polysemic and plays upon ambivalences. Psychoanalytically situated, and in relation to the Transferential structures outlined above, fantastic literature is *the* material expression of the unconscious: the unsaid and the unsayable of the repressed. George Bataille has described the fantastic as a "tear, or wound laid open in the side of the real."[109] In these terms the fantastic speaks in the gaps and silences that are present in literary Transference: it is the literature of alterity, the literature of the "(m)other," the "non-thetic" of Kristeva's definition: the pull towards all that is opposed to dominant signifying practice.[110] The fantastic is here claimed as a manifestation of *the feminine* in these children's literature texts precisely because of its particular emphasis on the condition of corporeality, and the questions it raises about the status of the body as physical, ephemeral, or supernatural. The fantastic expressed in these focus texts, therefore, houses the unsayable of psychic phenomena expressed in themes of: dreams, dissolution and rebirth of the self in scenes of metamorphosis, quasi-mystical experiences with bodily and psychic transformations, encounters between self and the Other played out in narrative themes of specularity and doubling, split-subject, ghosts, mirrors and shadow-selves, themes of abjection in images of the grotesque, witchcraft, madness,[111] and sorcery. All of these narrative phenomena occur and recur across and within the focus texts.

To these one could add Jackson's list of "transgressive energies" expressed through the fantastic, of: "eroticism, violence, laughter, nightmares, blasphemy, lamentation, uncertainty, and female energy, excess."[112] In response to some of the obviously inherently violent aspects of some of the narrative phenomena in Jackson's list, which could easily fit uncomfortably within the tradition of children's literature, Leo Bersani has explained that the desire which is at the heart of fantastic narratives is intrinsically violent because,

> Desire itself is an activity within a certain lack, and the logic of our desiring fan-
> tasies leads ultimately to the annihilation of all Otherness. . . . Desire is intrinsically
> violent both because it spontaneously assumes this annihilation of everything alien
> to it, and because its fantasies include a rageful recognition of the world's capacity
> to resist and survive our desires.[113]

Such expressions of rage and violence are identified as one of the narrative contents structuring subjectivity, especially in relation to child/mother relations in
The Tricksters, The Other Side of Silence, and *Dangerous Spaces*.[114]

McHale has identified the relationship between the fantastic and the postmodern when he says that:

> In the context of postmodernism, the fantastic has been co-opted as one of a number
> of strategies of an ontological poetics that pluralizes the "real" and thus probleme-
> tizes representation . . . developing the fantastic genre's inherent potential for onto-
> logical dialogue into a vehicle for postmodernist ontological poetics.[115]

Rosemary Jackson described the fantastic as a dialogical mode, existing on the
hinterland between the "real" and the "imaginary" (I should say the Imaginary)
and interrogating monological forms of representation.[116] In this sense, and
within these narratological strata the focus texts are positioned not only as narratives of the fantastic, but also as types of postmodern—more specifically as types
of *the feminine* postmodern—generic characteristics in children's literature as
pursued below.

In the fantastic, which McHale has described as the place where the world
and "other worlds" mingle, fictional space is simultaneously constructed and
deconstructed by the use of technical strategies such as: "superimposition,"
"interpolation," and "misattribution." These strategies describe various states of
spatial proximity and relationship, boundaries and structures, and temporal relations between zones, which may be either compatible or incompatible with each
other. For example, "Superimposition," describes two familiar spaces being
placed one on top of the other; their "tense and paradoxical coexistence" produces a third space identifiable with neither of the other two zones, such as we see
in the place called Viridian in Mahy's *Dangerous Spaces* and conceived of here as
not so much a real as a psychic landscape. "Interpolation" describes the strategy
of introducing an alien space *within* a familiar space, such as, for example, the
room which becomes a "crossways of many lines of space and time," during
Laura's initiation in *The Changeover*. "Dual ontology" arises when characters are
ambivalently situated as either supernatural or real and intrude upon the real as in,
for example, *The Tricksters*, where characters of an ambivalent status intrude into
the world of Carnival's Hide without resolution or explanation. "Misattribution,"
describes narrative intention to displace or to disrupt automatic associations as,

for example, is exemplified in the disruptions and distortions of the familiar fairy-tale associations of "Little Red Riding Hood" in Gillian Cross's *Wolf*; or, at the level of language, the dissonance between signified and signifier in the utterances and thoughts of old Sophie West's demented mind in Mahy's *Memory*.

All of these terminologies provide a vocabulary with which to describe the narratological complexities of literary subjectivity as inscribed in what is here being claimed as *the feminine* fantastic in these texts of children's literature, precisely because of their otherness (not their Otherness) in the scheme of narratives, and these ideas will recur through the chapters that follow. They are framed in heterotopia between the natural and supernatural, and feature the collapse of ontological and generic boundaries that Cixous, Irigaray, and Kristeva all argue is the place of the pre-Symbolic: the place of the repressed, indeed, the place of *the feminine* in so-called legitimate discourse (see especially, in this respect, chapter 3 and Kristeva's idea of abjection). Within these fictional zones, structures of fantasy and reality interplay and coexist: whether through the interpolation of an alien space within a familiar space, or worlds, and/or characters, as in *The Tricksters*, and *The Changeover*; whether between states of dreaming and waking as in *Wolf*, and *Dangerous Spaces*; or through the eruption of unconscious contents, and mnemic traces onto the plane of language and conscious in the Symbolic as in *The Other Side of Silence*, and *Memory*; or through unconscious contents displaced into material signifiers such as Peter's otter in Cross's *Pictures in the Dark*.

Despite Todorov's absolute denial of the psychoanalytic dimension in the fantastic, the narratives of the focus texts, when positioned in *the feminine* fantastic, cannot be conceived in terms other than psychoanalytic, because it is their raison d'etre to express a desire for the Imaginary in a game of the impossible, and to seek to overthrow and to disrupt Symbolic unities—yet another reason for claiming their status *as* narratives of *the feminine* fantastic. In Lacan's terms the pull towards the Imaginary *is* fantasy. Upon such a literary canvas the idea of character as conceived in the classical tradition as immutable and monadic is displaced into a texture of faces, facades, and multiple, "polypsychic" identities. As such, the term *character* gives way to subject because it is only in the concept of the *subject* that we can invoke the displacement of identity across the textual strata of the written text as metaphor for psychic structures.

In her essay "The Character of 'Character,' "[117] Cixous deconstructs classical conceptions of character in an effort to expose the reading subject's subjugation to the idea of character in traditional patterns of reading. " 'Character,' " she says:

> Is the servant of a certain order that parades itself across the theater of writing . . . with the prospect of traditional reading that seeks a potential identification with such and such a "personage." . . . So long as we do not put aside "character,"

everything it implies in terms of illusion and complicity with classical reasoning will remain locked up in the treadmill of reproduction.[118]

According to Cixous, "Character," when it is read in the mode of identification, positions the reading subject in the syndrome of role-playing and becomes what the word character implies: a mask, a simulacrum, effacing the idea of the subject as an effect of the unconscious. Identification is a narcissistic process of learning to look at an idealized other (an *ego ideal*, in Lacanian terminology) which returns its own idealized image, a dual process in which the reader simultaneously identifies as both subject and object of the narrative gaze mediated through character and narrative voice. However, in the psychoanalytic literary mode of the fantastic, and in the readership mode of Transference described above, the literary subjects in, and of, the text are denied the possibility of this mode of identification, because they are encoded in a spectrum of differences which deconstruct the "sign" of unified character and, "by being several and insubordinable, can resist subjugation."[119] All the focus texts inscribe a decentered discourse of the subject,[120] and address the "writtenness of character," who, as is evident in Mahy's work, are often themselves writers of fiction. The thrill, and the skill, of them is that they achieve all this in the generic dissonance caused by their being positioned ambiguously between elements of the fantastic and realism to achieve the especially *feminine* subjectivity that it is this book's purpose to demonstrate.

The chapters which follow will build on all the above themes and foci, as the conceptual framework against which to develop the idea of *the feminine* as a dialectic of literary subjectivity through the focus texts, by showing the determinative interrelationship between the subjects *in* and *of* literature in an aesthetics of reading in the mode of *the feminine*.

SUMMARY

This chapter raises the idea of *the feminine* both in terms of its being an alternative signifying system of corporeality, and as a mode of literary engagement in a certain generic strain of children's literature, of which the focus texts of this book are proposed as paradigms. It claims that *the feminine* opens up an otherwise unnamed, and therefore unacknowledged, critical dimension in the discourses of children's literature which will be pursued and developed through the book.

A psycho-textual model of text/reader relations, and a semioticized subject *of* and *in* the children's literature texts, is proposed as a dynamic framework through which to engage with *the feminine* in the literary exchange, and is operational both in the readings of the focus texts and in readings of other children's literature texts of *the feminine* definition that are implicated (and sometimes named) in the book, but are outside its immediate scope. The chapter then describes the multiple textualities across which the idea of *the feminine* is dispersed, and why an appropriation of a Lacanian model of subject formation is an inevitable consideration in the spectrum of readings in *the feminine* because Lacan proposed a semiotic subject inscribed in the Other of the Symbolic Order, and because, on the basis of the Lacanian model of subject formation, we have an understanding of how language transcends any individual subject (*énoncé* versus *énonciation*) but, at the same time, how language cannot be considered apart from the subject.[121] Lacan, for all his masculinist orientations, nevertheless offered a spatial semioticized and dynamic model of subject formation and refuted the humanist idea of a monadic subject in favor of a subjectivity that is fractured and decentered by the quaternary divisions that take place in and through the subject's entry into language (in his Schema L), in which process the unconscious is a continuous source of disruption.

The Lacanian topology of subject formation has been simultaneously adopted and critiqued by the three French critics whose voices are raised here to counter much of what has been perceived by feminist criticism generally to be the masculinist orientation of classical psychoanalytic pronouncements on subject formation in the work of both Freud and Lacan. The French school of feminist criticism, as exemplified by the work of Cixous, Irigaray, and Kristeva, is introduced and will be developed through the book, because it extends the parameters through which we can understand and define language, and because the idea of *the feminine* emanates from their work and counters what they perceived to be the masculinist basis of Lacan's theories of the subject, which are not, in Cixous's view, gender-specific, to take account of the structures of sexual difference. These three critics inevitably have raised questions about the ambiguous and marginal status of women in the Symbolic Order of the Lacanian definition, and the problematics of the female subject's access to signification. So, though not exclusively, it is the case that women and girl children, as subjects of, and in the literature of, children's literature, are an important consideration through which to theorize *the feminine* in these focus texts. Subjectivity in *the feminine* has thus been presented as plural, circular and unfixed, identified in alterity and difference, with a specificity in the Imaginary (Kristeva's "Semiotic") that disrupts the linear temporality and logic of the Symbolic. Kristeva's "Semiotic," Irigaray's *"le parler femme,"* and Cixous's *"l'écriture féminine,"* taken together have reformulated the question of sexual difference in a positive light, and have repositioned women in terms which transcend what has been perceived to be masculinist notions prevailing in classical psychoanalytic definitions of subject formation, that is *her* as the negative pole of *the men*. The chapters which follow will both build on and develop these ideas through the focus texts.

Finally, this chapter identifies and reclaims for *the feminine* Todorov's idea of the fantastic in literature, not only because elements of the fantastic/uncanny are generically distinctive features of all the focus texts from which it may be possible to generalize from the particular in the quest to identify children's literature texts of *the feminine* definition, but also because, by its very definition, the fantastic resides in the unsaid and unsayable of legitimate discourse and corporeality, and therefore is disruptive of stability and unity, is subversive of linear temporality, is structured in the tensions between the pre-Symbolic Imaginary and the logic of the Symbolic and, for all these reasons, bears the hallmarks of *the feminine* as it will be pursued through the subsequent chapters of this book.

NOTES TO CHAPTER 1

1. Luce Irigaray, "This Sex Which Is Not One," in *This Sex Which Is Not One*, trans. Catherine Porter (Ithaca: Cornell University Press, 1985), 23–33; Hélène Cixous and Catherine Clément, *The Newly Born Woman*, trans. Betsy Wing (Minneapolis: University of Minnesota Press, 1986), 97.
2. For a lucid overview of the critical debates between the Anglo-American and French schools of feminist criticism see Alice A. Jardine, *Gynesis: Configurations of Woman and Modernity* (Ithaca: Cornell University Press, 1985), 13–87.
3. To have brought these three critics together in a single study in this way is potentially problematic. But to have done so is not to have neutralized, nor disregarded their differences, nor to suggest that their individual pronouncements on the speaking/writing subject are definitive and unproblematic. Their work has been debated and critiqued across the spectrum of feminist criticism, from the macro-debates between the Anglo-American and French schools, to those micro-debates that continue between and across the various factions of feminist criticism, each with its own partisan position and point of view. However, the intention here has not been to return to, nor reenter these debates, but to acknowledge them as points of departure, and for these reasons this book draws attention to some of the main critiques and criticisms of the work of these three French critics in footnoted commentaries and references rather than in the main body of the work.
4. Technical terms, such as "Symbolic," "Imaginary," "Mirror," "Transference," "Semiotic," and so on are signaled by the use of initial capitalization to distinguish their meanings from more common usage.
5. Hélène Cixous, "The Laugh of the Medusa," trans. Keith Cohen and Paula Cohen, *Signs: Journal of Women in Culture and Society* 1, no. 4 (1976): 875–93.
6. See Susan Sellers, *The Hélène Cixous Reader* (London: Routledge, 1994), xxix. Cixous herself focuses almost exclusively on literary works written by men (Genet, Hölderlin, Kafka, Kleist, and Shakespeare) with, only recently, the exception of Clarice Lispector.
7. See Margaret Whitford, ed., *The Irigaray Reader* (Oxford: Basil Blackwell, 1991), 24.
8. It has not been my intention here to explore definitions of what is or is not "children's" literature, nor the nature and substance of the child audience that is implied in the generic definition, because I feel these matters have been, and are being, extensively explored and debated elsewhere in children's literature criticism. See, for example, my article "The Dilemma of Children's Literature and

its Criticism," *File* 95, no. 3 (1995): 1–7; Karin Lesnik-Oberstein, "Defining
Children's Literature and Childhood," in *The Routledge International Companion Encyclopedia of Children's Literature*, ed. Peter Hunt (London: Routledge,
1996), 17–31; Karin Lesnik-Oberstein, *Children's Literature: Criticism and the
Fictional Child* (Oxford: Clarendon Press, 1994); Zohar Shavit, *Poetics of Children's Literature* (Athens: University of Georgia Press, 1986); Barbara Wall,
The Narrator's Voice: The Dilemma of Children's Fiction (London: Macmillan,
1991); Peter Hollindale, *Signs of Childness in Children's Books* (Stroud: The
Thimble Press, 1997).

 9. Jacques Derrida, *Of Grammatology*, trans. Gayatri C. Spivak (Baltimore: Johns
Hopkins University Press, 1976).

10. Fredric Jameson, *The Political Unconscious: Narrative as a Socially Symbolic
Act* (Ithaca: Cornell University Press, 1981).

11. James M. Mellard, *Using Lacan, Reading Fiction* (Urbana and Chicago: University of Illinois Press, 1991), 143.

12. Diana Fuss, *Essentially Speaking: Feminism, Nature and Difference* (London:
Routledge, 1990), 57. For critiques of Kristeva see: Jacqueline Rose, "Julia Kristeva: Take Two," in *Coming to Terms: Feminism, Theory and Politics*, ed. Eliza-
beth Weed (London: Routledge, 1989) 17–33; Judith Butler, "The Body Politics
of Julia Kristeva," *Hypatia* 3 (Winter 1989) 104–18; Cynthia Chase, "Desire and
Identification in Lacan and Kristeva," in *Feminism and Psychoanalysis* eds.,
Richard Feldstein and Judith Roof (Ithaca: Cornell University Pres,1989), 65–83;
Janice Doane and Devon Hodges, *From Klien to Kristeva: Psychoanalytic Feminism and the Search for the 'Good Enough' Mother* (Ann Arbor: University of
Michigan Press, 1992); Kelly Oliver, *Reading Kristeva Unraveling the Dou-
blebind* (Bloomington: Indiana University Press, 1993). Irigaray's use of the term
"woman" has been much criticized: see, for example, Janet Sayers, *Biological
Politics* (London: Tavistock, 1982); Juliet Mitchell and Jaqueline Rose, eds. *Feminine Sexuality: Jacques Lacan and the École Freudienne* (London: Macmillan,
1982), 54–6. In an interview with Jennifer Wallace, "The Feminine Mystique,"
The Times Higher, 18 September 1998, 19, Irigaray defended herself against the
feminist charge of "essentialism": "I think one belongs to sex or gender not
before one's birth—that would be the stereotype that I should not inevitably
adopt—but I think you are marked by a gender, or you have gender more precisely, after your birth. It is right to question the stereotypes that exist before our
birth but it is also right to live in accordance with who we are." In *This Sex Which
is Not One*, Irigaray metaphoricizes her use of the term *woman*: "I can answer
neither *about* nor *for* "woman" . . . it is no more a question of my making woman
the *subject* or the *object* of a theory than it is of subsuming the feminine under
some *generic term* such as "woman." The feminine cannot signify itself in any
proper meaning, proper name, or concept, not even that of woman," 156–7. Margaret Whitford points out, however, that Irigaray's project is the symbolization of
sexual difference, "She is speaking not of biology but of the *imaginary*, in which
one may make male *or* female identifications, regardless of one's biological sex.
A distinction needs to be made between (a) woman as biological and social enti-
tles and (b) the 'female', or 'other', where 'female' stands metaphorically for the

genuinely other in relation to *difference* (as in the system consciousness/unconsciousness) rather than opposition. Irigaray is privileging women and the morphology of the female body in her symbolization of the other." in "Luce Irigaray and the Female Imaginary: Speaking as a Woman," Margaret Whitford, *Radical Philosophy* 43 (1986): 3–8, 7.

13. See, for example, Patricia Waugh on "object relations theory" in Patricia Waugh, *Feminine Fictions, Revisiting the Postmodern*, (London: Routledge 1989), 83–4; *Motherhood: Psychoanalysis and the Sociology of Gender* (Berkeley: University of California Press, 1978).

14. Sue Vice points out that "Lacan is currently probably the most influential psychoanalytic writer, with his work cited in or underlying literary theory, art, film studies, social and cultural theory and feminism," in *Psychoanalytic Criticism: A Reader*, ed. Sue Vice (Cambridge: Polity Press, 1996), 15–6.

15. For the purpose of giving some continuity to the interpretation of Lacan, I shall use, as my baseline of Lacanian interpretation, translations of his works into English by Mitchell, J. and Rose, J. eds., *Feminine Sexuality*, Alan Sheridan's translation of Jacques Lacan: Jacques Lacan, *Écrits: A Selection*, trans. Alan Sheridan (London: Routledge, 1977), and commentaries by Ellie Ragland-Sullivan and Anika Lemaire: Ellie Ragland-Sullivan, *Jacques Lacan and the Philosophy of Psychoanalysis*, (London: Croom Helm, 1986), Anika Lemaire, *Jacques Lacan and the Philosophy of Psychoanalysis*, trans. David Macey (London: Routledge, 1970), because they are universally acknowledged as authorities on Lacanian interpretation, and because they appear to offer some stability of interpretation and translation.

16. For example, Anika Lemaire has identified five different uses of Lacan's own use of the term "Other," and four different interpretations of the term "*objet a*" alternating with "*objet petit a*." Anika Lemaire, *Jacques Lacan*, 157, 174–5.

17. See, for example, Jane Flax, "Signifying the Father's Desire: Lacan in the Feminist Gaze," in *Criticism and Lacan: Essays and Dialogue on Language, Structure and the Unconscious*, eds. Patrick Colm Hogan and Lalita Pandit, (Athens and London: The University of Georgia Press, 1990), 109–19; and Norman Holland, "I-ing Lacan," *Criticism and Lacan*, ed. Hogan and Pandit, 87–108.

18. Jacques Lacan, *Écrits*, 193.

19. Ibid.

20. Mellard, *Using Lacan*, 7. See also, Jane Gallop, *Reading Lacan* (Ithaca: Cornell University Press, 1985), 55.

21. Lacan, *Écrits*, 4.

22. Jacques Lacan, "Cure psychanalytique à l'aide de la poupée fleur," Comptes rendus, réunion 18 Octobre, *Revue francaise de la psychanalyse* 4, (October–December, 1949): 567; Mitchell and Rose, *Feminine Sexuality*, 31.

23. Jacques Lacan, "Cure psychanalytique à l'aide de la poupée fleur," 567, quoted in Mitchell and Rose, 30.

24. Ragland-Sullivan, *Jacques Lacan*.

25. Anika Lemaire, *Jacques Lacan*, 40.

26. Elizabeth Wright, *Psychoanalytic Criticism: Theory in Practice* (London: Routledge, 1987), 110.

27. Wright, *Psychoanalytic Criticism*, 110.

28. Jacques Lacan, "Lacan and the Discourse of the Other," in *The Language of the Self: The Function of Language in Psychoanalysis*, trans. Anthony Wilden (Baltimore: Johns Hopkins University Press, 1968) 159–311; 160.

29. Mellard, *Using Lacan*, 12.

30. Ibid.

31. Ragland-Sullivan, *Jacques Lacan*, 74.

32. Ibid.

33. Terry Eagleton "Enjoy," *London Review of Books* 19, no. 23, 27 November, 1997.

34. Ragland-Sullivan, *Jacques* Lacan, 35.

35. Lacan later replaced the term "*l' objet petit a*" with the term "*l' objet a*," when he reinterpreted Kleinian theories about the object relation; see Jacques Lacan, *The Language of the Self*, 163.

36. Richard Boothby, *Death and Desire: Psychoanalytic Theory in Lacan's Return to Freud* (London: Routledge 1991).

37. Mitchell and Rose, *Feminine Sexuality*, 38–9.

38. See, for example, Jacques Lacan, "God and Jouissance of the Woman," Mitchell and Rose, *Feminine Sexuality*, "There is woman only as excluded by the nature of things which is the nature of words," 137–48;140. However, Jacqueline Rose is at pains to point out that the phrase, "by the nature of words," has been displaced by some feminist critics to mean "*from* the nature of words," who, thereby, have recast the problem in terms of women having an entirely different language (from men), see Mitchell and Rose, *Feminine Sexuality*, 49.

39. See, for example, Rosalind Coward, *Patriarchal Precedents* (London: Routledge and Kegan Paul, 1983); Jane Flax, "Signifying the Father's Desire: Lacan in a Feminist's Gaze," *Criticism and Lacan: Essays and Dialogue on Language, Structure and the Unconscious*, eds. Patrick C. Hogan and Lalita Pandit (Athens and London: The University of Georgia Press, 1990), 109–19; Luce Irigaray, *Speculum of the Other Woman*, trans. Gillian C. Gill (Ithaca: Cornell University Press, 1985); Alice A. Jardine, *Gynesis: Configurations of Woman and Modernity* (Ithaca: Cornell University Press, 1985); Jane Gallop, *Reading Lacan* (Ithaca: Cornell University Press, 1985); Susan Rubin Suleiman "Writing and Motherhood," *The (M)other Tongue: Essays in Feminist Psychoanalytic Interpretation*, eds. Shirley Nelson Garner, Claire Kahane, and Madelon Sprengnether (Ithaca and London: Cornell University Press, 1985) 352–81; Elizabeth Gross, "Love Letter in the Sand: Reflections on *Feminine Sexuality: Jacques Lacan and the École Freudienne*," edited by Juliet Mitchell and Jacqueline Rose, *Critical Philosophy* 1, no. 2 (1984): 69–87.

40. Mitchell and Rose, *Feminine Sexuality*, 41.

41. Jacques Lacan, "Seminar of 21 January, 1975," *Feminine Sexuality*, eds. Mitchell and Rose, 165.

42. Lacan, *Écrits*, 149.

43. Ibid., 65

44. Ibid., 154.

45. Émile Benveniste, *Problems in General Linguistics*, trans. Elizabeth Meek (Miami: University of Miami Press, 1981).

46. Jacques Lacan, *The Four Fundamental Concepts of Psycho-Analysis*, trans. Alan Sheridan (Harmondsworth: Penguin, 1979), 206. Also, Mellard, *Using Lacan*, 11.

47. Lacan, *The Four Fundamental Concepts*, 206. Also, Mellard, *Reading Lacan*, 16–7.

48. Ragland-Sullivan, *Jacques Lacan*, 200.

49. See Wright, *Psychoanalytic Criticism*, 111. See also, Lemaire, *Jacques Lacan*, 199–207.

50. Lemaire, *Jacques Lacan*, 32–4.

51. See Christopher Norris, *Deconstruction: Theory and Practice* (London: Routledge, 1990), on Jacques Derrida's logocentrism in opposition to phonocentrism and on *"différance"* as disturbance at the level of the signifier, 18–55.

52. Emile Benveniste, *Problems in General Linguistics*, trans. Elizabeth Meek (Miami: University of Miami Press, 1981), 225.

53. Jacques Lacan, *The Language of the Self*, 57.

54. Mitchell and Rose, *Feminine Sexuality*, 32.

55. Lacan, *Écrits*, 24.

56. Ibid.

57. William J. Richardson, "Lacan and the Subject of Psychoanalysis," in *Interpreting Lacan*, eds. Joseph H. Smith and William Kerrigan, vol. 6, *Psychiatry and Humanities* (New Haven and London: Yale University Press, 1983), 56–63: 58.

58. Benveniste, *Problems in General Linguistics*, 225.

59. Lacan, *Écrits*, 165–6.

60. Jardine, *Gynesis*, 115: "Evidence for this (silencing) ranges from the privileging by psychoanalysis on the focus on female hysterics to the emphasis by contemporary philosophy on those bodies which have escaped Western society's definition of 'the normal male': the insane, the criminal, the male homosexual. In modern 'fiction' the expanse of female alterity also extends from spaces, through pronouns to characters . . . As Kristeva puts it, 'The feminine other appears clearly in the feminine characters, that is, when, put to death as addressee, 'you' becomes a fictional third person: 'she.' "

61. Benveniste, "Subjectivity in Language," *Problems*, 223–30, 209, 224–5, and passim.

62. I am using the word "suture" here to describe the relationship between the reading subject and the text as described by Kaja Silverman, who says that "suture" is often used to describe the relationship of the viewing subject to film, and comes from Jacques-Alain Miller, in the wake of Lacan, to mean "the moment when the subject inserts itself into the symbolic register in the guise of a signifier, which closely resembles the subject's inauguration into language." Silverman, *The Subject of Semiotics*, 200.

63. Peter Brooks, "The Idea of Psychoanalytic Criticism," *Critical Inquiry* 13 (Winter 1987): 334–48; 341.

64. Ellie Ragland-Sullivan, "The Magnetism between Reader and Text: Prolegomena to a Lacanian Poetics," *Poetics* 13 (1984): 381–406.

65. Brian McHale, "In the Zone," in *Postmodernist Fiction* (London: Routledge, 1987), 43–58. McHale also uses the terms: "Reconstructed Worlds" and "Intertextual Space," which I use in Chapter 4.

66. Roland Barthes, *The Pleasure of the Text*, trans. R. Miller (London: Cape, 1976), 16.

67. Ibid., 56.

68. See, for example, respectively, Wolfgang Iser *The Act of Reading: A Theory of Aesthetic Response* (Baltimore: The Johns Hopkins University Press, 1978); Gérard Genette, *Narrative Discourse*, trans. Jane E. Lewin (Oxford: Blackwell, 1980); and Jonathan Culler, "Semiotics as a Theory of Reading," in *The Pursuit of Signs: Semiotics, Literature, Deconstruction* (London: Routledge and Kegan Paul, 1981) 47–79.

69. In discussing the generation (the origin) of the literary text and the psychoanalytical field's (both Freudian and Lacanian) privileging of a concept of the father and the Law, David Carroll pointed out that: "In both positions the text is the obedient and servile offspring, the father in one way or another its truth." David Carroll, *The Subject in Question: The Languages of Theory and the Strategies of Fiction* (Chicago and London: University of Chicago Press, 1982), 27.

70. I have borrowed the terms "text as psyche," "psyche as text," from Elizabeth Wright, *Psychoanalytic Criticism*, 122.

71. Ibid.

72. See Mellard, *Reading Lacan*, 5.

73. Ragland-Sullivan, "What is 'I'?" *Jacques Lacan and the Philosophy of Psychoanalysis*, 59.

74. Ragland-Sullivan, "Magnetism," 381–406; 381.

75. Ibid., 383.

76. See Mellard, *Using Lacan*, 46.

77. Lacan, *The Four Fundamental Concepts*, 106.

78. Elizabeth Wright, "Another Look at Lacan and Literary Criticism," *New Literary History* 19, no. 3 (Spring 1988): 617–27; 621.

79. Roland Barthes, *The Pleasure of the Text*, trans. Richard Miller (London: Jonathan Cape, 1975), 5.

80. Barthes, *Pleasure*, 27. See also Roland Barthes, A *Lover's Discourse: Fragments*, trans. Richard Howard (Harmondsworth: Penguin Books, 1979).

81. Julia Kristeva, *Tales of Love*, trans. Leon Roudiez (New York: Columbia University Press, 1987).

82. John Lechte, "Art, Love and Melancholy in the Work of Julia Kristeva," in *Abjection, Melancholia and Love: The Work of Julia Kristeva*, ed. John Fletcher and Andrew Benjamin (London and New York: Routledge, 1990), 24–41; 30.

83. Ibid., 30.

84. See, for example Toril Moi, "Patriarchal reflections: Luce Irigaray's looking-glass," in *Sexual Textual Politics* (London: Methuen, 1985), 127–49; Irigaray, *Speculum*; John Berger, *Ways of Seeing* (London and Harmondsworth: The British Broadcasting Corporation, Penguin, 1972), 45–64; Laura Mulvey, "Visual Pleasure and Narrative Cinema," *Screen* 16, no. 3 (Autumn 1975) 6–18; Lorraine Bamman and Margaret Marshment, eds., *The Female Gaze: Women as*

Viewers of Popular Culture (London: The Women's Press, 1988); Ann Kaplan, "Is the Gaze Male?" in Ann Snitow et al., *Desire: the Politics of Sexuality* (London: Virago, 1984), 321–38. The idea of the gaze has been appropriated to a reading of *The Tricksters* in Chapter 2, "The Gaze."

85. Wright, *Psychoanalytic Criticism*, 117.

86. See Brian McHale, *Postmodernist Fictions*, 45: McHale's "zone" is the juxtaposition in written texts of spaces which, he says, "real-world atlases or encyclopedias show as noncontiguous and unrelated.

87. See Wright, *Psychoanalytic Criticism*, 111.

88. Shoshana Felman, "Turning the Screw of Interpretation," in *Literature and Psychoanalysis: The Question of Reading Otherwise*, ed. Shoshana Felman, (Baltimore: The Johns Hopkins University Press, 1982), 94–207; 133.

89. Silverman, *Subject*, 50.

90. Mellard, *Using Lacan*, 5.

91. Ibid., 55.

92. Jacques Derrida, *Of Grammatology*, trans. Gayatri Chakravorty Spivak (Baltimore and London: Johns Hopkins University Press, 1976).

93. Elizabeth Grosz, *Sexual Subversions*, 26.

94. Jonathan Culler, "Textual Self Consciousness and the Textual Unconscious," *Style* 18, no. 3 (Summer 1984): 369–76; 369.

95. Ibid., 371, 372.

96. Ibid., 369.

97. See, for example, Linda R. Williams, *Critical Desire: Psychoanalysis and the Literary Subject* (London: Edward Arnold, 1995), 53–6, and Barbara Johnson, "The Frame of Reference: Poe, Lacan, Derrida," *Yale French Studies*, 55–6 (1977): 457–505.

98. See, Peter Brooks, *Reading For the Plot* (New York: Knopf, 1984).

99. See Juliet Flower MacCannell, *Figuring Lacan: Criticism and the Cultural Unconscious* (Lincoln: University of Nebraska Press, 1986), 90–117.

100. Peter Brooks, "Freud's Master Plot: Questions of Narrative," *Yale French Studies* 55–56 (1977): 280–300; 293.

101. Elizabeth Wright, "Another Look", 621.

102. Elizabeth Wright, *Psychoanalytic Criticism*, 201.

103. See the conclusion to this book.

104. Tzvetan Todorov, *The Fantastic: A Structural Approach to a Literary Genre*, trans. Richard Howard (Ithaca and New York: Cornell University Press, 1975); see also, Tzvetan Todorov, "The Fantastic in Fiction," *Twentieth Century Studies* 3 (1970) 76–92; Tzvetan Todorov, "The Categories of Literary Narrative," trans. K. Kester, *Papers on Language and Literature* 16, no. 1 (1980): 3–37; Tzvetan Todorov, "The Origin of Genres," *New Literary History* 8, no. 1 (Autumn 1978): 159–70.

105. Christine Brooke-Rose, *A Rhetoric of the Unreal: Studies in Narrative and Structure Especially of the Fantastic* (Cambridge: Cambridge University Press, 1981), 63.

106. Rosemary Jackson, *Fantasy: The Literature of Subversion* (London: Methuen, 1981), 20.

107. Ibid., 3.
108. Todorov, *The Fantastic*, 120.
109. Jackson, *Fantasy: The Literature of Subversion*, 22.
110. See Jackson, *Fantasy*, 76, in relation to Sartre's distinction between the *thetic* and the *non-thetic*, "The 'non-thetic' can have no adequate linguistic form, for it exists before, or outside, human language."
111. Michel Foucault draws analogies between "madness" and the "fantastic." Michel Foucault, *Madness and Civilization: A History of Insanity in the Age of Reason*, trans. R. Howard (London: Tavistock, 1989), 93, 110.
112. Jackson, *Fantasy*, 177.
113. Leo Bersani, *A Future for Asyntax, Character and Desire in Literature* (Boston and Toronto: Little, Brown, 1976), 13.
114. See, for example, Sandra Gilbert and Susan Gubar, *The Madwoman in the Attic: The Woman Writer and the Nineteenth-Century Literary Imagination* (New Haven: Yale University Press, 1979); Shoshana Felman, "Women and Madness: The Critical Phallacy," *Diacritics* 5, no. 4 (Winter 1975): 2–10; Shoshana Felman, *Writing and Madness*, trans. Martha Noel Evans and Shoshana Felman (Ithaca: Cornell University Press, 1978).
115. McHale, *Postmodernist Fictions*, 75, 79.
116. Jackson, *Fantasy*, 35–6.
117. Hélène Cixous, "The Character of 'Character'," trans. Keith Cohen, *New Literary History* 5, no. 2 (Winter 1974): 383–402.
118. Ibid., 385, 387.
119. Ibid., 387.
120. Irene Bessiere, *Le récit fantastique: la poétique de l'incertain*, (Paris: Minuit, 1974), quoted in Jackson, *Fantasy*, 103 "Fantastic narrative constitutes a decentered discourse of the subject."
121. See Silverman, *Subject*, 194, 195.

2

Writing the Subject in Children's Literature: *l'écriture féminine*

THEORETICAL INTRODUCTION TO THE CHAPTER

In *The Newly Born Woman*[1] Hélène Cixous explored the relationship between the *the feminine* text and the "woman writing herself," and described it in terms of reconnecting with "*the feminine Imaginary*" that speaks through the agency of the body. Language, she says, is a body function:

> Woman, writing herself, will go back to the body that has been worse than confiscated, a body displaced with a disturbing stranger . . . Write yourself: your body must make itself heard. Then the huge resources of the unconscious will burst out. Finally the inexhaustible feminine Imaginary is going to be deployed.[2]

It is in this sense of "writing the body" that *the feminine* can be understood as an aesthetic of corporeality; this particular dimension is the focus of this chapter, worked out through a concentration on Mahy's *The Tricksters* and *The Other Side of Silence*.

In "Coming to Writing," Cixous further explains her understanding of feminine writing as both body and text:

> Language is a translation. It speaks through the body. Each time we translate what we are in the process of thinking it necessarily passes through our bodies.[3]

In her seminal work, *The Laugh of The Medusa*,[4] and in subsequent works, Cixous pursues ideas of sexual difference and subjectivity in ways which echo Kristeva and Irigaray but, unlike Kristeva and Irigaray whose main focus is on speech, Cixous is first concerned with the specificity of women's *writing*, in what she has called "*l'écriture féminine*."[5] Celebrating Derrida's assumption of *différance*,[6] which Cixous claims has liberated *writing* from its binary oppositions of male and female, she has seemingly pursued the idea of a form of bisexuality in the human subject, a position she claims is present in both men and women but, whereas it has been repressed in men, women necessarily already adopt it.[7]

> For historical reasons, at the present time it is woman who benefits from and opens up within this bisexuality beside itself, which does not annihilate differences but cheers them on, pursues them, adds more: in a certain way *woman is bisexual*—man having been trained to aim for glorious phallic monosexuality. By insisting on the primacy of the phallus and implementing it, phallocratic ideology has produced more than one victim.[8]

In her theory of writing, Cixous instates women's writing in what she has called the "affirmation of difference" celebrating *the feminine* as emerging from "*the feminine Imaginary*":

> An adventure, an exploration of woman's powers: of her power, her potency, her ever-dreaded strength, of the regions of femininity. Things are starting to be written, things that will constitute a "feminine Imaginary" (*sic*) the site, that is, of identifications of an ego no longer given over to an image defined by the masculine, but rather inventing forms for women on the march . . . There is work to be done on female sexual pleasure and on the production of an unconscious that would no longer be the classic unconscious.[9]

The "classic unconscious" Cixous says, is always the repressed of culture that tells women the old stories they have heard before in a language that is a "savage tongue."

   Cixous's idea of "*the feminine Imaginary*" together with Kristeva's notion of the "Semiotic" (see below) as subversive and equal constituents of the Symbolic, must then, be included in a notion of *the feminine* literary subjectivity. This feminine literary subjectivity seeks to liberate the subject from the constraints and repressions imposed by the Symbolic as it has been defined in Lacanian epistemology; it resides not in opposition to the Symbolic but as an in-mixing, even while recognizing the need to maintain the fundamental dynamic of discontinuity between the Imaginary and the symbolic.

   In her work on *l'écriture féminine*, Cixous determined that *the feminine* texts are not decided by the sex of the author but by the nature of the writing:

> Great care must be taken when working on feminine writing not to get trapped by names: to be signed with a woman's name doesn't necessarily make a piece of writ-

ing feminine. It could well be masculine writing, and conversely, the fact that a piece of writing is signed with a man's name does not in itself exclude femininity.[10]

This is the position that is adopted here in relation to *the feminine Imaginary*. Cixous has explored how the male and female experiences of loss are displaced into women's writing as a site of corporeal filtration:

> Man cannot live without resigning himself to loss. He has to mourn. It's his way of withstanding castration. . . . Woman, though, does not mourn, does not resign herself to loss. She basically *takes up the challenge of loss* . . . [it] makes her writing a body that overflows, disgorges, vomiting as opposed to masculine incorporation.[11]

Here, Cixous has reversed and modified Lacanian ideas of female repression and the male domination of the signifier, by giving women *expression* through writing (language) and by positioning man's experience of loss in an image of *repression* (incorporation). Cixous's thesis of writing *the feminine* is predicated on the female body as the agency through which women will write themselves, "in white ink," out of repression and, by signifying their own bodies,[12] inscribe themselves as subjects, not objects, in the Symbolic:

> By writing her self, woman will return to the body which has been more than confiscated from her . . . Censor the body and you censor breath and speech at the same time. . . . It is by writing, from and toward women, and by taking up the challenge of speech which has been governed by the phallus, that women will confirm women in a place other than that which is reserved in and by the symbolic.[13]
>
> In writing, women will affirm woman somewhere other than in silence, the place reserved for her in and through the symbolic.[14]

Luce Irigaray has also explored an idea of *"the feminine Imaginary,"* and has described it as the "repressed 'unconscious' of culture."[15] Its characteristics, she says, bear many of the features which resemble the unconscious: fluidity, mobility, and an indifference to the laws of logic, manifested through the body and expressed in *"le parler femme"* which is both writing and speech. In her works devoted to the primal elements: earth, air, fire, and water,[16] and in "The 'Mechanics' of Fluids,"[17] she has related these elements to manifestations of the *the feminine* Imaginary and described them as indicators of subjectivity in a perpetual process of becoming and, therefore, in a continuous state of flux. In her two major works: *This Sex Which is Not One*,[18] and *Speculum of the Other Woman*,[19] and in her subsequent writings, we have a much more radically iconoclastic approach than either Freud or Lacan's work on subject formation. In these two works she raises her voice against the singular failure of both Freud and Lacan to theorize the female subject:

One thing has been singularly misunderstood, hardly sketched out in the theory of the unconscious: *The relationship of woman to mOther and the relation of women among themselves.*[20]

Irigaray, in these works, raises the question of the need for a feminine Imaginary marked by the morphology of the female body and symbolized in *le parler femme*:

I am trying, as I have already indicated, to go back through the masculine imaginary, to interpret the way it has reduced us to silence, to muteness or mimicry, and I am attempting, from that starting-point and at the same time, to (re)discover a possible space for the feminine imaginary.[21]

She concludes from this that the only possible subject position available to women in classical psychoanalysis is male, and that women's identity in the Symbolic is only available as either a defective or castrated male.[22] Irigaray problematizes Lacan's idea of the specular image as being an economy of "the same" based on the primacy of the male. In these phallocentric assumptions, she says, there is no space for the woman to represent herself, or to be represented, other than as a mirror reflection of the male in whose representational systems, and systems of exchange, women's bodies are already coded as lacking and passive. Furthermore, her "sex" is rendered invisible, non-identifiable, and unrepresentable:

The desire for the same, for the self-identical, the self (as) same, and again of the similar, the alter-ego, and, to put it in a nutshell, the desire for the auto . . . the homo . . . the male, dominates representational economy.[23]

According to Irigaray's thesis, then, the female body can be construed in terms that have inscribed it in social and historic discourses, but it is through the system of *language* and *representation* that women have internalized an image of themselves; and it is in *speech* that their perceptions and experiences are given meaning. In *Speculum*, Irigaray identifies the "blind spots" in patriarchy that have effaced a specifically female genealogy. Through her call to represent women "otherwise" she proposes the need for alternative forms of language (*langage* as distinct from the paternal *langue*);[24] the need to "speak woman" (*parler femme*); the need for new systems of knowledge; and the modification to the economic system of exchange as "indispensable for any social mutation." She calls for a "de-formation of language and discursive structures," "dichotomizing breaks," and for retroactive structures, including the break between:

Enunciation and utterance (*énoncé*). . . . Linear reading is no longer possible: that is, the retroactive impact of the end of each word, utterance or sentence upon its beginning must be taken into consideration in order to undo the power of its teleological effect . . . if we don't invent a language, if we don't find our body's language, it will have too few gestures to accompany our story . . . Asleep again, unsatisfied, we shall fall back upon the words of men.[25]

In answer to the charges of "essentialism" which Irigaray's theorization of the subject has provoked,[26] Irigaray herself has said: "What I want, is not to create a theory of woman, but to secure a place for the feminine within sexual difference,"[27] and, in the final analysis, she has acknowledged that indeed there are many essences of the female in this sex "which is not one." In *Speculum* she proposes a shift from male objectivity and outsidedness through which women are turned into objects through the agency of *"The look,"* "the logic of *The gaze"* to a subjectivity of interiority in *the feminine* that thus creates for women a self-reflective space of "specul(aris)ation."

Irigaray's main objective has been to take Derrida's idea of *différance* and to use it to deconstruct what she describes as the "economy of the same" in which phallocentric discourses have made unexamined assumptions of male as subject and female as object in systems of symbolic exchange that have silenced alterity. Derrida's deconstructionist thinking is especially evident in Irigaray's project to find a non-hierarchical female identity that is not founded on women being defined as an absence in relation to male presence, or as Other in relation to the male self, or as lack in relation to male possession (of the phallus). Neither has it been her project to replace these terms with a simple inversion of privilege, but to seek a new way in which to express *the feminine* which is different from what Irigaray has described as "the excluded middle": working both *with* and *without* what, post-Derrida, has become known in feminist thought as "pha*logo*centrism":

> Beyond the double negation of the first two [moments of deconstruction], woman is recognized and affirmed as an affirmative power, a dissimulatress, an artist, a dionysiac. And no longer is it man who affirms her. She affirms herself, and of herself, in man. Castration, here again, does not take place. And Anti-feminism, which condemned woman only so long as she answered to man from the two reactive positions, is in its turn overthrown.[28]

In the process of proposing other ontologies and alternative language systems that, she claims, better represent and express her female subjectivity, she has exposed just how unstable the theories are that would divide inner and outer realities. The subject of language and of speech is *also* constructed and defined by language and speech, and implied in them.

In her more recent work, Irigaray, like Kristeva, has reconnected the female to archaic language and cultural prehistory and, as already mentioned, has positioned her thesis of subjectivity and *the feminine* in the primal elements of earth, air, water, and fire, which are claimed as the natural materials making up our bodies and our passions:

> The passions are to do with fire and ice, light and night, water and submersion, earth
> and the discovery or loss of ground, respiration in its most profound and most
> secretly vital sense.[29]

By refusing the binaries of male/female polarities and the paradigms of scientific linearity in language, and in her call for women to speak and *write* from the "excluded middle," "in meanings that are tactile as well as conceptual," she reconnects the body and materiality to notions of subjectivity and the unconscious in a way that Lacan and classical psychoanalysis could not. At the same time she identifies a mode of discourse that takes account of sexual difference but which also situates both male and female in oxymoronic relations of harmonic discord.

Much of the critical writing of Cixous, Irigaray, and Kristeva, then, is dedicated to reinstating *the feminine* definition to the order of language and, between them, they have amassed a sufficient body of criticism to establish an idea of the woman's body as an alternative signifying system. Collectively, they have reinstated the Imaginary as a player of equal and significant status in the game of language, even though, as each has pointed out in her distinctive theorization of the subject, the Imaginary has been repressed and marginalised by theory. However, to be repressed is not to be absent: "the repressed is omnipresent as an unconscious force within the psyche [which] haunts both symbolic systems and the subject."[30] In the words of Jacqueline Rose the quest to redefine the relationship of women as the a priori subject of the Imaginary lies in the fact that they are:

> Assigned to a point of origin prior to the mark of the Symbolic difference and the
> Law. The privileged relationship of women to that origin gives them access to an
> archaic form of expressivity outside the circuit of linguistic exchange.[31]

A great deal of the works of these three critics is founded on an understanding of an idea of female archaism which is pursued further in chapter 3.

Kristeva works largely uncritically within the basic premises of Lacanian psychoanalysis to achieve her philosophy of the subject, in that she accepted Lacan's a priori *male* subject, but Cixous and Irigaray have challenged (have deconstructed) its very premise. Indeed, Irigaray has called for an alternative genealogy of the subject that takes account of *the feminine* function through language in her idea of *"le parler femme."*[32] And Cixous has sought to establish alternative forms of feminine expression in which to give voice to *the feminine* through writing that inscribes the pre-Symbolic relations and experiences she believes have the power to undermine and reformulate the existing binary structures through the inclusion of other experiences in her idea of "*l'écriture féminine,*"[33] as is the specific focus in this chapter.

SUMMARY

The fact that this alternative language system, expressed through speech and writing, originates and is situated in the primary relations between woman and child make it especially relevant to children's literature. First, because children, like women, have been excluded and silenced in language except to speak in the language of the Father's Law. Second, because in the system of literature, children's literature, like the theorizations of women's literature in patriarchal discourse, is positioned as Other—as all that is repressed and disavowed and struggles to find a meta-language. Third, because children's literature, particularly the kind of young adult literature featured here, is often very much about the primary relations between women who are usually, but not exclusively, mothers and their children, or is about young adult girl-children such as we see featured in these texts who, as either readers or discursive constructs, are present in the process of the literary exchange. Finally, all of this is relatively untheorized in the field of children's literature studies.

The chapters that follow, therefore, develop and build on the work of these three feminist critics. They speak in an "other" language that manifests the eruption of Imaginary contents onto the plain of the Symbolic. In this sense, *the feminine* in children's literature is discursively present as a motivating force in the readings of the focus texts. This chapter takes the critical perspectives and explores through Margaret Mahy's *The Tricksters* and *The Other Side of Silence,* how *the feminine* is actualized through a transferential reading as described in chapter 1. These fictions, in common with many other children and young adult's fictions, feature central female subjects who realise a subjective transformation in *the feminine* through their own writing which gives this chapter its focus on *l'écriture féminine.* This chapter also shows how these narratives bear the quality of discursive fluidity and open structure that Hélène Cixous and Luce Irigaray have appropriated to their respective descriptions of *the feminine* in writing and in speech. In this sense, what follows in this book is a demonstration of how reading in *the feminine* opens up the interstices of the text to a new form of literary experience. In *The Tricksters,* for example, Irigaray's primal elements of earth, air, fire, and water, especially the element of water, are shown to be agents for liberating a *feminine* Imaginary in the central subject, the ambiguously named, Harry, and the entire narrative is shown to be embedded in the language and imagery of corporeality, physicality, and transformation.

In *The Other Side of Silence,* the central female character is also known by a significantly ambiguous name, Hero, and her self-imposed silence is theorized here as a literal manifestation of feminist criticism's pronouncements in the silencing of women in Symbolic patriarchy. Through a series of bodily and psychical encounters with her projected double in the shape of Rinda Credence, Hero, like Harry in *The Tricksters*, connects with *the feminine* through the agency of her own writing and emerges from her silence into a new form of language no longer circumscribed by the Symbolic. This process is signaled in the narrative when Hero burns her autobiographical book (which effectively has been the book which the reading subject has engaged with, thus giving a metafictional dimension to the narrative), and by the shift from first to third person narration: "Silence reinvented, repossessed, and magical."[34] These, then, are the manifestations of the *l'écriture féminine* that are pursued through this chapter.

THE TRICKSTERS

The feminine *in Metafictional Mode*

The Tricksters is a novel which foregrounds the textuality of narrative fiction, and inscribes *the feminine* in its fictional subjects, who are self-consciously aware of their status as fictions. Set in New Zealand, it is a cameo of the lives of the Hamilton family—Jack and Naomi, and their four children, Christobel, Harry, Serena and Benny—who are taking their summertime Christmas vacation at their ancestral beachside summer home, "Carnival's Hide." They are joined in the narrative present by three others who act as counterpoints to the family's mores and routines: Anthony Hesketh, an English botanist on a study trip to New Zealand, Christobel's friend Emma, and her illegitimate child, Tibby. In addition, they are visited variously throughout their sojourn at Carnival's Hide by Christobel's boyfriend, Robert, and his friend, Charlie, who arrive and leave by boat. The house once belonged to their great-grandfather, Edward Carnival, who built and lived in it with his wife, Ann, and their two children, Teddy and Minerva, who are mythologized in Carnival family history, not least because of the mysterious drowning and disappearance of young Teddy.

Discursively, this novel is an example of the kind of writing Cixous identified as "*l'écriture féminine*," characterized as writing of open structure that is varied, rhythmic, and multiple. These discursive effects are mirrored in the story through the central character, the gender-neutrally, and significantly, named Harry, who realizes *the feminine* both in Cixous's sense of *l'écriture féminine*, and in Irigaray's sense of *le parler femme*, through her encounters with her family history and relations, but especially through the agency of her own writing.

Of *l'écriture féminine*, Cixous has said:

> She lets the other writing speak—the language of 1,000 tongues which knows neither enclosure nor death . . . Her language does not contain, it carries, it does not hold back, it makes possible.[35]

The Tricksters demonstrates its open structure by beginning with a retelling of the ancient, familial story of the drowning and mysterious disappearance of Teddy Carnival and ending with a beginning, in the chapter titled, "Once upon a Time."[36] Early in the novel, Harry, in conversation with her young sister Serena, identifies the potentiality for fluidity, the self-reflexive nature of narrative fiction, and her own (and the reading subject's) status of textuality within narrative, when she says:

> "I'd like a book," she said slowly, dabbling in a rock pool. 'It's a special book, this one. . . . As you read my book you alter the world. You read Chapter One, look up from its pages and—hey presto—things have changed. . . . When you got to the end of the book, you'd feel there was a face watching you through the last page, and when you turned the last page you'd find that you were a book yourself. . . . You were a book, and someone else was reading you. Story and real would take it turn and turn about, you see. . . . ' Then, Harry fell silent. (23)

Harry has spoken like the oracle and, in this statement, she not only recognizes the fictional status of herself as subject in process of becoming, she also fore-grounds the meta-discursive issues in which both she and the reading subject, as textual effects of the narrative, are inscribed, and around which this novel is structured. In comparison Cixous writes in relation to her idea of *l'écriture féminine*:

> Life becomes text starting out from my body. . . . I go where the 'fundamental' language is spoken, the body language into which all the tongues of things acts, and beings translate themselves, in my own breast, the whole of reality worked upon in my flesh intercepted by my nerves, by my senses, by the labor of all my cells projected, analyzed, recomposed into a book.[37]

In this context of textuality, in *The Tricksters*, a group of characters converge on what is, effectively, the stage-set Carnival's Hide. The house is the scene of their Christmas vacation, and in it they play out their parts as actors in their own lives, in search of not so much an author as an identity. This novel depicts the labyrinthine constructions of fiction founded in both space and time, but where time and space norms collapse into the narratives of past and future and converge on a tenuous present of silences, secrets, and duplicity; where the boundaries of fantasy and reality are continuously reversed, inversed, and confounded, and where familial memory is played out in a psychic drama by characters of unstable identity.

As in a Pirandello play, in *The Tricksters* there is repeated reference to the fictional status of characters, to the role of authorship, and questioning about what is real: " 'You're only a sort of invention of mine . . . I wrote you, and I can cross you out' " (125). " 'Well maybe I do look like a character in your book' "

(125). " 'You're not real people' " (125). " 'Who is whose invention?' " (126). " 'You and Hadfield have made yourselves up out of my ideas' " (126). " 'My father—now there *was* an author! Wrote us in. Wrote us out' " (127). " 'Why bother to act? 'To deceive others' " (182). " 'None of you is anything but a fiction to Ovid' " (196). " 'It's a fairy tale—a real fairytale—peopled with monsters, as well as fairy godmothers' " (215). " 'Have I made love with a ghost?' 'It's what writers do, isn't it? Make love with ghosts' " (220). " 'I'm going to force happy endings out of all this' " (260). In this fictional world everything is unstable: history, time, the family, and family relations; there is continuous slippage between words and their meanings, between words uttered and intention, between inner and outer psychic realities, and metaphorical statements are interpreted literally, all of which are manifestations of the disruptive power of *the feminine* in these texts of *the feminine* definition.

The characters who populate this drama are never what they seem and this is another metafictive mode of doubleness, duplicity, and of mutability of character as subject in *the feminine* that reemphasizes their elusive role in the masquerade of identity and their fictional status. " 'They're not what they say they are . . . though God help me, almost nobody is, I suppose' " (72). " 'I'm not what I seem' " (152). " 'He's tremendous this side, but Felix doesn't really look like that and Felix isn't his real name' " (178). " 'This mild exterior hides powerful ambitions' " (186). "Behind the burnished surface she was troubled by the contradictions in herself" (184). Each is playing a part in his or her own life; each has an unutterable secret, the keeping of which is the psycho-dynamic agent of plot: Emma Forbes, posing as the mere friend of Christobel Hamilton, is silent about the paternity of her child, Tibby, and conspires to deceive everyone to believe that Tibby is the product of a past love affair with Sam; Jack and Naomi Hamilton conspire to keep silent about Jack's fathering Tibby during an illicit love-affair with Emma in order to present the solid front of a stable and unassailable love to their children; Ariadne Hamilton (known as Harry) keeps silent about knowing the truth of Tibby's paternity. Harry presents a face to the world that is never completely knowable, in much the way that her mythical namesake, Ariadne, has been described by Nietzsche as, "A riddle. Who knows except me what Ariadne is! . . . She is a riddle, an answer to solar solitude."[38] Anthony Hesketh, posing as a disinterested visiting scholar on a forestry scholarship to New Zealand from England, keeps silent about being the great-grandchild of Minerva Carnival, sister of Teddy Carnival. Minerva's secret about the death of Teddy Carnival is that he was murdered by their father Edward, and not mysteriously drowned in the way inscribed in Carnival family mythology. Finally, Teddy haunts the family home for want of closure, and is soaked in the memory of the walls of Carnival's Hide (12).

The narrative resides in *the feminine*, in its absence of closure, and in these kinds of textual silences, these familial secrets that are here defined as motivated by the unsaid, or the unsayable, of unconscious desires. Through these narrative features the reading subject of and in *the feminine* connects with traces of the textual unconscious[39] that is the characteristic marker of *the feminine*. The emphasis is on subjects in process, of their "becoming" rather than "being," echoing the feminist critique of the social construction of identity. It is also the kind of writing as "open structure" that is characteristically symptomatic of Kristeva's idea of the adolescent novel and Irigaray's and Cixous's idea of *the feminine* expression through writing,[40] adolescence being conceived by Kristeva as being "Less an age category as an open psychic structure. . . . The adolescent structure opens itself to the repressed at the same time that it initiates a psychic reorganization of the individual."[41]

This masquerading of characters exemplifies the extreme discontinuity between selves and their social Other, that has been identified as a paradigm of the search for identity in contemporary fiction by women.[42] Psychoanalytically, it is a fictional representation of the working out of repressed familial memory where the "compulsion to repeat,"[43] is played out in the need ceaselessly to retell the Carnival family history. But Teddy Carnival, "was never found" (21), and the entire narrative thus circulates round the open ending to the life of Teddy Carnival.

Most secret of all, and central to the Christmas-time drama played out at Carnival's Hide, is the revelation that Harry Hamilton is the secret writer of a fictional romance so unspeakably torrid that she knows her story to be unshareable. Her story is a parody of classic romance, peopled with archetypal, mythical figures, and is the kind of stereotyped writing of clichés that Kristeva identified as symptomatic of the borderline fictions of the adolescent Imaginary, opening up, as she says, the repressed, and is the point of psychic reorganization.[44]

So, writing as open structure is inscribed at three narrative levels in this novel: first, at the level of the story itself as the working out of the familial unconscious in the telling, retelling and reworking of the story of Teddy Carnival and the Carnival family history; second, in the fictional story being written by one of its protagonists; and, third, at the discursive level of the novel itself. The *eclipsing* of these fictional levels opens up the spaces for indeterminacy in readerly engagement because the reading subject in *the feminine* is always ambiguously situated between them, and is another indicator of the characteristic fluidity in *l'écriture féminine*.

The reading subject alone, who has been excluded from all other textual secrets, is privy from the beginning of the novel to the secret writing life of Harry Hamilton, in shared voyeurism, known only to herself and the privileged reader, that is in the mode of literary Transference and is positioned in ambivalence. The narrative exploits the ambiguous spaces which open up among, in this case, the writing life of Harry Hamilton, the textual status she shares with the other characters in the narrative, and the "writtenness" of her own character creations: " 'I wrote you and I can probably re-write you, or even cross you out if I have to' " (125).

Harry Hamilton is both thrilled and ashamed of the deeds she invents for her romantic villain: Belen, the predatory, winged man, part man, part bird, and the product of her own pen, becomes her secret lover:

> Christobel, Emma, Anthony, Jack and Naomi became ghosts of her imagination. . . . Suddenly her true life was lived in the moments when the tip of her pen met the white paper. (14)

These examples of inversion of real and imaginary contents are symptomatic of the metafictional mode and are examples of some of the many ways in which the narrative transgresses ontological boundaries, blurring the distinction between fiction and reality and weakening the boundaries between art and life. Ultimately, Harry is to wonder whether she has been the "victim of an intricate illusion, which had filled her with memories indistinguishable from the memories of real events" (255).

Desire in Writing

As well as drawing attention to the self-conscious fictionality that operates in this text and implicates the reading subject in a textuality that is subversive of realist forms, the critical pointer of *the feminine* subjectivity in this narrative is the way in which Harry's own writing has the double function not only of generating the plot of *The Tricksters*, but also is a paradigm of the woman writer's quest for a form of writing in which to express *the feminine* Imaginary in Cixous's idea of *l'écriture féminine*. Harry's writing initially is the projection of her repressed desire for ego-recognition, a textual unconscious[45] mirroring her own unconscious, and a type of metonymical transfer in which she endows objects, the characters of her story, with her unconscious desires. "Behind the written lines was a space she longed for" (14). She longs to become something other, which is also a manifestation of her questing for the other, *the feminine*: to be an enchantress, to be Ariadne the mythical figure of her name-sake, to be beautiful, to be a sexual being, to be desired and desirable, to be both loveable and loved, to be Christobel. All of these conjecturings of her projected selves are realized in the slippage between the signifiers of her writing and the signified of the "world" it conceives it, between, the narrative tells us, "the black bars of writing" and "the whole world beyond," and is here interpreted as the pull between the discourses of the Symbolic and the lost (repressed) Imaginary contents of the other.

During her primordial and transformational underwater encounter with the grotesque body of the dead Teddy Carnival—a gaping body oozing water and blood through its orifices[46] that contrasts sharply with the beautiful, classical body of her fictional hero Belen—Harry begins her process of transformation when she recognizes the space that lies behind her writing as the same space that exists behind Teddy Carnival's rock. Describing it, at this point, as an "alien" space, it is the space of her alterity.

The entrance to the rock into which Harry inserts her hand can be explained in terms of the gaping jaw described in Bakhtin's notion of the grotesque image of the body as "A wide entrance leading into the depths of the body. The bodily depths are fertile; the old dies in them, and the new is born in abundance."[47] In these senses, Harry's encounter with the ghost of Teddy Carnival is an out-of-time, out-of-body, experience, and is the watery place where she begins to connect with *the feminine* Imaginary. In the space behind her writing, Harry begins to project herself as other because it is here that she begins to engage with the space of Imaginary alterity otherwise circumscribed in the Symbolic by language and the Law. But, paradoxically, she constructs a narrative that is situated in male fantasies, carrying dominant literary images imposed on her by masculinist conceptions of literary heroes, and depicting images of women through the male gaze. Harry imagines herself in her character of the beautiful and desirable, Lady Jessica as a vision of angelic beauty, desired by Belen's male idealization of women, but secretly hiding lascivious (carnal!) passions and intentions to seduce him.

Harry's writing epitomizes the woman writer's struggle to resolve the problematic nature of the relation between sexual and artistic identity and, typically of the woman writer, she believes herself to have gone mad: " 'I've gone mad from imagining things' " (28). Sandra Gilbert and Susan Gubar in their *Madwoman in The Attic* pointed out, in relation to the plight of women writers in history who have dared to take up the pen, that "for women in particular patriarchal culture has always assumed mental exercises would have dire consequences";[48] and Cixous has suggested the paralyzing effects on potential women writers of patriarchal oppressions:

> Where is the ebullient, infinite woman who, immersed as she was in her naiveté . . . , hasn't accused herself of being a monster? Who, feeling a funny desire stirring inside her to write, to dare to speak, in short to bring about something new, hasn't thought she was sick? Well her shameful sickness is that she resists death, that she makes trouble.[49]

Harry's love affair with her story is a textual *jouissance* worked out in the act of writing. "The text is a fetish object," Roland Barthes tells us, "and *This fetish desires me*. The text chooses me, by a whole disposition of invisible screens . . . and lost in the midst of a text there is always the Other, the author."[50] Cixous too has linked female writing with love: "writing is a gesture of love."[51] Thus, Harry Hamilton is able to claim that her text is writing her: " 'Here I am!' something was saying. 'Write me down. Let me live' " (15). Writing makes her powerful and through it she believes she is able to transcend the here-and-now identity inflicted by years of being hemmed in as nothing but the silent, undistinguished "middle one" of the Hamilton family: a marginal, docile, taken-for-granted, and overlooked family figure, viewed by herself, and by everyone else, as lacking any sense of agency.

> In family life all the best possibilities (beauty, cleverness and the power to go out and have adventures) had been taken over before she was born and were being used up by others. . . . She was sick of feeling closed in by people above and people below, of being good old Harry, not wonderful Ariadne. (14, 22)

The sensual, sexual self that is named "Ariadne" has been repressed in process of learning to play the role of the subject position inscribed in her nickname "Harry." Ariadne is, she believes, liberated in her writing: in her writing, "A wild part of herself was set free" (14).

Also typical of the woman writer, Harry is aware of her own contradictions, narrated as the division between her private (artistic) and public (domestic) selves: "inside her she was divided, the homely familiar world behaving in a normal way on one side, and on the other a prospect of madness" (26). In this we have a very clear depiction of the polarities of female entrapment: on the one hand, as 'Harry' she is "the Angel in the House,"[52] a domestic image of women idealized through patriarchy, "seen as a passive, docile and above all *selfless* creature.[53] She also is a paradigmatic author who dares to transgress received norms of artistic creativity because she "has a story to tell,"[54] in which duplicitous art lies the monster of patriarchy and female fear of madness. It is significant that Harry conducts her writing "under the roof," (in the attic) of Carnival's Hide, recalling the title of Sandra Gilbert and Susan Gubar's famous critical work, *The Madwoman in the Attic*. Harry believes herself to have been liberated through her writing, but, in fact, at this stage of its development, she is paradoxically circumscribed by the male-inspired images she uses. As another form of female entrapment she writes in the words and images already available to her: "the already said" of literature. Her attempts at self-definition are, as Gilbert and Gubar have pointed out, complicated "by all those patriarchal definitions that intervene between herself and herself."[55]

The feminine *Fantastic*

From within these ambivalent narrative spaces the Tricksters emerge as characters of uncertain origins: a trinity of personas who might be the material manifestation of Harry's fiction, or alternatively, an incarnation of the ghost of Teddy Carnival or, indeed, both of these possibilities. The Tricksters' origins and identities are never fully resolved, and are potentially plural when viewed either through the focalization of Harry, or judged through the filtering perceptions of the narrative voice, or through the actions and reactions of all the characters who are not Harry.

The Tricksters are "hypodiegetic" characters created by the storytelling character, which disturb ontological hierarchies.[56] In a truly fantastic mode the Tricksters exist between two worlds and *hesitate* in the gap between two explanations. In these ways the narrative again keeps open a plural reading, splitting the reading subject between two points of uncertainty and suspending their ontological status in the kind of ambivalence that Todorov described as fantastic.[57] In their potential to disrupt the unities, logic and meanings of common discourse they bear the characteristic of *the feminine*.

Either as real or supernatural figures, the Tricksters are unquestionably carnate as trickster heroes for the duration of this narrative, and are manifestly real to all who lay eyes on them, masquerading both as magicians with superhuman powers, and as seductive, corporeal, and erotic lovers. Together, Ovid, Hadfield, and Felix (arbitrarily self-named in their fictional roles from fragments of fictions on the Hamilton's bookcase) are the mythical figures of three-in-oneness such as we see contained in the mythologies of the Godhead, or in Robert Graves's conception of the White Goddess,[58] manifesting their individual natures while uniting as opposites in an intense melee, " 'jostling each other for a place in the sun' " (194). Individually, they present themselves as the manifestation of three rival, erogenic potentialities: head, heart, and instinct (224). In keeping with the fantastic definition, the Tricksters are figures of ambivalence: they may be a reincarnation of the dead Teddy Carnival, or they may be projections of Harry's own story. Ovid can be seen as the projection of her Prince Valery, and the "entantiomorphs" Felix and Hadfield are, "exactly like (her) marvelous winged man Belen" (73). Regardless, they conduct themselves in an unrelenting struggle for supremacy of one part over the other, worked out in physical abuse, and in emotional and psychological blackmail. There are discourses on their origins as triplets from the same maternal egg (70, 85). Meanwhile, the twins Felix and Hadfield are seen as manifestations of the split, apparently schizoid, nature of Teddy Carnival's personality, suggested by his being "amusing in a malicious way," and given to "moods of violence" (35). As potential manifestations of the ghost of Teddy Carnival, the Tricksters are time-travelers in Brian McHale's sense of a "transhistorical identity," in which characters, apparently from disparate historical eras, are brought together at a single locus and implicated in the theme of illusion and reality in an obviously Bakhtinian carnivalesque motif.[59] They are self-consciously fictional characters constituted in language, constructing an identity and a history for themselves through the language of storytelling and through a game of wordplay, double meanings, and irony: " 'Well, we're traveling brothers. . . . And we're wandering along on one of those fantastic quests, hoping to save the world from the powers of darkness.' " " 'Checking up on family history as we go.' " " 'To find our beginnings,' " " 'And endings. Either will do' " (62-3). They are " 'Carnivals . . . relatively speaking' " (56). " 'Carne levare' (that's "a leaving off of meat").' " " 'Carne vale' — 'Carnival.' " " 'The only real men in a world of spirits, but that's human nature' " (65, 6).

The feminine *Carnivalesque*

All of these self-references and verbal conjuring tricks that provoke ambivalent laughter are symptomatic of the carnivalesque and are examples of the way in which the Tricksters play on their status as carnivalesque, ephemeral beings. They also hint at their origins in another time/space dimension reminiscent of the grave: " 'We come from a lonely place' " (66–7, 9), they announce as Harry simultaneously identifies the "shocking scar" along Ovid's hairline and likens it to a "hieroglyph of death" (67).

The principle of the carnival is that it is an interruption to, and a suspension of, everyday life and that it is founded in bodily excess and feasting. It is another indicator of the narrative's inscription in a language of corporeality:

> Carnival in its widest, most general sense embraced ritual spectacles, such as fairs, popular feasts and wakes, processions and competition, comic shows, mummery and dancing, open-air amusement with costumes and masks; it included comic verbal compositions (such as parodies, travesties and vulgar farce).[60]

The Tricksters are Carnivals with a carnivalesque mission in the iconoclastic, Bakhtinian sense,[61] to transgress boundaries and to disrupt prevailing truths of the Carnival/Hamilton family. It is in this sense that they connect with Harry's experience of Teddy Carnival's watery, grotesque body, and become the unwitting agents of Harry's transformations in *the feminine* by opening up the spaces of her liberation. The idea of Carnival shares many of the subversive characteristics of *the feminine* function in language: "Carnival," Bakhtin tells us,

> Celebrated temporary liberation from the prevailing truth and from the established order . . . Carnival was the true feast of time, the feast of becoming, change, and renewal. It was hostile to all that was immortalized and completed.[62]

Bakhtin also points out the importance of the relations of carnival feasting to time, both cosmic and biological time, and to moments of crisis:

> The feast is always essentially related to time, either to the recurrence of an event in the natural (cosmic) cycle, or to biological or historic timeliness. Moreover, through all the stages of historic development feasts were linked to moments of crisis, of breaking points in the cycle of nature or in the life of society and man.[63]

Thus, the Tricksters converge on the Hamilton household at a time of feasting, festivity and corpulent excess, at a time combining the New Zealand coincidences of the festivals of Midsummer, Christmas, and New Year, by which the three Parts of the novel are named, and bringing together occasions of vacation based on ancient fertility festivals that were the excuse for carnival.[64]

The Tricksters are themselves a parody of carnivalesque motifs, exploiting opportunities for open-air feasting and celebration that culminate on the beach and around the water's edge at the time when the Hamilton family is displaced in a place they discover this Christmastime that they can no longer regard as the homely place they had once thought it to be.

Carnival's Hide harbors secrets much darker and much more treacherous than the Carnival family could ever have imagined, not insignificantly among which is another example of bodily function that is revealed in the truth about Jack's paternity of the youngest of the family's line, Tibby, now laid bare in the revelations precipitated by the presence of these timeless visitors seemingly from nowhere. Thus, the place of "*das heimliche*" which, in the Freudian definition means in one sense, "homely," "agreeable," "familiar," "cheerful," and "comfortable" but, in another sense, and without being contradictory, means also, "what is concealed and kept out of sight,"[65] becomes literally *das unheimliche*, of the Freudian definition, meaning "strange," "threatening," "frightening," and "uncanny," when the terrible Carnival secrets of murder, and an act approximating incest, are exposed. This is the realm of the uncanny which Freud tells us is "that class of the frightening which leads back to what is known of old and long familiar," and which Cixous described as: "a relational signifier. . . . For the uncanny is in effect *composite*, it infiltrates itself in between things, in the interstices, it asserts *a gap* where one was likely to be assured of unity."[66]

The Incest Taboo

The Tricksters' mission, as tricksters in the mode of *the feminine* fantastic, is to unseat and destabilize established truths; to prise open a gap between signifieds and signifiers in a concerted effort to destabilize, once stable (comfortable?) meanings. In so doing they expose two ancient and repressed familial memories: first the repressed secret of "what was known of old," and has lain hidden for generations in the crumbling walls of Carnival's Hide: that Teddy Carnival was killed, not accidentally drowned. Second, they expose a more recently repressed memory of an age-old transgression which is the law prohibiting incest, broken by Jack's fathering Emma's child. The narrative tells us that Emma had "adopted" and been "adopted by" the Hamilton family (37, 9). So, by fathering Emma's child, Jack has transgressed the primal taboo inscribed by the Symbolic function of the Law in the Name-of-The-Father:

> 'The Law of the Father,' as Lacan sees it, is the threshold between the 'Kingdom of culture' and 'that of nature abandoned to the law of copulation.' It is not a function of Real biological blood relations, but of systems of nomenclature or kinship systems. One is forbidden sexual access to those who one *has named* as family. The question of paternity is in fact a matter of *naming* of the Father's Name not his blood.[67]

In *Écrits* Lacan, says of the incest taboo:

> The primordial law is therefore that which in regulating marriage ties superimposes
> the kingdom of culture on that of nature abandoned to the law of mating. The prohi-
> bition of incest is merely a subjective pivot. This law is revealed clearly enough as
> identical to an order of language. For without kinship nominations there is no power
> capable of instituting the order of preferences and taboos.[68]

And Anika Lemaire commenting on the work of Lacan says:

> The prohibition of incest superimposes the realm of culture, whatever its local
> forms may be, upon that of nature by means of sexual restrictions and by the cre-
> ation of links of solidarity.[69]

Jack has transgressed the Law of the Father which is the pillar of language in the
Symbolic. But, more than this, there is an ironic connection between the killing of
Teddy Carnival and the conception of Tibby in a literal play on the word "carnival" that is both the "leaving off" of flesh (Teddy's death), and its obverse, the
"taking on" of flesh (Tibby's birth).

In the scene in which the secret of Harry's secret writing is laid bare in the
presence of the entire family, where her book is read aloud to the tune of Christobel's withering contempt and the mocking laughter of the assembled Carnivals,
we have another ironic association through laughter, this time between Jack's
incest and Harry's writing. Laughter is a carnivalesque motif associated with the
"material bodily principle" which is why it is so intrinsically important to the idea
of the corporeality of language in *the feminine* and the recovery of a *feminine*
Imaginary and is described by Bakhtin as the unveiling of the womb. Ruth Ginsburg discusses the relations between the "material bodily principle" and the
womb, not as entrance and exit, as viewed by Freud and Bakhtin, but as an internal space:

> Indeed, both Freud and Bakhtin jointly cover their ambiguous longing to be swal-
> lowed by the womb once again. This is expressed in the joke of home-sickness by
> Freud, and in the joke of medieval laughter for Bakhtin. But jokes for Freud and
> laughter of Bakhtin are those serious phenomena that reveal the undercurrents of
> human life. They make possible the verbal expression of incest.[70]

Harry has "mothered" her creation which is her own writing in much the same
way that Jack has fathered Tibby:

> Having brought them to half-life, she [Harry] now says they were crippled creatures
> and wished to abandon them like a heartless mother. . . . Her father had said the

ability to reproduce was terrible, and in a small way it was a writer's gift as well as a father's (134).

The convergences of "mothering," "fathering," and allusions to the womb and incest, incorporate multiple images of the body and embody the three points of the Oedipal triangle: mother, father, and offspring. They have further ramifications for the relationships between Jack and Christobel, and for Naomi's role as mother in relation to them both that is pursued further in chapter 3.

The Gaze

Clothes, dressing, dressing-up, and masquerade are intrinsic to the carnival; clothing the body, such as we see being brought to fruition in the "fancy dress" Christmas Eve beach party, is intimately connected with *the feminine* in terms of the masquerade: changed identity, changed self-image, becoming beautiful, and all manner of transformation. These associations are implied by the title of the book from which Ovid takes his name: Ovid's *Metamorphoses,*[71] are yet another manifestation of *The Tricksters*'s texture of textuality.

Emma is made beautiful, is "transformed," like Cinderella, for the Taverner's Midsummer party by being dressed in Christobel's clothes and thus becomes a quasi-literal daughter to Jack. " 'I know clothes don't matter, but I always used to enjoy dressing up' " (117). She has allowed herself to become the family's dressing-up doll, their spectacle to stand back and admire. In this dressing-up she prefigures Christobel's being adorned as the object of Ovid Carnival's gaze when later he makes her into the "mineral girl." More significantly, by dressing up in Christobel's clothes Emma metaphorically *becomes* Christobel: the father's desired daughter (his object of desire) with whom he seeks to father a child, and who is himself desired *by* the daughter:

> 'I'll tell you what,' she [Christobel] said. 'I don't care how reasonable Ma makes it sound, I utterly hate the idea that Emma knows something about Jack that we don't. She knows him as a man, and I only know him as a father.' (258)

Harry too feels she can become Christobel, become "transformed," when she steals Christobel's red silk dressing gown and projects her as an *ego ideal*, a symbolic representation of her psychic transformation in *the feminine*. "She could become Christobel for a little while. She could try out what it might be like to be beautiful (119)."

However: "Beauty was not enough for Christobel, she wanted to be noticed in every way" (35). Cristobel's entire existence is a dramatic spectacle of herself as man's specular image; and while Harry is overlooked, she thrives on being looked at, by being admired, and on being desired by men. As the great-great granddaughter of Minerva Carnival, she represents the figure of Minerva in the classical Greek manifestation as the goddess Athena, whom Irigaray has identified as the mode of representation of ourselves for man's desire. Athena epitomizes the image of woman formed in man's image, described by Irigaray as:

> Adorned femininity—manifestation of the father's idea of feminine power. Appropriating the mother's power, swallowing it up, introjecting it, . . . a simulacrum assumed by the God to help him in his work, to establish his empire. An empire of pretence . . . Preferring young men, but shunning marriage, her father's virgin. The inspiration and guardian of institutions. It should not be doubted that she is virile, if she drops her tunic. Armed: femininity. Playing with all the disguises. Childish, if necessary, without having known childhood; fraternal, the better to betray confidence; simulating friendship for women and leading them to retire willingly into cellars.[72]

" 'Make me completely amazing' " (190), Christobel implores Ovid when he transforms her into the veiled and alluring object and ultimate manifestation of his male fantasy, as the "mineral girl," making her the "marionette of his dreams," "a toy of precious but lifeless treasure," his "puppet" (191). Caught up in the gaze of Ovid Carnival, and in the spirit of Teddy Carnival who used people as his play things, Harry observes that Christobel has metamorphosed " 'into a sort of doll,' " with whom Ovid is playing (195). Thus Harry can speculate with some justification, and with ramifications at many narrative levels, about whether or not there was "really a live sister left at the core of that beautiful puppet" (191). By his artistry Ovid has transformed Christobel into the image of Teddy Carnival's (his own!) sister, Minerva. Like the veiled goddess, Minerva, she is the fetishized object who symbolizes the image of the woman as man's creature, generated by man, and whose blinding female powers and inspiration are the threat to patriarchal dominance that is metaphorically harnessed behind the veil.

Gilbert and Gubar have discussed the veiled Minerva as one example among many of the long and complex history of literary paternity and as part of the patriarchal mythology that has defined woman as: "By, from, and for, men. . . . Whether she is beautiful or hideous, the veiled woman reflects male dread of women."[73] The narrative is a mirror-maze of glances, with multiple viewpoints, and with references to mirrors, eyes, seeing and being unable to see, reflections, watching and being watched, looking and being looked at. By allowing herself to be re-made as the object of Ovid's fantasy Christobel has been de-sexed and immobilized in his gaze, dramatizing the split between herself as subject and herself as object. In his essay, "The 'Uncanny' "[74] Freud theorized the male gaze as:

> A phallic activity linked to the male desire for sadistic mastery of the object, enacting the voyeur's desire for sadistic power in which the object of the gaze is cast as its passive, masochistic, feminine victim.[75]

" 'Everyone will be able to swim but you' " (191), Ovid tells Christobel in the pronouncement that reveals her desiccated, subjugated status and his complete mastery over her by denying her the freedom of the water. As Harry's projected *ego ideal*, the mannequined Christobel symbolizes Harry's arid status as writer for which water is to be the elemental agent of her liberation into *l'écriture féminine*.

The feminine *Intertextual Space*

This novel is rich with intertextual references, which are another form of foregrounding of its intrinsic concerns with textuality, and its position in what Roland Barthes has described as "the network of codes," in which the reading subject is intersubjectively implicated. The promiscuously allusive quality of the narrative which denies the reading subject a straightforwardly linear experience of narrative engagement is another marker of *the feminine* because as a narrative it invites the type of paradoxical centripetal and centrifugal readerly engagement that is typical of the nonlinear experience of *the feminine* textuality. The narrative also recalls the allusive qualities of contemporary women's writing from, for example, Angela Carter and Margaret Atwood.

The range of intertextual references is promiscuous: classical, biblical, and literary, rather than cryptically structured upon a mythical prototype, they are significant because each carries implications for Harry's transformation into *the feminine*. There are, for example, many references to water and drowning structured round the death of Teddy Carnival and, according to Irigaray, water is the most "amniotic" of elements, the most primordial, therefore, the most closely related to *the feminine*:

> The marine element is therefore both the amniotic fluids, the deepest marine element which can't simply be an appearance . . . and it is also, it seems to me, something which represents feminine jouissance quite well, including in a movement of the sea, of going and returning of continuous flux which seems to me to be quite close to my jouissance as a woman, and completely foreign to what an economy of erection and detumescence represents. My movement let us say of feminine jouissance is more maritime than scaling or descending a mountain.[76]

Thus, Harry imagines herself as both desirable and terrible in death as "a mermaid or a beautiful drowned girl whom people would find washed up in the morning" (46), evoking Ophelia in death and hinting at Harry's death wish in her desire for a state of inorganicism, her desire to get to the space beyond the chain of signifiers of her writing which is hindering her self-realization, her desire to reach her Thanatos: "A place of her own, to go out between the water lilies to a land where no one (except possibly Felix Carnival) could follow her" (179). Belen as a winged man, and references to the aspirant Taverners as winged (115), recalls the

myth of Icarus, a winged boy who fell from the sky and was drowned; Teddy Carnival is himself compared explicitly to *Lycidas*, Milton's poem about a drowned
man whose poetic subject was also an Edward. Harry's mock-marriage to the sea:
"There, I've married the sea. I'm Mrs. Oceanus" (24), invokes the mythical
Oceanus, brother of Kronos who devoured his own children. Christobel's mocking comment: " 'And here's old Harry home from the Sea,' " recalls Stevenson's
"A Song of the Road": "This is the verse you grave for me: / 'Here he lies where
he longed to be; / Home is the sailor, home from the sea.' "[77] Yet another invocation of Harry's death-wish is her unconscious desire: she is often to be seen lying
on her back under the starry sky at the water's edge, or on the water, gazing at the
constellation Orion (46, 89, 97, 242). Water is Harry's element; it is where she
encounters the numinous in her meeting with Teddy Carnival. She marries the sea
in the mock ceremony using a shell ring; it is the sea that feels more sensuous,
and makes her feel even more beautiful than when she was wearing Christobel's
red silk dressing gown (263). When Felix Carnival—who is Teddy Carnival's
aspect of love—becomes transfigured in the moment of recognizing their mutual
love (151), it begins to rain: "Then the sky opened and the rain poured straight
down" (151). As Grosz has said of Harry's mythical namesake, Ariadne,

> She speaks from the watery, fluid realm of the oceans, confronting Nietzsche's land-
> scape of earthly heights and planes. She speaks as the multiple and fluid, a fluidity
> Irigaray has already posed as feminine in "The 'Mechanics' of Fluids."[78]

There are also allusions to *The Tempest*, with Harry implicitly acting like a
Miranda, whose latinate name means "wonder": "she wanted to draw wonder up
out of herself" (188), wondering at the beauty of the washed-up men, the Bringers
From The Sea of family secrets, and encountering one-believed-drowned-but-
reincarnated, like Ferdinand, the spirit of Teddy/(Ariel) imprisoned by a wicked
parent. Hints of the Odysseus legend also permeate, "Ovid looked like a spirit of
the bloody sea" (101). In *The Odyssey*, men come out of the sea as Odysseus did
to many women, including Nausicaa, for whom he was, as the Tricksters are on
one occasion, naked (100). In *The Odyssey* the sea is *"oinops"*—often translated
as "wine dark," (bloody); and in her fictional description of Jessica, Harry writes
that " '*Her hair fell over her naked shoulders like black wine*' " (218).

   The midsummer setting, which evokes fertility rites associated with the carnivalesque, also signifies Harry's bodily transformation from maiden to woman in
her first sexual encounter with Felix, and evokes images of Dionysian feasting
and festivity. It also evokes the midsummer madness of Strindberg's *Miss Julie*,
where inappropriate couplings and copulations are attributed to the intoxications
of midsummer's eve. More specifically it relates to *A Midsummer Night's Dream*
with explicit reference to transforming love-juice, " 'Everyone will get flower
juice squeezed into their eyes and fall in love with the first person they see' "

(117). Thus, there is a subplot of exchanged lovers and a changeling child, as well as puckish conjuring tricks with Ovid/Oberon as a master of magic ceremonies; furthermore, Robert exchanges Christobel for Emma and then behaves like the rejected, melancholic, lover (114); and, finally, Harry is seduced by, and falls in love with, Felix on midsummer's eve when her vision is myopic because Felix insists on removing her glasses.

The novel also abounds in embedded, unattributed quotations; for example, a fragment of Cornelia's song from Webster's *The White Devil* when Christobel taunts Anthony that he is " 'trying to find a forest at the end of the world where robins will cover him over with leaves' " (36).[79] This latter connects with Felix imaged as a wolf (87) who—as the Tricksters do to Teddy Carnival—dig up the "unburied bodies" of "friendless men." " 'I'm alongside the wolves maybe,' " Felix tells Harry, " 'But bleating not howling' " (88), evoking yet another reference to drowning in the lines from Stevie Smith's poem "Not Waving but Drowning."

Other unattributed sources, for example the seemingly random shower of quotations spontaneously springing from Harry's thoughts on waking (51), are both oceanic and epiphanic, adumbrating the changes taking place in Harry, and the monumental changes in the Carnival family history precipitated by the arrival of the three Tricksters: "Dull would he be of soul who could pass by," from "Lines Composed upon Westminster Bridge,"[80] is Wordsworth's epiphany of the urban new transformed into innocence; "no longer at peace under the old dispensation" from Eliot's "The Journey of the Magi," marks the coming of the new dispensation in the Christmas transition from the Old to the New Testament. The three Tricksters, who come at Christmas and know the baby's secret paternity, and signal the end to the old Carnival family dispensation, are likened to the Magi: " 'There go the three wise men' " (94), and " 'He came bearing gifts,' Naomi said. 'Gold, frankincense and myrrh,' finished Christobel" (105). (Elsewhere Anthony is likened by Naomi to the Messiah, " '*You're* the one whom we heard was coming' " [208].) "The Sea! the Sea!" comes from Xenophon's "Anabasis"[81] marking the rejoicing of his returning mercenary Greek army after years of fighting in land-locked Central Asia; the sight of sea marked not only their homecoming but also the restorative property the sea held for their identity and existence. Other quotations from Lewis Carroll's "Jabberwocky," and Edward Lear's "A Book of Nonsense," are matched by the wit and wordplay issuing from the lips of the Tricksters.

Most obviously there are parallels to the mythical women Ariadne and Minerva; all of these mythical references being united in the character and in the name of Ovid and his *Metamorphoses*: Minerva Carnival, whose mother died in bearing her and, therefore, is herself ostensibly motherless, is explicitly named as the Goddess of Wisdom (204), and she parallels the Greek Minerva (Athena/Pallas) the motherless Goddess of Wisdom, plucked fully grown from the head of her father Jupiter; her totemic owl is a pervasive image throughout *The Tricksters* (15, 139, 189, 193); Ariadne/Harry, daughter of King Minos/Jack (with a guilty secret about the paternity of the minotaur), who falls in love with first Theseus/Felix, and is married by Bacchus on the island of Naxos.[82] The Christmastime revels among surrounding hills at the water's edge and in the summer breeze, to the music, not of the Bacchic trumpet, but of the flute played by Hamish Price's young wife, captures the spirit of Bacchus and invokes Keats's "The Song of the Indian Maid," of the arrival of Bacchus to the place where, like Harry, the "enamored bride Cheated by shadowy wooer from the clouds," sits weeping her tears into "water-lily cups."[83]

The Elemental **féminine**

These numerous watery references are commonplace in that body of children's literature which resides in *the feminine*. Irigaray has dedicated a trio of works[84] to the exploration of an alternative subjectivity that takes account of women's corporeal specificity in the primal elements of water, earth, air, and fire and to different, nonhierarchical modes of existence between the two sexes. She has turned to medieval alchemy[85] and the transmutation of elemental substances into the primal ingredients of subjectivity, the harmonious intermingling, or discordant repulsion of which, according to the laws of Empedocles' pre-Socratic philosophy, are an infinite process, determining either Love or Strife.[86] She says:

> I wanted to go back to this natural material which makes up our bodies, in which our lives and environment are grounded: the flesh of our passions. . . . The passions are to do with fire and ice, light and night, water and submersion, earth and the discovery or loss of ground.[87]

"The 'elsewhere' of feminine pleasure," Irigaray writes, "can be found only at the price of crossing back through the mirror that subtends all speculation."[88] And, like Alice, who went through the mirror to find a looking glass logic in words that did not function in the dichotomous structures of binary oppositional terms, Harry, and the reading subject of the narrative, finds her "elsewhere" of Irigaray's thesis of *the feminine* in the space behind the formal properties of her writing. It is an alternative subjectivity that frees her elemental self in the speculative mirror of the Imaginary in a conceptual realm that lies beyond the law of the *Logos*:

> At last, Harry thought, at last she had actually squeezed not just a hand but her whole self between the lines of her book and found space for wild and sweeping games, magical acts with no one crowding around her. (202)

The Tricksters have acted in this respect as agents of the plot. Just as they have used Harry as a vehicle for *their* existence (224), she has used them as *her* vehicle for an alternative subjectivity in *the feminine*, realized through her written character, Felix, in a space outside of time. In the combination of elements there are no fixed boundaries. Elizabeth Grosz, speaking on Irigaray's idea of the elemental feminine says, "all bodies, heavenly or celestial, terrestrial and corporeal have permeable relations capable of being reconceived and acted out in different terms."[89] In these terms it is possible for Harry, as a supposedly corporeal being, to fall in love, and to make love, with the textual Felix Carnival as a supposed "spirit" or "ghost" because Felix is her love affair with her own writing, which is, equally, the reading subject's experience of lure and capture in the Transferential relations of reading in *the feminine*.[90] The narrative is rich with marine, celestial, volcanic, and organic imagery and experiences, signifying the elemental meta-morphoses by which Harry's subjectivity becomes alternatively defined: "earth, fire and water had once played turn and turn about" (74); there are significant and minor earthquakes signifying bodily and psychic transformation (143, 264), and a thunder storm: "The rain poured down around them and they stood there a little, poised over the inky sea while the hilltops flicked with lightning" (152); even more explicitly, "She thought she might be pushed into becoming a spirit of fire, incandescent. . . . Her hair quite black except for the single hairs at the edges which caught the light and burned like threads of fire" (172).

When Harry takes to the hills with Felix Carnival for their act of open air lovemaking, it is as if "on the high horizon, a place that was neither earth nor sky would open for them" (202). When she burns her book it is a moment of narrative realization in which she recognizes that the "black bars of writing" have been only the *vehicle* for her metamorphosed subjectivity and are now redundant, and as she does so it is against a background of apocalyptic images of the elemental particles that have now become transmuted into her own being:

> No stars, no moon, low clouds, only the wind occasionally lifting its voice around the house, but almost indistinguishable from the sound of the sea. . . . drifting down the path, her abused book clasped to her once more, she came face to face as always with the sea and also with the rekindled fire. . . . The thousand separate voices of the sea made one voice, and it was the sound of time itself, lapping at the edge of the land. . . . Suddenly she felt the fire bite her. . . . She lay back on the sand and looked up at the sky . . . she saw Sirius and Canopus. Orion climbed up to lie above her. The easterly wind lifted the ash beside her and tumbled it off into the night. . . . They became part of the sand and the sea and air. (242–4)

In and through these senses, and by the fact of her having made love with her char-acter, Felix Carnival, Harry has used her writing as a corporeal experience, to con-nect with *the feminine* Imaginary and a subjectivity that is mutable, plural, and in process of a perpetual becoming. It is a process like the combinatory particles and atoms that constitute the primary elements of which she is a part, and are part of her, and mirror the experience of the literary subject reading in *the feminine*.

l'écriture féminine

The plot of *The Tricksters* is paradoxically open-ended and circular. In these respects it is a narrative of *the feminine* for its manifestations of illogicality and circularity, especially so when its final chapter is a beginning, titled: "Once upon a Time" (249). By the end of the story Harry realizes the Christmas wish she has voiced at the beginning of the story: to have a book which turns into herself, by which process she becomes the textualised subject of her own narrative. When Christobel gives her a new book of blank pages in which Harry begins to write her new story, the transmutation of *the feminine* in herself and *in* her writing is now laid bare. Instead of the "black bars of writing" which characterized her unreconstituted subjectivity in the Symbolic economy of her earlier writing, her pen has now given way to a fluidity, and simultaneous discontinuity, suggesting Irigaray's idea of the elemental feminine and Cixous's description of *l'écriture féminine* as an "endless circulation. . . . It is always endless, without ending: there's no closure, it doesn't stop."[91] In *the feminine* mode Harry's writing is now described for its qualities of:

> Looping lines . . . a world line like the one left behind by the tide. . . . words were uncertain, but their uncertainty was what made them magical. . . . Once the words were written she had plenty to think about, for they might lead in any direction. (266)

Harry has connected with the elemental feminine in herself and to her relation with "nature, matter, the body, language and desire."[92] Thus, through her physical encounters with her writing, she has connected with *the feminine* Imaginary, in the sense of Irigaray's redefinition through the body in *le parler femme*, and Cixous's invocation for the erotics of writing to derive from the body in her idea of a "feminine textual body"[93] in the *l'écriture féminine*:

> Write your self. Your body must be heard. Only then will the immense resources of the unconscious spring forth . . . To write. An act which will not only "realise" the decensored relation of woman to her sexuality, to her womanly being, giving her access to her native strength; it will give her back her goods, her pleasures, her organs, her immense bodily territories which have been kept under seal.[94]

In *l'écriture féminine*, the writer "brings back to light the life that's been buried."[95]

> Writing is the passageway, the entrance, the exit, the dwelling place of the other in me—the other that I am and am not, that I don't know how to be, but that I feel passing, that makes me live—that tears me apart, disturbs me, changes me, who?[96]

Thus it is that Harry rewrites her subjectivity, and what appears to be an ending is in fact a beginning, and the marker of *the feminine* subject in process, in the perpetual process of becoming that the *the feminine* requires as a condition of literary subjectivity in, and of, the narrative.

The next section focuses on *The Other Side of Silence* in which *the feminine* Imaginary is achieved through a process of fictional autobiography and in the refusal of speech and the Law.

THE OTHER SIDE OF SILENCE

Just as Harry Hamilton lives her "true" life in her own writing, Hero, as the principal subject of Mahy's *The Other Side of Silence*, lives a divided life between her "real life" of family relations in her family house in Edwin Street, and her "true life" in the fantasy world she creates for herself in the house of the mysterious Miss Credence in Credence Crescent. The novel is structured in alternating chapters headed "True Life" and "Real Life" that signal Hero's movements between these two houses, and are the metaphorical markers of her psychic territories; in her movement between them Hero effects a dramatization of her alienated condition as subject. She moves between, on the one hand, the *moi* and the *je* of her social self in her family life with the Rappers where she is inscribed as Other in the Symbolic, masculinist economy of language and, on the other, an Imaginary silence achieved by refusing speech and rejecting the subjectivity that language in the Symbolic would impose upon her, played out behind the walls of "Old Squintum's" (Miss Credence's) garden. " 'Real,' " Hero says, " 'is what everyone agrees about. True is what you somehow know inside yourself' " (27). In her life with the Rapper family, she has elected to be silent. Annie, her mother, is a new-woman academic who specializes in children's language development. Her father Mike is the new-man househusband who cares for and nurtures the family. Three other siblings represent the spectrum of academic aspiration and failure, and each one of them is embroiled in and identified through their capacity to manipulate language: Genevra, the brilliant, child-prodigy dropout older sister now earns her living as a dragster, crashing cars; the older brother, Athol, is permanently studying for the MA that will keep him at home, well-fed, and dependent on his parent's support, and younger sister Sapphira (known as Sap) speaks in the language and rhythms of poetry and aspires to be a writer.

As with *The Tricksters*, this narrative features an ambiguously gendered female whose name also symbolically embodies both female and male attributes as in the female "(Her)o," and the use of the male "o" signifier in "Her(o);" and, like *The Tricksters*, it has a metafictional textuality that narrates the same ephemeral distinctions between everyday life and the fictive nature of fiction. In *The Other Side of Silence*, however, the diegetic level has shifted one step closer to the reading subject because it is presented as a quasi-autobiographical account, narrated in the first person by Hero as the principal voice and focalizer, and as the speaking subject "I" (and hero in her own story), telling the story of a younger version of herself: "Back then when I was twelve" (3).[97] She "writes" herself as the fragmented textual ego and through this quintessential act of writing she ultimately recovers an alternative voice and subjectivity which speaks and moves in a language recouped from the other side of the silence that is Hero's own. The entire narrative is in this sense a Transference statement where the subject, who is Hero, talks-out her "cure"[98] through the agency of her biographical writing to her intimately situated, and attentive, reader/analyst as the "subject-presumed-to-know." In this model of readership as Transference,[99] the reader-cum-analyst in turn feeds back to the narrative (her) responses by way of interpretation in a reciprocal process of Transference and counter-Transference. In this interpretative mode, the events narrated by Hero as "True Life" are a manifestation of her Imaginary projections, and become the psychic space where she confronts her alienated self as double through encountering the grotesque body of Rinda Credence.

Hero continuously refers to the fictional status of her own biographical account (which is, as in *The Tricksters*, the book the reading subject is now reading) referring to it as, "my own story" (138). She perceives herself as a text that is being written and that is not yet completed; she is to be read as a text by herself and by others, and in her allusions to fictionality we have a double textualization: first, of Hero as a character in her own story; and, second, as a textualized self *through* her own story. For example: "I was always trying to match my own life with one story or another" (121); "I must push the story on, and then I really could close the book and leave it behind me. I must solve the mystery" (138); "I still felt I was in a story, but it was my story once more. I didn't have to sit there waiting to be rescued. I could alter the end" (154); " 'Run home! Run home now! Real life, not true!' But it just wasn't possible. Once begun the story had to be fulfilled" (140). She speculates about the many other fictional lives she could have had if she had been a different kind of book which are significantly grounded in fantasy and language: "Supposing *I had been* turned into a book back then, I would have wanted to turn into *The Jungle Book*, the story of Mowgli, a boy who lived in the jungle and talked the language of the animals. Or I might just have made do with *The Secret Garden*. But I would probably have turned into *Old Fairy Tales*, which is the book everyone read to me when I was small" (8).

The first person narration exemplifies how these types of quasi-autobiographical fictional narratives that occur regularly in children's fiction, and are, typically, and historically, the woman's mode, are a meeting point for textual egos, the place where the "I" who speaks encounters the "I" who is spoken.[100] Here, the reading subject is effectively positioned in the focalization of Hero, with no other objective or objectifying view of events than those that are filtered through her narration. The reading subject is therefore, knowingly positioned in the story and apprehended as a fiction. In addition, Hero's narration destabilizes any readerly aspiration to believe the authenticity of her story when she suggests that her "true life" was partly invented (3); and, that "Squintum might have been a man or a woman, the house might have been real or imaginary" (22). Hero is therefore discursively inscribed as a potentially unreliable narrator in Ellie Ragland-Sullivan's sense that "We are always unreliable, when—as an 'I'—we try consciously to explain or narrate our 'True' selves."[101] The reading subject is, thus, ambivalently situated between the events that are narrated as "True Life," and events narrated as "Real Life"; between, in other words, the conscious and unconscious contents of the narrating subject that is the terrain across which questions of the *the feminine* literary subjectivity are raised and where it is constituted in the dynamic of literary exchange.

Language, Madness, and **The feminine**

In a family that operates on, and defines its successes by, the skillful manipulation of words, a family that, as Hero explains, lets "words flow away like wasting water," silence "is an alternative authority" for Hero (164). Gilbert and Gubar pointed out how in history women have rebelled against the silence imposed on them by patriarchy.[102] But, in a neat, ironic act of inversion, *The Other Side of Silence* presents Hero's elected silence as a perverse kind of power and control, a verbal anorexia with which she mutilates not her body but her speech in an act of personal rebellion.[103] In this metaphorical anorexia, Hero as author of her own biography parallels Gilbert and Gubar's description of the woman writer whom they describe as "anorexic":

> resolutely closing her mouth on silence (since—in the words of Jane Austen's Henry Tilney—'a woman's only power is the power of refusal') even while she complains of starvation.[104]

Hero's unconscious rage against a world of words is to have no words, and as the silent subject, she makes herself present through a different set of signifying practices. The "madwoman" of Gilbert and Gubar's thesis is the creative female artist who, they say, has been numerously represented in myths and fairy tales as silent or silenced:

> The male child's progress toward adulthood is a growth toward both self-assertion and self-articulation: "The Juniper Tree" implies a development of the powers of speech. But the girl child must learn the arts of silence either as herself as a silent image invented and defined by the magic looking glass of the male-authored text, or as a silent dancer of her own woes, a dancer who enacts rather than articulates. From the abused Procne to the reclusive Lady of Shallot, therefore, women have been told that their art, like the witch's dance in "Little Snow White," is an art of silence.[105]

It is significant for these issues of female language and silence in fairy tales that Hero imagined herself, in another kind of story of her life, as a character in her childhood storybook, *Old Fairy Tales*. The moment when Hero begins the process of her "cure" through which she reconnects with her own lost childhood, is dramatized in her own narrative when she comes face to face with Rinda Credence in the tower room of Credence House as her mute, antithetical double, her Other, "waiting for me like a terrible kind of twin" (141). As Hero's second self, Rinda Credence is indeed in Cixous's words, "The hysteric, whose body is transformed into a theatre of forgotten scenes, relives the past, bearing witness to a lost childhood that survives in suffering."[106] In these moments she suffers a traumatic sense of disorientation when, first, her "true life," instead of being her freedom, becomes her prison: "I was locked in what I had once thought of as true life" (143), and, next, becomes indiscriminately merged in the "Real/True" by which the chapters are subsequently named. In this moment of her "cure," Hero begins to speak aloud in a newfound tongue and is forced to construct a rationale for her own silence as being a form of madness:

> Deep down I had always known that Miss Credence was mad. But then, what about me, for that matter? What sort of person stops talking. Real people all talk. Perhaps the silence that had made a special person of me in my talking, arguing family really showed that I was a little mad, as well (148).

Hero's idea that a willingness to talk defines "real" people, and that a failure to do so is an indicator of madness, is symptomatic of a cultural logic subscribing to psychoanalytic models in which the signifier, (the name, the pronoun)[107] grants the subject full access to subjectivity via the Symbolic Order. Michel Foucault has claimed that madness is, primarily, a lack of language, an:

> Absence of production, the silence of a stifled, repressed language that is civilization's gesture of exclusion; madness and language are mutually exclusive because madness can only be discussed in the language of reason.[108]

For Derrida the very status of language is its break with madness, the "general condition and constitutive foundation of the very enterprise of speech."[109]

> Sentences are normal by nature. They are impregnated with normality, that is, with meaning. . . . They contain normality and meaning, no matter what the state of health or madness of the utterer may be.[110]

Miss Credence as sorceress and Hero as hysteric are, therefore, juxtaposed as "the abnormal ones,"[111] two women positioned on the margins as outsiders in their respective social circumstances. In their mutual conditions of madness they sit side by side in their individual states of imprisonment. Cixous says that these female roles, the roles of sorceress and hysteric (which, incidentally, are dramatized numerously and variously in children's literature), are both ambiguous and antiestablishment, and exist between symbolic systems, "in the interstices":

> They are the people afflicted with what we call madness, anomaly, perversion and between them [the hysteric and sorceress], provide, somehow, the guarantee that locks the symbolic systems in, taking up the slack that can exist between them, carrying out, in the Imaginary, roles of extras, figures that are impossible at the present time.[112]

In the characters of Hero Rapper and Miss Credence, then, we have the manifestation of the double aspect of language and madness. Silent Hero who ratifies her own identity by choosing not to speak sits in opposition to mad Miss Credence, a woman who defines herself through meaningless utterances and whose subscription to patriarchal language has paradoxically silenced her intellectual genius. Words flow out from her in a non-stop monologue:

> Gabbling—gabbling all the time, retelling an old story. . . . Sliding from comma to comma, full stops occurring only when she needed to take a particularly deep breath. (145–6)

Hero's derisive description of Miss Credence as "gabbling" in this linear stream of words where the movement from "comma" to "comma" is also the sliding from "signifier to signifier" in the chain of words that exemplifies the paradigm of "scientific linearity" in patriarchal language, is precisely the reign of language that *the feminine* seeks to counter in Irigaray's conception of *le parler femme*. It is as if Miss Credence were speaking the book she could have written to make her as famous as her dead father in whose Oedipal grip she is still held prisoner. Because of it, she has been metaphorically silenced in the Symbolic through her father's oppressions, and has passed them on in the line of succession by the literal silencing of her own daughter to whom she has been (and illustratively) physically brutal and abusive in a way that parallels the not-so-visible psychological brutality and abuse imposed on her by her Father's rule and Law:

> I was a clever girl, well, I am, clever, I'm in the top two and a half per cent . . . I could have flown. My father . . . well, of course he was proud of me, but he knew that the world is hard on clever women, and I think, when he pulled me back, that he might have been trying to protect me. (151)

Miss Credence, despite her ability to use many words, has been metaphorically silenced by being conceived of as not so much a real person as "a distraction on the edge of her father's life" (148). She is the double aspect of Annie Rapper and, like her, she is the maimed female embodiment of the destructive effects of the imposition of the Father's Law of language and logic. The ultimate and ironic conclusion to these struggles to achieve subjectivity in *the feminine* is that at the moment when both Rinda Credence and Hero Rapper recover speech, Miss Credence, as the embodiment of the destructive consequences of the Law of the Father, is silenced, forever when, towards the end of the narrative, she attempts unsuccessfully to shoot herself with her father's gun. By committing this last desperate act of self-destruction she fulfils the role into which the witch/sorceress figure in history has been cast, that is, to be "hanged burned, quartered, exorcised,"[113] or in other ways silenced. At the same moment in the narrative, Hero, the "hysteric," returns to the bosom of her family speaking her new-found alternative kind of language which transcends both the power of her silence and the powerfully silencing effects of patriarchal language.

> The tarantella dancer lapses into fatigued acquiescence; the sorceress is hanged—or burned, quartered, exorcised—leaving only 'mythical traces,' and the hysteric 'ends up inuring others to her symptoms', the family closes around her again, whether she is curable or incurable.[114]

Fictional Selves/Self as Fiction

Hero repeatedly contrasts her own life with the life of fictional heroes in fairy tales, while in her own story she unwittingly acts out and alludes to those same fairy tale tropes and archetypal patterns. These examples of doubleness in the narrative structure are reflected in the structuring of narrative subjects as doubles and are symptomatic of those narratives that reside in *the feminine*.

In her movements between home and the Credence Forest, Hero alludes to, for example, such fairy tale characters as Little Red Riding Hood, Bluebeard, and Rapunzel. Through the experiences of these fairytale characters, Hero speaks prophetically about the events and experiences of her own life: "In fairy tales girls and boys leave their homes in mills or castles or hovels and set off into forests where they find wonder. It is dangerous, in there among the trees, but amazing things happen to fairy-tale children"(9); "Miss Credence could ask who was knocking at her door. 'Lift up the latch and walk in' " (123); "In fairy stories the girl who goes into the forbidden chamber will meet a terrible doom" (139); "I wished I had a great braid of hair, thick as a rope, to throw across to him" (157); "She hadn't become a nightingale like Jorinda in the story, and she wasn't any kind of Rapunzel. No rescuing prince could ever have climbed her thin, brown, straggling hair" (142).

As well as comparing herself to fairy tale heroes, Hero also compares the Credence house to a "house in a storybook," with Miss Credence herself as the owner of the forest, always to be seen, from Hero's treetop vantage point, surrounded by birds, and clothed as if in the image of a witch as she sports the trappings of her dead father's clothing, "She always wore a long black cloak, and a black hat, the wide, bent brim hiding her face from anyone looking at her from above" (4). *Old Fairy Tales* is the book of Hero's childhood, the book, she says, she would most probably like to become, containing the Grimm's fairy tale of "Jorinda and Joringel." Miss Credence renames Hero Jorinda, the "bird child" of the Grimm's tale, which both literally and metaphorically evokes Hero's life behind the walls of the Credence garden. It is a story about an old woman ("She was a witch") living alone in her wild forest castle, who captured and turned young girls into nightingales, locking them up in cages in her castle room, where they could not speak but only make birdsong.

The story of "Jorinda and Joringel" also recalls Ovid's myth of Philomel (Procne)[115] who had her tongue cut out by Tereus the Thracian king, and who spoke in an unintelligible bird's voice, "a wild, unquenched, deep-sunken, old-world pain,"[116] and eventually transformed herself into a nightingale. Between them the story of Jorinda and Philomel are feminist icons for the silencing of the female tongue in history; they embody the story of women's exclusion from language, ironically evoked here in Miss Credence's question to Hero:

'Can't you talk?' Miss Credence asked me. . . . 'Not at all?' she persisted. 'Well . . . how sad for you Jorinda, and for your parents, too. No wonder you want to turn into a bird. I always think flight is a kind of language. Not that I fly myself.' (20)

As Patrick Fuery says,

Silence is not the absence of the voice or noise, but the inability to be heard. . . . If, within the definitional paradigm, subjectivity is indicated through the voice, the question then arises as to how the silent subject is indicated. The answer is through a set of signifiers articulated in a system which is not heard within a certain paradigmatic and syntagmatic register.[117]

Fuery describes precisely feminist criticism's definition of the inscription of women in patriarchy as silenced when he says, "through a set of signifiers articulated in a system which is not heard within certain paradigmatic and syntagmatic registers." Bakhtin perceives the status of being heard as a dialogic relation: "This follows from the nature of the word which always wants to be heard."[118] Cixous, in the context of women's exclusion from the Symbolic, and evoking in this context both Hero and Miss Credence, says that:

Silence: silence is the mark of hysteria. The great hysterics have lost speech, they are aphonic, and at times have lost more than speech, they are pushed to the point of choking, nothing gets through. They are decapitated, their tongues are cut off and what talks isn't heard. . . . She (the woman) is given *images* that don't belong to her, and she forces herself, as we've all done, to resemble them.[119]

Hero's silence is the symptom of her rage at her inability to be heard in family relations where the reign and rule of the Father's Law is paradoxically expressed through her mother who is the object of her rage, and this issue of female rage is taken up again and pursued in chapter 3.[120]

The-Name-of-The-Father

Fredric Jameson, citing Lacan, points out that the naming function of language has profound consequences for the subject:

> For the acquisition of a name results in a thorough-going transformation of the position of the subject in his (sic) object world. . . . The pronoun, the first person, the signifier, results in a division of the subject which drives the 'real subject' as it were underground and leaves a 'representative'—the ego—in its place. . . . Thus, the discontinuity insisted on by linguists between the énoncé and the subject of the enunciation corresponds to the coming into being of the Unconscious itself, as that reality of the subject which has been alienated and repressed through the very process by which, in receiving a name, is transformed into a representation of self.[121]

Miss Credence renames Hero "Jorinda, Queen of the Bird People" (17), recalling both the silenced Philomel who turned into a bird and Jorinda, silenced and locked in a tower, and she recites her own distorted version of Jorinda's story while Hero works to restore the dead and overgrown Credence garden to life. Names and naming are unquestionably indicators of identity in this narrative: Miss Credence is named as "Miranda Star Credence" in the birthday book that Hero finds while cleaning out the Credence study. But elsewhere she is known as "Miss Credence," and although leading a double life between her home and her work, she has no identity other than the name she bears as her father's daughter. She bears her identity through her father's name, wearing his hat and cloak, the ironic garb of patriarchy and the source of her own oppression. She has a duplicitous identity that is split between her public and private selves:

> On the other side of the gate, in Benallan, she kept up an appearance which nobody had ever bothered to question, but out in her garden, she turned herself into her father's ghost by wearing his cloak and smoking the same kind of cigarettes that he had smoked. (147)

Hero conceives of herself as nameless during her tree life above Squintum's garden, and this, she reveals to us the reading subject as her intimately positioned analyst, is her way of obliterating the identities imposed on her by naming:

> I had been able to climb and scramble through Squintum's Forest, leaving all names behind me. Being nameless had been a kind of freedom. . . . The name was a leash that could be used to twitch me into place. (23)

Characters are structured as negative reflections of each other: Hero, Jorinda, Rinda, and Ginevra—all bear names that are the different aspects of Hero. Ginevra is presented as Hero's "Ideal-I," and as the prototype "word child" of her mother's creation (" 'Ginevra, my oldest daughter, is definitely our word child' " [69]), while Rinda is the somatic symptom of Hero's psychic repression. Kristeva articulates this split between the Semiotic and Symbolic subject when she says:

> We are confronted with a limit that turns the speaking being into a separate being who utters only by separating—from within the discreteness of the phonemic chain up to and including logical and ideological constructs.[122]

Hero's rejection of speech is the struggle to reclaim her alienated other, which has been repressed by being named in the Father's Law, a gesture to reconnect with her pre-Oedipal, preverbal, *the feminine* Imaginary sacrificed in the primary process of separation from her mother in the necessary transition to the Symbolic that has been rejected, and reified in the horrific image of herself as Rinda Credence.

The feminine *and Abjection*

Fuery points out that voice, "is one of the key discursive practices through which the body is inscribed as a (possible) presence within the desired site of subjectivity."[123] It follows, then, from this, that not only is the body identified as the key vehicle and agent of human subjectivity, but that the absence of voice excludes access to subjectivity through the agency of the body, and this is one way that the idea of *the feminine* is an expression of the language of corporeality. For Kristeva, the body is coded and inscribed in language as the eroticized "clean and proper body" of desire. It follows, therefore, that the absence of voice carries also all the implications of Kristeva's idea of the abject; it is, in Elizabeth Gross's interpretation:

> The space of the body in its pre-oedipal, pre-social organization. . . . It is the expression of a contradictory self-conception, one in which the subject is unable to reconcile its (imaginary, felt, fragmented) experience of itself with it idealized image. Abjection is the subject's revolt against the corporeality of subjectivity.[124]

The abject is everything that the speaking subject of the Symbolic excludes from its definition of self; it requires the disavowal of corporeality in order to attain a status that confers it, in its own terms, stable identity and, therefore, is the necessary condition of language:

> Language acquisition implies the suppression of anality; in other words, it represents the acquisition of a capacity for symbolization through the definitive detachment of the rejected object, through its repression under the sign.[125]

The Abject is the underside of the Symbolic and, therefore, like Foucault's idea of silence and madness, it stands in opposition to language and the Law. It is the inverse of all that is required to qualify for full subjectivity in the Symbolic; and the "rejected object" (the body) is the primal process of separation from the maternal body, "its abjection of self is its only signified."[126]

The dumb Rinda Credence's disgusting and dirty body, oozing snot, her cheeks striped scarlet with the blood from her own gouging as she "tried to scratch herself out of existence" (150), personifies Kristeva's notion of the abject. Rinda acts in this narrative as the corporeal agent across which Hero connects with the other.

> These body fluids, this defilement, this shit are what life withstands. . . . There I am at the borders of my condition as a living being. . . . Such wastes drop so that I might live, until, from loss to loss, nothing remains in me and my entire body falls beyond the limit—cadere, cadaver.[127]

Rinda Credence is the "border," the "in-between," the "ambiguous"[128] figure that threatens identity; it is she through whom Hero peers into the abyss of horrific self-recognition at the silenced, abject, self that disgusts her. As the embodiment of abjection, Rinda Credence is the creature who threatens to shatter the stabilizing bar between the signifier and the signified of spoken discourse: she threatens to erupt onto, and to disturb, the plane of the Symbolic. She exists on the threshold of the Symbolic embodying all that must be expelled, and is the image of pre-subjective existence before the mother "enacts the Law for the frightened body."[129] Kristeva says it is the mother's body that stands between nature and culture and mediates the Symbolic Law (of the Father):[130] "that order, that glance, that voice, that gesture."[131]

> Abjection preserves what existed in the archaism of pre-objectal relationship, in the immemorial violence with which a body becomes separated from another body in order to be—maintaining that night in which the outline of the signified thing vanishes and where only the imponderable affect is carried out.[132]

The birth of Rinda Credence signifies the ever-present threat of disruption that the abject poses to the Symbolic:

> The abject *recurs* and threatens the subject not only in those events Freud described as the "return to the repressed"—that is, in psychical symptoms—they are also a necessary accompaniment of sublimated and socially validated activities, such as the production of art, literature, and knowledges.[133]

Rinda is the product of her own mother's temporary lapse into sexual pleasure, now sublimated into (her father's, and the Law's) socially validated activities of art, literature, and knowledge that are her mother's pastimes. Kristeva has pointed out that, "Even in the most sacrosanct, purified, and socially sanctioned of activities, the unclean and the improper must be harnessed."[134] As the consequence of her mother's sexual activities, and thus as the mark of Miss Credence's "sin," Rinda Credence must be herself abjected from her mother's body and psyche. Miss Credence contemplated killing her daughter at birth: "I thought of killing her when she was born" (162). Rinda is saved from death only because she is also the perverse mark of her mother's narcissistic crisis and because, however imperfect, she is the Oedipal child the mother desired of her father, a desire displaced onto her fleeting liaison with her father's only friend and academic equal, Clem. Preserving Rinda in the attic room of Credence House as a distorted kind of love object has been Miss Credence's way of preserving her father's memory, and her relationship with him.

l'écriture féminine

In the concluding chapters the narrative shifts from first to third person narration, effecting a distance between the narrating and reading subjects. In these concluding chapters, Hero takes her final stand against her subjugation to language in the Symbolic Law of patriarchy, and the imposition of an alien identity sustained through matriarchal oppression in the figure of her mother, by burning her autobiographical book that has been the instrument of her "cure." When her mother finds and reads Hero's book, declaring " 'And Hero—you're a *writer*. You really are.' She said the word 'writer' as if she were announcing a great victory for Hero" (173). Hero realizes that like the patriarchal speech she has rejected, the physical presence of her book threatens to become another instrument of her mother's oppression: "Annie wants to edit it and send it to a publisher. She's thrilled with me. At last I am what I ought to be . . . At last, she thinks, I am going to be my true self" (181). So, by destroying the story of her life in the flames of the wood stove, and by deleting it from the screen and memory of her word-processor, she finally discovers that she is able to rid herself of the patriarchal

Other and is able to take possession of "a different sort of silence even more magical than the first" (180). In a *feminine* other, Hero is able to say no to Annie's idea
of her, and thus, a further refusal of the Father's Law.

> The imaginary is lifted into the symbolic, the transitional objects can now be signi-
> fied, and the imaginary is inscribed as what it is, a function of the Other, through the
> sublimation of the maternal site in the paternal metaphor operated by language.[135]

No longer the object who is spoken in a representing utterance (the subject of
énoncé),[136] she forecloses on the Symbolic and speaks in a *feminine* tongue
recovered in speech through a process of Transferential writing that has been
equally experienced by the reader.

NOTES TO CHAPTER 2

1. Hélène Cixous and Catherine Clément, "Sorties," in *The Newly Born Woman*,
   trans. Betsy Wing (Minneapolis: University of Minnesota Press, 1986), 63–132.
2. Ibid., 93
3. Hélène Cixous, "Coming to Writing," in *"Coming To Writing" and Other
   Essays*, trans. Sarah Cornell, Deborah Jensen, Ann Liddle, and Susan Sellers
   (Cambridge, Mass. and London: Harvard University Press, 1991), 1–58.
4. Hélène Cixous, "The Laugh of the Medusa," *Signs: Journal of Women in Culture* 1, no. 1 (Summer 1976): 875–93; reproduced in *New French Feminisms*,
   eds. Elaine Marks and Isabelle de Courtivron (Brighton: Harvester, 1981),
   245–64.
5. Cixous's idea of *l'écriture féminine* has been much discussed and much criticized: see, for example, the bibliography of Cixous's critics listed in *The New
   Feminist Criticism*, ed. Elaine Showalter (London: Virago, 1986), 390–2; also
   Toril Moi, *Sexual Textual Politics* (London and New York: Methuen, 1985),
   102–6.
6. Each of the three critics in focus unquestionably has been influenced conceptually by Derrida's deconstructionist theory, in which he sought to dismantle the
   metaphysical and rhetorical structures at work in Western metaphysics in general, but in the written text in particular. He also sought, in his concept of *différance*, to expose the oppositional binary logic and inherently hierarchical
   premises upon which these binaries operate. These binaries, he says, are located
   in, for example, the structures of: "good/bad," "same/other," "subject/object,"
   "male/female," "mother/father," "presence/absence," and so on. Derrida rejects
   the oppositional principles of these binaries that dictate that the meaning of a
   word exists only in relation to its opposite. Instead he favors an idea of relational
   difference where meaning exists in a structural network determining that a word
   (or a phoneme or a concept) is intrinsically meaningless until it is used as a signifier in relation to and *different* from other words, and because its meaning
   comes into play only in as much as it *defers* to other elements that succeed and
   surround it. In relation to binary logic, he says: "One of the two terms controls

the other . . . holds the superior position: to deconstruct the opposition is first to overthrow [*reverser*] the hierarchy." In what Derrida has described as "the next phase of the deconstruction," the reversal is displaced into a new term used without the status of the privilege its opposite once possessed, in a process he calls "the irruptive emergence of a new 'concept': a concept which no longer allows itself to be understood in terms of the previous régime." Jacques Derrida, *Of Grammatology*, trans. Gayatri Chakrovorty Spivak, (Baltimore and London: The Johns Hopkins University Press, 1976), l.xxvii).

7.   See Susan Sellers, ed., *The Hélène Cixous Reader* (London: Routledge, 1994), 40.

8.   Cixous and Clément, *Newly Born*, 84–8.

9.   Cixous, "Castration or Decapitation?," 52.

10. Ibid.

11. Ibid., 54.

12. Jane Flax is concerned that in Cixous's idea of "writing from the body": "Discourse *becomes* a closed system in which the writer becomes a prisoner of the oppositions she intended to deconstruct . . . The end point of this logic seems to be woman *qua* woman would once again be consigned to silence." Jane Flax, *Thinking Fragments: Psychoanalysis, Feminism, and Postmodernism in The Contemporary West* (Berkeley and Los Angeles: University of California Press, 1990), 178.

13. Cixous, "The Laugh of the Medusa," 880.

14. Cixous and Clément, *Newly Born*, 93.

15. Luce Irigaray, *Parler n'est jamais neuter* (Paris: Les Éditions de Minuit, 1985), 55.

16. Luce Irigaray, *Amante Marine: de Freidrich Nietzsche* (Paris: Les Éditions de Minuit, 1980), translated into English as *Marine Lover of Friedrich Nietzsche*, trans. Gillian C. Gill (New York: Columbia University Press, 1991); Luce Irigaray, *Le Corps-à-corps avec la mère* (Montréal: Les Éditions de la pleine lune, 1981); Luce Irigaray, *L'Oubli de l'air: Chez Martin Heidegger* (Paris: Les Editions de Minuit, 1983).

17. Luce Irigaray, "The 'Mechanics' of Fluids," in *This Sex Which Is Not One*, trans. Catherine Porter and Carolyne Burke (Ithaca: Cornell University Press, 1985), 106–18.

18. Irigaray, *This Sex*.

19. Irigaray, *Speculum*.

20. Irigaray, *This Sex*, 124.

21. Ibid., 164.

22. Luce Irigaray, "The Bodily Encounter With the Mother" in *The Irigaray Reader*, ed. Margaret Whitford (Oxford: Basil Blackwell, 1991), 34–46; 45.

23. Irigaray, *This Sex*, 26–7

24. Irigaray, "Bodily Encounter," 45.

25. Irigaray, *Speculum*, 124.

26. See, for example, Janet Sayers, *Biological Politics* (London: Methuen, 1982); also, Jacqueline Rose, *Feminine Sexuality*, eds. Mitchell and Rose, 54–6. For a defense of Irigaray's position see Margaret Margaret Whitford, "Re-Reading Iri-

garay: Luce Irigaray and the Female Imaginary: Speaking as a Woman," *Radical Philosophy* 43, nos. 3–8 (1986): 3–8; 6–7.

27. Irigaray, *This Sex*, 195. See also Naomi Schor, "*Introducing Feminism*" in *Paragraph*, vol. 8 (Oxford: Oxford University Press, 1986), 93–101; 99.

28. Jacques Derrida, *Spurs: Nietzsche's Styles*, trans. B. Harlow (Chicago: University of Chicago Press, 1979), 97.

29. Luce Irigaray, *Divine Women*, trans. Steven Muecke, *Sydney Local Consumption Occasional Papers*, no. 8 (1986).

30. Jane Flax, *Thinking Fragments*, 218.

31. Mitchell and Rose, *Feminine Sexuality*, 55.

32. Irigaray, *This Sex*, 79–80.

33. Cixous and Clément, *Newly Born*, 95–6.

34. Mahy, *Silence*, 183.

35. Hélène Cixous, "The Laugh of the Medusa." *Signs: Journal of Women in Culture* 1, no. 4 (Summer 1976): 876–93; 180

36. See later in this chapter.

37. Hélène Cixous, *Coming To Writing*, 52–3.

38. Friedrich Nietzsche, *Ecce Homo: How One Becomes What One Is*, trans. R. J. Hollingdale (Harmondsworth: Penguin, 1979), 110.

39. See chapter 1 "The Textual Unconscious"

40. See Irigaray, *Parler n'est jamais neutre*; also Cixous and Clément, *Newly Born*.

41. Julia Kristeva, "The Adolescent Novel," in *Abjection, Melancholia and Love*, eds. John Fletcher and Andrew Benjamin (London and New York: Routledge, 1990), 8–23; 8.

42. See, for example, Nancy A. Walker, *Feminist Alternatives: Irony and Fantasy in The Contemporary Novel by Women* (Jackson and London: University of Mississippi, 1990), 75–6.

43. See chapter 5; also, Sigmund Freud "Beyond the Pleasure Principle," in vol. 18 of *The Standard Edition of The Complete Psychological Works of Sigmund Freud*, ed. James Strachey (London: The Hogarth Press, 1953–74), 7–64.

44. Kristeva, *Adolescent Novel*, 9–10.

45. See chapter 1 "The Textual Unconscious."

46. See Peter Stallybrass and Allon White, *The Politics and Poetics of Transgression* (London: Methuen, 1986), 21–3: Stallybrass and White discuss the discursive norms of the grotesque body as featuring "gaps," "orifices," "the gaping mouth," "disproportion," "protuberant distension," and as a "mobile, split, multiple self" in contrast to the governing principles of the classical body as "elevated, static and monumental," "closed," "homogeneous," "centered," and "symmetrical."

47. Mikhail Bakhtin, *Rabelais and His World*, trans. Hélène Iswolky (Bloomington: Indiana University Press, 1984), 339.

48. Sandra M. Gilbert, and Susan Gubar, *The Mad Woman in The Attic, The Woman Writer and The Nineteenth-Century Literary Imagination* (New Haven: Yale University Press, 1979), 55.

49. Cixous, "Laugh of the Medusa," 876.

50. Roland Barthes, *The Pleasure of The Text*, trans. Richard Miller (London: Jonathan Cape, 1976), 27.

51. Cixous, *Coming to Writing*, 42.
52. Virginia Woolf, "Professions for Women," in *The Death of The Moth and Other Essays* (New York: Harcourt, Brace, 1942), 236–8; 58. "Before we women can write, we must kill the angel in the house."
53. Moi, *Sexual Textual.*
54. Ibid., 58.
55. Gilbert and Gubar, *Madwoman*, 17.
56. See McHale, *Postmodernist Fictions*, 121.
57. Todorov, *The Fantastic.*
58. Robert Graves (first published 1948), *The White Goddess: A Historical Grammar of Poetic Myth* (London: Faber, 1997).
59. McHale, *Postmodernist Fictions*, 17.
60. Peter Burke, *Popular Culture in Early Modern Europe* (London: Temple Smith, 1979), 178–204.
61. Bakhtin, *Rabelais.*
62. Ibid., 10.
63. Ibid., 9.
64. Peter Stallybrass and Allon White, *The Politics and Poetics of Transgression*, 9.
65. Sigmund Freud, "The 'Uncanny'," in *From The History of an Infantile Neurosis and Other Works*, vol. 17, *The Standard Edition*, ed. James Strachey (London: The Hogarth Press, 1953–74), 219–52.
66. See Freud, "The Uncanny," 220. Also, Hélène Cixous, "Fiction and its Phantoms: A Reading of Freud's Das Unheimliche (the 'Uncanny')," *New Literary History* 7, no. 3 (Spring 1976): 525–48.
67. Elizabeth Grosz, *New Literary History* 7 no. 3 (Spring 1976): 525–48.
68. Lacan, *Écrits*, 16. See also, Sigmund Freud, "Totem and Taboo," in vol. 13 of *The Standard Edition*, 1–162.
69. Lemaire, *Jacques Lacan*, 84.
70. Ruth Ginsburg, "The Pregnant Text. Bakhtin's Ur-Chronotope: The Womb," in *Bakhtin: Carnival and Other Subjects, Selected Papers from The Fifth International Bakhtin Conference, The University of Manchester, Critical Studies* 3, nos. 2–4, ed. David Shepherd (Amsterdam-Atlanta: Rodopi, 1993), 173.
71. Ovid, *Metamorphoses*, trans. Mary M. Innes (Harmondsworth: Penguin, 1955), 9. "In his *Metamorphoses*, Ovid (43BC-AD17) draws on Greek mythology, Latin Folklore and legend from even further afield to create a series of narrative poems, ingeniously linked by the common theme of transformations."
72. Luce Irigaray, "Veiled Lips," *Mississippi Review* 11, no. 3 (1983): 102; also, Luce Irigaray, *Amante Marine: de Friedrich Nietzsche.*
73. Gilbert and Gubar, *Madwoman*, 12, 472.
74. Freud, "Uncanny."
75. Moi, *Sexual Textual*, 134.
76. Luce Irigaray, *Le corps-à-corps avec la mère.* This extract is taken from Elizabeth Grosz's English translation in Elizabeth Grosz, *Sexual Subversions*, 49. The original reads: "L'élément marin, c'est donc à la fois les eaux amniotiques, le plus profond du marin que ne peut pas faire simplement apparence, . . . et c'est aussi, il me semble, quelque chose qui figure assez bien la jouissance

féminine, y compris dans un mouvement de la mer, d'aller-retour, de flux continu qu me semble assez proche de ma jouissance en tant que femme, complètement étrangere à ce qu'est une économie de l'érection et de la détumescence. Mon mouvement, disons de jouissance féminine, est plus maritime que l'escalade sur la montagne et la descente de la montagne." I include this French script as an example of a work of Irigaray that has not yet been wholly translated into English, to show the rhythm and flow of the language in the original French, and Irigaray's use of "*le féminin.*"

77.   Robert Louis Stevenson, "Requiem," *The Oxford Book of Victorian Verse*, ed. Arthur Quiller-Couch (Oxford: Oxford University Press, 1912), 741. "*Under The wide and starry sky / Dig The grave and let me lie / Glad did I live and gladly die . . . This is the verse you grave for me: / 'Here he lies where he longed to be; / Home is The sailor, home from the sea.'* "

78.   Grosz, *Subversions*, 167.

79.   The extended quotation reads, "*Call for The robin redbreast, and The wren, / Since o'er shady groves they hover, / And with leaves and flowers do cover / The friendless bodies of unburièd men, / For with his nails he'll dig them up again. They would not bury him because he died in a quarrel.*" John Webster, *The White Devil*, 5.4. 97–105, in *Three Jacobean Tragedies* (Harmondsworth, Penguin, 1965), 242.

80.   William Wordsworth, "Lines Composed upon Westminster Bridge," in *William Wordsworth*, ed. Stephen Gill (Oxford: Oxford University Press, 1984), 285.

81.   Xenophon, "The March to the Sea," *The Persian Expedition*, bk. IV, ch. 7, trans. Rex Warner (Harmondsworth: Penguin, 1949), 131–72.

82.   Ariadne is abandoned by Theseus on the island of Naxos and is rescued by Bacchus (Dionysus) who subsequently marries her. On her death Bacchus threw into the sky the seven-starred crown that was his marriage gift to her where it was fixed as the constellation known as Ariadne's Crown or Corona. H. A. Guerber, *The Myths of Greece and Rome: Their Stories, Signification and Origin* (London: George G. Harrap, 1907).

83.   John Keats, "The Song of the Indian Maid," "Endymion," in *The New Oxford Book of English Verse*, ed. Helen Gardner (Oxford: Oxford University Press, 1973), 602–5. "*And as I sat, over The light blue hill/There came a noise of revelers: The rills. / Into The wide stream came of purple hue — 'Twas Bacchus and his crew! / The earnest Trumpet spake, and silver thrills / From kissing cymbals made a merry din—/ 'Twas Bacchus and his kin! / Like to a moving vintage down they came, / Crown'd with green leaves and faces all of flame; / All madly dancing through the pleasant valley.*"

84.   Luce Irigaray, *Amante Marine*; *Passions Élémentaires* (Paris: Les Editions de Minuit, 1982); *Elemental Passions*, trans. Joanne Collie and Judith Still (London: The Athlone Press, 1992); *L'Oubli de l'air: Chez Martin Heidegger*.

85.   Margaret Whitford has noted the similarity of Irigaray's use of the primary elements to Gaston Bachelard's works, especially his *L'Air et le songes* (Jose Corti: Paris, 1943): "Reading her work alongside his, it is difficult to believe that there has not been a Bachelardian influence at some stage. . . . In a number of works, Bachelard classes these images in terms of the four elements: earth, air, fire and water, and argues that these are primitive and basic categories of the imagining

mind." Margaret Whitford, "Luce Irigaray and the Female Imaginary: Speaking as a Woman" *Radical Philosophy* 43 (1986): 4.

86.   This infinite process of repetition anticipated Nietzsche's idea of "eternal recurrence," which he has described as: "the unconditional and endlessly repeated circular course of all things." *Ecce Homo*, 81.

87.   Luce Irigaray, *Divine Women*, trans. Stephen Muecke (Sydney: Local Consumption Occasional Papers, 8. 1986): 1.

88.   Irigaray, *This Sex*, 77.

89.   Grosz, *Sexual Subversions*, 170.

90.   See chapter 1.

91.   Cixous, "Castration or Decapitation?," 53.

92.   Irigaray, "Women on the Market," in *This Sex*, 170–91.

93.   Cixous, "Castration or Decapitation?," 53.

94.   Cixous, "Laugh of the Medusa," 880.

95.   Cixous, *Coming To Writing*, 51.

96.   Cixous and Clémont, *Newly Born*, 85–6.

97.   Gérard Genette describes the distinction between what he calls "extradiegetic," "heterodiegetic," and "homodiegetic" narrational levels, (with diegesis being the level of the story narrated), taking the extradiegetic to mean a narrator's position above the level of the story which is also heterodiegetic if the narrator is absent from the story and approximating the "omniscient" narrator, and "homodiegetic" to mean a narrator who also participates in the story. Gérard Genette, *Narrative Discourse*, trans. Jane E. Lewin (Oxford: Blackwell, 1980), 255–6. In *The Tricksters*, narration is generally *focalised* through Harry and is omniscient (extradiegetic), whereas in *The Other Side of Silence* narration is in the first person, homodiegetic, mode, but with a significant shift to third person, extradiegetic, narration in part five of the novel.

98.   This relates to Feud's famous "talking cure" which rests on the confidence that repressed events are able to be recollected in vivid detail, and the feelings attached to them expressed in words and gestures of dramatic speech. See David Farrell Krell, *Of Memory, Reminiscence and Writing: On The Verge* (Bloomington and Indianapolis: London: Macmillan, 1981).

99.   See chapter 1 "Text/Reader Relations."

100. See chapter 1 "*Moi* and *Je*."

101. Ragland-Sullavan, "Magnetism," 387.

102. Gilbert and Gubar, *Madwoman*, 43. See also Irigaray, *The Irigaray Reader*, 43–4: "It is important for us to guard and keep our bodies and at the same time make them emerge from silence and subjugation. . . . It is therefore desirable, for us, to speak within the amorous exchange."

103. This idea is pursued in more detail in chapter 3, which focuses on the mother.

104. Gilbert and Gubar, *Madwoman*, 57–8.

105. Ibid., 43

106. Cixous and Clément, *The Newly Born Woman*, 5.

107. See Silverman, *The Subject of Semiotics*, 200.

108. Michel Foucault, *Madness and Civilization: A History of Insanity in The Age of Reason*, trans. Richard Howard (New York: Vintage Books [Random House], 1973).

109. See Shoshana Felman, *Writing and Madness* (Ithaca, Cornell University Press, 1985), 44.

110. Jacques Derrida, "Cogito and the History of Madness," *Writing and Difference* (Chicago: Chicago University Press, 1978) 31–63; 44.

111. Cixous and Clément, *Newly Born*, 9.

112. Ibid., 5, 7.

113. Ibid., *xii*.

114. Ibid.

115. Ovid, *Metamorphoses*, 146–153.

116. Matthew Arnold, "Philomela," in *Poetry and Criticism of Matthew Arnold*, ed. A. Dwight Culler, (Boston: Houghton Mifflin, 1961), 144.

117. Patrick Fuery, *The Theory of Absence: Subjectivity, Signification and Desire* (Westport and London: Greenwood Press, 1995), 106, 103.

118. Mikhail Bakhtin, *Speech Genres and Other Late Essays*, trans. Vern W. McGee (Austin: University of Texas Press, 1986), 127.

119. Cixous, "Castration or Decapitation?," 49, 47.

120. The ideas of the daughter's rage against the mother are explored further in chapter 3.

121. Fredric Jameson, "Imaginary and Symbolic in Lacan," 362–3.

122. Julia Kristeva, *Revolution in Poetic Language*, 46.

123. Fuery, *Absence*, 105–6.

124. Gross, "The Body of Signification," in *Abjection*, 94.

125. Kristeva, *Revolution*, 152.

126. Ibid.

127. Kristeva, *Revolution*, 3. Also, Toril Moi, "Language, Femininity, Revolution," in *Psychoanalytic Criticism: A Reader*, ed. Sue Vice (Cambridge: Polity Press, 1996), 158-64: "In a sense, then, Kristeva does not have a theory of 'femininity,' and even less of 'femaleness.' What she does have is a theory of marginality, subversion and dissidence." See also Kristeva's article on dissidence: Julia Kristeva, "Un nouveau type d'intellectuel: le dissident," *Tel Quel* 74 (Winter 1977): 158–64: "In so far as women are defined as marginal by patriarchy, their struggle can be theorized in the same way as any other struggle against a centralized power structure."

128. Julia Kristeva, *The Powers of Horror: An Essay in Abjection*, trans. Leon S. Roudiez (New York: Columbia University Press, 1982), 9, 10.

129. Ibid., 10.

130. Kristeva, *Revolution*, 95.

131. Kristeva, *Powers*, 10.

132. Ibid.

133. Elizabeth Gross, "The Body of Signification," 87.

134. Ibid.

135. Ibid., 229.

136. Kristeva, "The True-Real," in *Kristeva Reader*, 214–37; 214.

3

Reading the Mother in Children's Literature: *le parler femme*

THEORETICAL INTRODUCTION TO THE CHAPTER

In her essay "About Chinese Women,"[1] Kristeva elaborates her perceptions of the Symbolic as a process of language *learning* in "The-Name-of-the-Father." Predicated on the rejection of pleasure as the necessary process of detachment from the mother's body, the Symbolic, she says, gives way to training, and prohibitions. The Symbolic is the clock of objective time and a "*system of speech* that involves an increasingly logical, simple, positive and 'scientific' form of communication, that is stripped of all stylistic, rhythmical and 'poetic ambiguities.' "[2] She has already, in the same essay, identified the Symbolic Order as linear and temporal because what she calls the "speaking animal" is given temporality by being able, in speech, to distinguish a before, a now, and an after:

> If *I* don't exist except in the speech I address to another, *I* am only *present* in the moment of that communication. . . . There is no time without speech. Therefore, there is no time without the father. That, incidentally, is what the Father is: sign and time.[3]

Lacan confirmed his belief in the linear temporality of speech in the Symbolic when he acknowledged in the game of *Fort!-Da!* the child's ability to symbolize absence of the lost object (the mother) at the level of the signifier in a chain of words. He viewed speech as a linear movement towards something and as an attempt to fill gaps making speech not only the agent of desire, but also dependent on a notion of loss, or absence, in much the same way that he theorized desire as a *consequence* and *condition* of loss.[4]

Luce Irigaray also has challenged what she perceives to be the masculinist linearity of language in her call for the representation of women "otherwise" in new systems of meaning and knowledge structures which authorize different forms of discourse:

> *Overthrow syntax* by suspending its eternally teleological order, by snipping the wires, cutting the current, breaking the circuits, switching the connections, by modifying continuity, alternation, frequency, intensity.[5]

For Kristeva, however, all language is not masculinist. In "Revolution in Poetic Language," she says that on the plain of the Symbolic the poetic erupts, and the archaic is retrieved, synchronically, as the working out of drives: ("appropriation/rejection, orality/anality, love/hate, life/death"). John Lechte, speaking about the works of Kristeva, has said "It is the mother who is at the point where the drives become manifest as the material base of language, art and all subjectivity.[6] In the view of all of these critics, the Imaginary becomes synonymous with the feminized space of alterity. In the words of Elaine Showalter, it is an attempt to repossess:

> All the space of the Other (*sic*), the gaps, silences and absences of discourse and representation, to which the feminine has traditionally been relegated.[7]

Julia Kristeva coined the term "Semiotic" to refer to this archaic, alternative language system which exists in the pre-linguistic, pre-Mirror relations with the mother. The Semiotic describes a pre-signifying, polymorphous, space (or "chora") of anarchic impulses and energies (pulsions) which precede the regulatory influences induced in the onset of the Mirror Phase. It is an uninterrupted, symbiotic, space of both love and *jouissance* between mother and child.[8]

Positioning the Semiotic as a direct oppositional challenge to the masculinist orientation of the Symbolic, Kristeva maintains that it is this "repressed, instinctual, maternal element," that is reactivated in what she calls the "poetic subject of language." In conjecturing these oppositional dimensions of the Semiotic and the Symbolic, Kristeva links subjectivity to textuality and maps the conditions under which the subject achieves representational and symbolic definition. In chapter 12 of her thesis, *Revolution in Poetic Language*,[9] she effectively textualizes these two conditions and oppositions by introducing the terms "genotext" (related to "process") and "phenotext" (related to "unity") to evoke the Semiotic and the Symbolic respectively.[10] Elizabeth Grosz points out that, in her later work, Kristeva maintained that socio-political and historical constraints:

> Repress the processes of *production* of signification by focusing only on the finite product, the text produced. The phenotext tries to minimalize genotextual intrusions

disrupting and over-coding its desire for univocal communication. The text tries to obliterate its own materiality so that meanings, messages, can be transmitted without acknowledging the *inherent* polyvocity and plurality, the materiality and ambiguity of all texts.[11]

In language (texts generally, but including speech), according to Kristeva, the Semiotic shows up as poetic tropes such as the displacement and condensation contained in metaphor and metonymy and rhetorical figures, but they are always subordinate ("subjacent") to language's principal function of naming, the sign, and syntax.[12]

> Like the repressed, the semiotic can return in/as irruptions within the symbolic. It manifests itself as an interruption, a dissonance, a rhythm Semiotic unsubsumable in the text's rational logic or controlled narrative. The semiotic is thus both the precondition of symbolic functioning and its uncontrollable excess.[13]

From this theoretical position Kristeva explores the intersection of textuality and psychoanalysis in subjectivity. She concludes that the appropriation of the maternal territory in the Symbolic, "simultaneously prevents the word from becoming mere sign, and the mother from becoming an object like any other: forbidden."[14] She describes the poetic, whose rhythm provides the interplay with the sign, as "one of the most important factors producing interplay within the structure of meaning as well as a questioning process of subject and history."[15] Kristeva therefore asserts that the Semiotic erupts in the Symbolic to act as a destabilizing agency to undermine the ontological verities which the Symbolic would impose on the speaking subject, and that it (the Semiotic) becomes a signifier of *the feminine* in Symbolic discourse. We must conclude from this theorization that the poetic as it exists as both text and subject, in Kristeva's epistemology, is feminine. This is her thesis on the arts and literature, particularly the literature and art of the avant-garde that, paradoxically for Kristeva, is an exclusively male preoccupation in as much as she uses only male works of art and literature as her examples; but insofar as she controversially perceives masculine and feminine to coexist equally in both the male and the female, her thesis is sustainable. In the avant-garde she identifies an explosion in the Symbolic of the otherwise repressed and unarticulated *jouissance* of the Semiotic. According to Kristeva, not only does the avant-garde challenge established forms of textual representation by interrogating the limits of language (and form) but, by permitting the Semiotic *jouissance* to rupture Symbolic discourse, it challenges and problematizes the nature of identity itself:

> Art—this semiotization of the symbolic— . . . represents the flow of jouissance into language. Whereas sacrifice assigns jouissance its productive limit in the social and the symbolic order, art specifies the means—the only means—that

jouissance harbors for infiltrating that order. In cracking the socio-symbolic order, splitting it open, changing vocabulary, syntax, the word itself, and releasing from beneath them the drives borne by vocalic or kinetic differences, jouissance works its way into the social.[16]

In her now famous essay, "Women's Time,"[17] Kristeva explores in more depth and detail the contingencies of time in the enunciation of language (speech), and she conjectures the space/time dimensions of language. On the one hand, she proposes time as linear teleology in the conventional sentence structures of Symbolic discourse (noun + verb; topic–comment; beginning–ending) reiterated here as masculine time, the time of history, or "cursive time." On the other hand, "women's time," or "monumental time," embraces both the repetitive cycles of gestation and the biological rhythms of cosmic time, as well as "a monumental temporality" that connects with eternity. This "monumental time," she says, is the mythical time of Kronos, and the time of resurrection myths, at least in so far as they embrace the cult of motherhood in, for example, classical mythology and contemporary Christianity:

> In which the body of the Virgin Mother does not die but moves from one spatiality
> to another within the same time via formation (according to the Orthodox faith) or
> via assumption (the Catholic faith).[18]

Lacan's psychoanalytic thesis of the subject perceived language in the Symbolic as the crucial and defining condition of subjectivity, but it left unanswered, and largely unaddressed, questions about the child's relations to corporeality: its relation to its own and its mother's body. Kristeva has theorized the pre-Mirror phase Semiotic as the site of a specifically maternal language, emanating from pre-lingual experiences of the mother's body, which challenges the dominance of the Oedipal *logos*.

> What follows is the aggressive and musicated discourse of a knowledge that attacks
> phallic power each time it sees it constituting itself under the aegis of the
> mother. . . . To rediscover the intonations, scansions, and jubilant rhythms preced-
> ing the signifier's position as language's position is to discover the voiced breath
> that fastens us to an undifferentiated mother, to a mother who later, at the mirror
> stage, is altered into a *maternal language*.[19]

Cixous subscribes to the view that "Women's speech is located in the body," and that her subjectivity is related to language not in autonomy but in fluidity and connectedness: It suggests the possibility of something outside the name-of-the-father.[20] Cixous also has identified the pre-Symbolic links between self and m/other and described it in terms of "Voice," as a voice that:

Sings from a time before the law, before the Symbolic took one's breath away and
reappropriated it into language under its authority of separation. . . . Within each
woman the first, nameless, love is singing.[21]

Lacan maintains that the child displaces these severed relations with the mother
into *objet petit a*, but Kristeva maintains that the child's accession to the Symbolic
can only be achieved by a process of renunciation, violent repression, and sacri-
fice of the kinds of maternal pleasures that are de facto inscribed in corporeality.
Both positions are simultaneously tenable, but Kristeva addresses, and goes some
way to answering, the question of what happens when corporeality is expelled
from Symbolic discourse. What is the consequence, in other words, of silencing
the maternal, which, she maintains, is the condition of Symbolic stability? In
short: how can the body signify in the premises of Symbolic discourse?

In her theory of "abjection,"[22] Kristeva identifies a space between language
and the speaking subject that is the repository for all that is delimited by the
child's need to achieve a condition of "the clean and proper body," to be constituted as a speaking subject and to gain access to symbolization. The abject is the
repository for everything that cannot be admitted to civilized discourse, the
boundary, or threshold, between nature and society; it is, in Kristeva's words:

A massive and sudden emergence of uncanniness, which, familiar as it might have
been in an opaque and forgotten life, now harries me as radically separate, loath-
some. Not me. Not that. But not other either. . . . A weight of meaninglessness,
about which there is nothing insignificant, and which crushes me. . . . It is thus not
lack of cleanliness or health that causes abjection but *what disturbs identity, system,
order* [my italics]. What does not respect borders, positions, rules. The in-between,
the ambiguous, the composite.[23]

This idea of "the clean and proper body" in relation to the abject takes us one step
further than Lacan's concept of "the normative subject." In fact, the abject deconstructs the premise of the "normative subject" by asking what must be rejected,
reviled, and expelled to achieve the condition of "normality." In Kristeva's theory
of abjection, the improper, the unclean, and the disorderly need to be expunged.
All that is ingested and ejected through bodily functions relating to oral, anal, and
genital functions: food, feces, urine, vomit, tears, blood, spit demarcate the outside and the "within" of the subject.[24] These are the fluids that emit from what
Lacan has called the "erogenic zones" (mouth, anus, eyes, ears, genitals). All the
childhood taboos, in fact, are relegated to the margins of consciousness, as object,
as other, as the abyss; but they continually threaten to invade the subjective sense
of "myself," the "I" of the socialized, *signifying*, and speaking subject. The abject
is signified in the speaking subject as repugnance and disgust, expressed as choking, retching, and vomiting; its contents are sublimated into symptoms named as

"a language that gives up, a structure within the body, a non-assimilable alien, a monster, a tumor (*sic*), a cancer."[25] To this list we could add the witch and the sorceress as distortions of maternal identity in the two faces of the mother that primal repression has caused the child to renounce; we could also add the criminal, all that occupies the margins, all that threatens the belief in stable identity, that threatens to transgress the psycho-social boundaries upon which normative society rests, and which ultimately provokes the horror of individual mortality. The abject is especially relevant to children's literature because of its threshold status not only in relation to its implied readership, the child, but also generically, in the system of literature that children's writers like Roald Dahl so successfully exploited. The abject is ambivalent, it occupies a space that is both inside and outside which Kristeva likens to the skin on the surface of milk. The most repugnant manifestation of abjection, however, is the corpse that is both in and out of life and is the ultimate waste, the border between living and dying that threatens the subject with a return to the abyss and is the subject's inescapable confrontation with corporeal decay and finitude.

Most importantly for the continuation of the theme of the mother in this chapter, the abject aligns with the Semiotic chora on the side of the maternal, as Kristeva has said:

> It confronts us . . . with our earliest attempts to release the hold of *maternal* entity even before ex-isting outside of her, thanks to the autonomy of language. It is a violent, clumsy, breaking away, with the constant risk of falling back under the sway of a power as securing as it is stifling.[26]

The abject, then, is the space of the subject's attempt to cling to pre-Mirror, pre-Oedipal mother/child relations and it is forever knocking at the door of the Symbolic Order as the unspoken underside, the obverse of rationality and linear sequence. For Kristeva, the mother's existence is defined by the rhythms of gestation, but, unlike Irigaray's work in this area, her subjectivity is defined only in terms of motherhood. Kristeva has been roundly criticised in feminist criticism[27] because she failed overtly to challenge Lacanian representations of the woman as anything other than the negative of the male, and because she left unchallenged Lacanian assumptions that the child is undifferentiated from the boy child in its pre-Oedipal relations with its mother in which process of subject formation the young child, defined de facto as male, is obtruded by *the feminine* like some sort of unwelcome, alien, but inevitable, tenant.[28] To work within Kristeva's theories of subject-formation, then, is to stay within the basic premises and terminologies of Freudian and Lacanian patriarchal psychoanalysis. But it is her theorization of the maternal body, which both Freud and Lacan failed even to acknowledge as anything other than absence and negativity, that marks Kristeva's work as different and separate from classical psychoanalysis. In her essays on motherhood, Kristeva has traced how patriarchal cultures have represented woman as both monster and angel: as Lilith, or the Whore of Babylon, or as virgins and divine mothers.[29] This complexity successfully describes the range of representations of mother-hood in these fictions, and implicitly anticipates the diversity of discourses through which they are constructed.

Like Kristeva's idea of the abject, Irigaray, in her way, challenges the reign of the "proper" as the necessary condition of entry into language and speech. Elizabeth Grosz has interpreted her thus:

> To speak as a woman means to undo the reign of the "proper" the proper name, property, propriety, self-proximity. It means to evoke rather than designate, to over-flow and exceed all boundaries and oppositions. It involves speaking from a posi-tion in the middle of the binaries (the so-called position of the 'excluded middle'), affirming both poles while undoing their polarization. To speak with meanings that resonate, that are tactile and corporeal as well as conceptual, that reverberate in their plurality and polyvocity.[30]

Irigaray also has addressed the question of the maternal function in psychoanaly-sis and culture,[31] and what she refers to as the "unacknowledged mother." She is critical of the way that the maternal role inflicted on women has subsumed woman's identity in motherhood and reproduction, and contained (restricted) her self-definition. As the mother in relation to her child she is restricted to the binary roles of over- or under-nurturing, and to an identity construed only as forms of mothering. Without a language in which to communicate with her children (because a priori in Irigaray's definition she has been defined in psychoanalysis as (a) male, and (b) therefore, able to speak only in the masculine tongue) she repre-sents herself to them in maternal gestures as either the "good mother" (of so many children's fictions) whose role is defined as the provider of food and a plenitude of love, or as her negative equivalent "the bad mother" who starves them of both love and nourishment (the witch of so many fairy tales). Either way she has the potential to extinguish her children with, either smothering nurturance and love ("You put yourself in my mouth and I suffocate"),[32] or the absence of both.

By submitting herself to the only role available to her in patriarchy, as the mirror image of the male, and as either the silenced or the "phallic" mother (see below), Irigaray maintains that woman erases all possibility of her own female identity. As a woman, she sacrifices all to her children who are the stand-ins for her absence. Irigaray is particularly interested in how these prescriptions affect rela-tions between women, especially when the other woman is her daughter. Her lyrical essay "And One Doesn't Stir without the Other,"[33] is a disturbing, daughter's-eye-view of the symbiotic paralysis between mother and daughter, and the mother's journey into the exile of motherhood. The daughter (who will herself become a mother) plays a double game with her mother: on the one hand she must violently sever her relationships with her own sex, her mother, to escape the social taboo of homoerotic relations and to take her place in the Symbolic Order as an object of sexual exchange. On the other hand, and paradoxically, the daughter must keep company with her mother to learn how to become a woman.

Irigaray argues, however, that because the woman has lost all conceptions of herself as a desiring female, she is unable to provide an adequate role model of womanhood so that the daughter can not learn anything more than to become the mother. The daughter, too, experiences exile by her inability to relate to her mother as a woman. The only escape from this impasse is for the daughter to relinquish her child's role in relationships with her mother. As an adult daughter, she will learn to reposition herself as a woman in relation to her mother, in a subject-to-subject relationship, and in an exchange of language: a new female language, in which the "I"/"you" polarities of patriarchy become the "we" of Irigaray's essay, "When Our Lips Speak Together":

> I love you, childhood. I love you who are neither mother (forgive me, mother, I prefer a woman) nor sister. Neither daughter nor son. I love you—and where I love you, what do I care about the lineage of our fathers, or their desire for reproductions of men? Or their genealogical institutions? What need have I for husband or wife, for family, personal, role, function? Let's leave all those to men's reproductive laws. I love you, your body, here and now. I/you touch you/me, that's quite enough for us to feel alive.[34]

The maternal discourse is also central to Irigaray's revision of the psychoanalytic paradigms through which she challenges what she has called Freud's (and Lacan's) "blind spot of the old dream of symmetry,"[35] and put the silenced mother in focus. From Irigaray's perspective the most influential effect on subject formation is not Oedipal castration, and accession to the Symbolic and the Father's Law, but Jocasta and the Imaginary (pre-Oedipal) severance of the umbilical cord.[36]

The term "phallic mother" originated in Freud's theories of sexuality[37] and underpins many feminist critiques on the question of motherhood. The phallic mother has been depicted in art and mythology as the female with male genitalia whose sexuality threatens to disrupt the Law of the Father and the economy of male domination:

> Faced with sexual differences, the man sees it as unfriendly to his own narcissistically conceived identity: femininity is dangerous because by "infecting" him, it might erase the distinction which buttresses his idea of masculinity.[38]

The phallic mother has been described as the woman who:

> Represents the absolute power of the female as autonomous and self-sufficient; at the same time she is woman reduced to the function of giving suck. She is neither

hermaphrodite nor androgyne, human nor monster, because she is emphatically Mother. . . . She is a fantasmatic caricature, and a caricature of the fantasmatic. Neither fully object nor fully subject she is, to use Freud's term for the symbolic-and-therefore-real contents of the unconscious, our most fiercely guarded 'psychical object,' as well as our role model and the very 'type' of the autonomous self. By having a penis, she defies the psychoanalytic 'fact' of woman's castration, as the same time she attests to the 'fact' of every other woman's castration but hers . . . In short, she has, she bears, she is, the fetish—but whose?[39]

In the phallic psychoanalytic economy, the mother is always and inevitably "monstrous" because, on the one hand, she is conceived as being already castrated and, in so being, carries within her the ever-present threat of castration of the male. On the other hand, she is monstrous because she has the capacity to refuse to subscribe to the phallocentric schism which symbolically has defined her as either the nurturing, and therefore asexual and non-desiring, mother, or as eroticized fetish.[40] In both cases she is seen as the object of male desire that would keep her silent and powerless, and always as Other to the male: "Behind the angel lurks the monster: the obverse of the male idealization of women is the male fear of femininity."[41] Kristeva starkly pointed out that "Either you stay spastic and aphasiac [as the castrated mother] Or you have this Phallic Mother enter into your language where she enables you to kill the master signifier."[42]

In *This Sex Which is Not One*,[43] Irigaray attempts to articulate an alternative discourse which reclaims for women the center ground, what she calls the "excluded middle" that lies between the polarities of male, binary logic, "between enunciation and utterance,"[44] and that challenges the singularity and "universality" of language and knowledges.[45] The issue for Irigaray is the psychoanalytic logic of "the same," by which women have been represented as the reflection of men: "woman serves as reflection, as image of and for man, but lacks specific qualities of her own."[46]

In Irigaray's idea of *le parler femme* women are liberated into a new psychic space that is beyond the law of the phallocentric *Logos*. Here the woman expresses herself in language that is both intellectual *and* emotional, and is conceptually postpatriarchal. *le parler femme* lies at the other side of the looking glass not simply as an inversion of patriarchal discourse and logic but as the new form of language:

Irigaray questions the structures of logic in which the female as concept has been suppressed, then displaces the whole system. Deconstructing structural polarities that assign priority to the first term and devalue the second, she attempts to leave behind the conceptual universe of the *Logos* and its symbolic policeman, the phallus. This new ideological place of Irigaray's writing could be described as preoedipal or post-patriarchal, or, as the place of a desire.[47]

le parler femme reproduces "The doubleness, contiguity and fluidity of women's sexual morphology and multi-centered libidinal energy that arises from them."[48] *le parler femme*, in other words, is language which speaks the body and is, like Irigaray's definition of female sexuality, "plural, autoerotic, diffuse and indefinable within the familiar rules of (masculine) logic."[49] The discourses of *le parler femme* emphasize tactile, corporeal sensitivities, Irigaray says, "It has nothing to do with the syntax which we have used to for centuries, namely, that constructed according to the following organization: subject, predicate, or, subject, verb, object."[50]

> 'She' is indefinitely other in herself. That is undoubtedly the reason she is called temperamental, incomprehensible, perturbed, capricious—not to mention her language in which 'she' goes off in all directions and in which 'he' is unable to discern the coherence of any meaning. Contradictory words seem a little crazy to the logic of reason, and inaudible for him who listens with ready-made grids, a code prepared in advance.[51]

For Irigaray, as with Cixous, and Kristeva, female sexuality in the phallic economy is circumscribed by images of women as:

> Mother, virgin, prostitute: these are the social roles imposed on women. The characteristics of (so-called) feminine sexuality derive from them: the valorization of reproduction and nursing; faithfulness; modesty, ignorance of and even lack of interest in sexual pleasure; a passive acceptance of men's "activity"; . . . neither as mother nor as virgin nor as prostitute has woman any right to her own pleasure.[52]

Irigaray has questioned the psychoanalytic economy of sexual *indifference*, and the system of representation that has depended on the repression of sexual difference. "Sexual difference," she says, "represents one of the questions or *the* question of our age."[53] She is concerned that the institution of motherhood in psychoanalysis and culture has subsumed women's subjectivity in the role of reproduction and nurturing, causing the woman to renounce her identity as a woman and a sexual being.[54] This affects not only the woman's self-regard but also the regard for her of her children, especially her relationship with girl children whom, she has pointed out in *Speculum of The Other Woman*,[55] both revere and revile, and simultaneously love and hate their mother's inscription in motherhood: "And what I wanted from you, Mother, was this: that in giving me life, you still remain alive."[56]

> The law of the same . . . required that the little girl abandon her relation to the origin and her primal fantasy so that henceforth she can be inscribed into those of men which will become the 'origin' of her desire. In other words, woman's only relation to origin is one dictated by men.[57]

The girl child's relations to her origins are, in Irigaray's terms, a matter of fantasy as a psychic reality. In her prose essay, "When Our Lips Speak Together,"[58] she has proposed an alternative modality to the Oedipal drama in a feminine myth of origin in which the daughter's relation to her mother is not founded on the phallic definition of lack, and where her subjectivity has not been subsumed in the role of mother. In this new relation the daughter speaks to her mother as woman, in a subject-to-subject, woman-to-woman, discourse of equivalence and equality as "we" and not in the phallic "I/you" which, she claims, is the language of separation and division conspiring to keep women apart from each other.

SUMMARY

This chapter focuses on the maternal function in children's literature and takes up the challenge to conventional language forms, particularly in the work of Kristeva and Irigaray, to explore the idea of *le parler femme* through the texts of *Pictures in the Dark, Dangerous Spaces, The Other Side of Silence, The Tricksters*, and *The Changeover*. These fictions, in common with a great many other works of children's literature, are embedded in family narratives in which the mother plays a key role. At their simplest they subvert convention by depicting families that are in some way dysfunctional, featuring dead or single, absent or adulterous, abandoning or psychotic, or irresponsible parents. Literary subjectivity in these fictions, as both character and readerly inscription, is en-gendered through forms of fantasy, dreaming, or some other kind of liminal space, in Oedipal relations, and in social and psychic positioning within familial metaphors. Generically, they subscribe to what Freud has called the "*Familienroman*" ("Family Romance"), to describe the imaginary narratives, the *fantasies*, by which individual family members, and with them the reading subject, interrogate and describe their origins, and the patterns of desire through which they interact with each other.[59] Julia Kristeva has said,

> Narrative is, in sum, the most elaborate kind of attempt, on the part of the speaking subject, after syntactic competence, to situate his or her self among his or her desires and their taboos that is at the interior of the oedipal triangle.[60]

The emphasis in this chapter is on the mother figure and on mother/child relations. But, more than a mere consideration of maternal characterization at the level of story, the idea of *le parler femme* here embraces also the whole sweep of narrative language, structure and temporality which is here claimed, in *the feminine*, as circular, fluid, open, and poetic in so far as it discursively reflects the rhythms and gestures of the maternal language advocated by Kristeva, and tactile in the sense that it is syntactically and stylistically fragmented and discordant.

We have seen how both Lacan and Freud in their work on human subject formation have described the father as synonymous with dominance, whether by virtue of the Lacanian Symbolic Law, or Freudian fantasies of the penis. In all cases, subject formation has been described with metaphors of fusion and separation circulating round the phallus as the core signifier and the sole object of the mother's desire. Feminist criticism's critique of classical forms of psychoanalysis have pointed out that in this phallic, Oedipal economy the mother has been defined only in terms of negativity, absence of meaning, and lack. The mother is seen as non-Being castrated by virtue of her non-possession of the phallus critiqued at length in Cixous's essays, "Castration or Decapitation?"[61] and "The Laugh of the Medusa,"[62] and more obliquely by Irigaray in her *Speculum of the Other Woman*, and other works that are drawn upon in this chapter. In the Lacanian, psycho-linguistic version of subject formation, this maternal absence translates into a maternal silence in relation to female exclusion from language in the Symbolic Order in the "myth of language" upon which edifice the Oedipal inscription of the subject rests:

> Language and culture depend on the death or absence of the mother and on the quest for substitutes for her. . . . Women are identified with the literal, the absent referent.[63]

Margaret Homans is here referring to the literal death, or absence, of the mother in Victorian fictions but the idea of absence is being used figuratively here to refer to the death and silencing of the mother in the Symbolic and the relationship of this silence to plot. In Irigaray's critique of this Oedipal modality, she says:

> The bond between mother and daughter, daughter and mother, must be broken so that the daughter can become woman. Female genealogy must be suppressed, in favor of the relation son-Father, of the idealization of the father and the husband as patriarchs.[64]

Motherhood and fatherhood imply both daughterhood and sonship. Both male and female children feature in these narratives but in all cases the parent/child dyad is considered within a framework that foregrounds the work of the three French feminist critics underpinning this book. So, for example, in considering Gillian Cross's *Pictures in the Dark*, which is, within a Lacanian/Freudian reading, an obviously Oedipal father/son narrative of the struggle for subjectivity via accession to the Symbolic and to the Law-of-the-Father, the emphasis is instead on the inverse implications of the Father's Law as a challenge to what Deleuze and Guattari have called the "imperialism of Oedipus."[65] In these terms *Pictures in the Dark* is considered as a narrative of "The Mother Tongue" and has been taken to include Kristeva's conception of the "thetic" because, as is argued, it is ultimately a narrative that inscribes the maternal body and is structured in the kinds of connectedness and fluidity that is axiomatic to *the feminine* subjectivity.

Likewise, the section titled *"le parler femme"* explores how far the very different representations of mother/daughter relations in *Dangerous Spaces* and *The Changeover* participate in what Irigaray has called "the fantasy of mutuality" in *le parler femme*.

"Monstrous Mothers" examines the representations of the especially ambiguous familial roles of mothers in Oedipal conflicts where, as already indicated, the "father" may as easily be female or male. Notwithstanding, it is the case that the actual father figures depicted in these fictions are always in some way inadequate by being either ineffectual, incompetent, absent, weak, or violent; and such negative traits, represented here as *male*, have their distinctive effects on these familial plot structures.

In the characters of Miss Credence in *The Other Side of Silence*, Naomi in *The Tricksters*, and Molly in *Dangerous Spaces*, it is possible to trace the spectrum of language by which maternal subjectivity is represented from the mother's being "silenced" by and in Symbolic patriarchy, to a realization of all that is implicated in Irigaray's idea of the *le parler femme*. Also, in the familial structures that inscribe these mother figures, it is interesting to observe how far both the institution and experience[66] of motherhood effaces their subjectivity as woman. This chapter also explores how the specter of the phallic mother is present, and is conflated, in the characters of Annie and her daughter Genevra in *The Other Side of Silence*, and positions her (in the Freudian thesis of female sexuality) as the pre-Oedipal, and, therefore, pre-castrated, type of *desiring* ("phallic") mother that has been the subject of much of the feminist critique raised here.

This, then, is the spectrum of familial narrative structures and relations that theorizes a notion of *le parler femme* and the maternal function in children's literature. Freud's patriarchal conception in his use of the term *Familienroman* (which Lacan failed adequately to challenge) is here transmuted into an emphasis on the maternal and *the feminine*. So, while there is an overarching question for this chapter about the way the mother figure is inscribed in familial narratives such as these, there is also a wider question about a poetics of *le parler femme* in literature for children.

PICTURES IN THE DARK

At first reading *Pictures in the Dark* is a father/son narrative relating the *impasse* in relations between a boy Peter, and his paranoid father; it is a narrative that is framed and *structured*, as if through the camera's eye, the aperture, of another boy, Charlie Wilcox, through whose passion for photography the story of Peter, Peter's family, and Peter's relationship with his father is exposed. But, more than this, it is an Oedipal story in which the mother is by definition implicated. It tells of a boy who escapes from his own body, by a process of dejection, and into the body of an animal, an otter, whose condition of existence is between earth and

water. So, it is appropriate and telling that this novel should be situated and discussed here in the language of corporeality that is available through *the feminine*
and, in this particular theorization, is located in the body of the primordial mother.
This is the Mother Tongue that speaks the language of the body that is presented
here as being otherwise repressed in Symbolic discourse.

Abjection and Return

Pictures In the Dark has been positioned as a narrative of *the feminine* because it
is of, and about, corporeality and, because, arguably in this context, Peter's
escape into the body of an otter is his *resistance* to submission to the Father's Law
in the Symbolic that is embodied in the overbearing presence of his father.
Equally and conversely, it is fundamentally a resistance to separation from the
mother, as well as a violent raging against her as the primary agent of separation.
The otter is theorized as a psychotic fantasy of return to the mother and as Peter's
attempt to reexperience a pre-Oedipal, pre-lingual, Semiotic *jouissance* that
stands in opposition to the Law, and is, as Kristeva has argued, on the side of *the
feminine*. In the phallic economy, the maternal *jouissance* and, with it, the discourses of the body, must be repressed to inaugurate full subjectivity in the Symbolic. The otter, in a Kristevan thesis of the maternal body and subject formation,
is theorized as the consequence and embodiment of abjection borne of the expul-
sion of/separation from the maternal object, which is the mother's body, and
founded in the fear of autoeroticism and the incest taboo. Abjection (the otter)
surfaces between subject (Peter) and object (the mother) in the condition that
existed in what Kristeva has described as the "archaism of pre-objectal relationships,"[67] but which is neither subject nor object. And Peter is inscribed in the narrative as the agent of abjection:

> The abject has only one quality of the object—that of being opposed to *I*. . . . what
> is *abject*, is radically excluded and draws me toward the place where meaning col-
> lapses. . . . It is a brutish suffering that 'I' puts up with, sublime and devastated, for
> 'I' deposits it to the father's account. I endure it, for I imagine that such is the desire
> of the other. . . . Not me. Not that. But not nothing, either. A 'something' that I do
> not recognize as a thing. A weight of meaningless, about which there is nothing
> insignificant, and which crushes me. On the edge of non-existence and hallucina-
> tion, of a reality that, if I acknowledge it, annihilates me. There, abject and abjection
> are my safeguards.[68]

Abjection, therefore, is the rejection of that which "I" becomes, and it is clearly
described in the narrative at those moments when Peter escapes into his "I" that is
the otter and, in a trance-like state of being, leaves the body of his "not-I" in a
corpse-like, non-seeing, non-feeling material body to be reborn into another

material dimension as the otter: "I give birth to myself through the exclusion of not-I."[69] The narrative tells that,

> He wasn't asleep. His body was tense, and his eyes were wide open and remote, staring into nothing. They didn't blink when Charlie shone the torch at them. And when he stretched out his hand, feeling sick and terrified, to touch the cold cheek, there was no reaction at all. Not even the automatic twitch of a sleeping person. (152)

Abjection is at the border of its condition, between subject and object and is brought on, Kristeva tells us, by "*Too much strictness on the part of the Other*, confused with One and the Other,"[70] which is here Peter's overbearing and repressive father who drives Peter into the "violence of mourning for an 'object' (the mother) that has always already been lost . . . from which, in order to *be* the ego has broken away."[71] The abject inhabits the same kind of space-time dimension that Kristeva has elsewhere described as the "thetic": that is "the place of the Other . . . a threshold between two heterogeneous realms,"[72] these are, in this case, the Semiotic and the Symbolic, and it can be mapped on to the abject in the issue of subject formation.[73]

The otter appears in the narrative in space but out of time (" 'But the otters aren't [here]. Haven't been any on this stretch of river for years' " [60].) It exists in a "thetic," anachronic, space/time dimension that is not entirely space nor time and conceptually evokes the ambivalent narrative realm in which Peter is structured as the deject in opposition to Charlie who is narratologically situated as his superego. ("To each ego its object, to each superego its abject.")[74] Charlie is the subject of the internalized Law-of-the-Father who redeems, and is himself redeemed by, the eruption of the Semiotic chora in the Symbolic through his art. Meanwhile, Peter's simpering, submissive and infantilized mother is inscribed as the silenced female upholder of the patriarchal Law.

The "deject," Kristeva says,

> Is the one by whom the abject exists . . . A devisor of territories, languages, works, the *deject* never stops demarcating his universe . . . A tireless builder, the deject is in short a *stray*. He is on a journey during the night, the end of which keeps receding.[75]

Thus Peter, who in his manifestation as the otter inhabits the condition of animality, is a nighttime "stray" lives close to the ground, maps his territory and knows, from an otter's-eye view, and from the *feel* and *smell* of the earth and water under him, every crevice and cranny, every turn, of the river and its banks. It is only by a leap of imagination that he is able to convert his knowledge into representational, symbolic form when he produces for Charlie the extraordinarily detailed map of the river that could only be the work of who one knows the river through the intimacy of animal instincts, one who has *lived* there. Peter is not allowed to go to the river, forbidden by his family. But it is from "This straying on excluded ground that he draws his *jouissance*."[76]

Kristeva has pointed out that the abject is not *the* place of the maternal *jouissance*, but is the depository that preserves all that existed in the idyllic archaism of the child's relations with the maternal body, in the amniotic experiences of the womb, and is the marker of all that must be ejected from that experience to allow the subject to accede to "proper sociality" of the "clean and proper body" of the Symbolic.[77] As upholder of the Law, Peter's father is obsessively preoccupied with ridding his family, and the family home, of the "unclean" and disorderly elements of corporeality, all that he reviles and that disgusts him: infection, pollution, and "germs." It is an ironically paranoiac endeavor of prohibition in which he works to keep himself and his home protected from the threat of an unclean invasion from the *outside*: "The whole place looked like a prison. The boarded gate at the front was clamped shut with a padlock and topped with barbed wire" (127). The father's loathing of defilement is his symbolic disavowal of his mother's body projected onto his son:

> Fear of the archaic mother turns out to be essentially fear of her generative power. It
> is this power, a dreaded one, that patrilineal filiation has the burden of subduing.[78]

Peter's father fails to recognize that his perception of the threat of infectious invasion from the outside already exists within him, and quite literally within the walls of his own house and family and is embodied in his repression and exclusion of his son: "Abjection is no longer exterior," Kristeva points out "it is permanent and comes from within." In her citation of the Levitican taxonomy of "unclean animals," the otter would qualify as impure because it is carnivorous, and because, by moving on both land and water, it crosses boundaries between habitats, does not confine itself to one element, and does not inhabit its "proper place."[79]

> Only birds which fly, fish which swim, have fins and gills, and only animals which
> walk on four legs, chew their cud and have cloven hooves are fit for sanctified con-
> sumption.[80]

The narrative describes the otter's movements on land in negative verbs that connote the ambiguity of its condition: it "slithered," "lollopped," "reared up," in a movement that was "neither climb nor jump" (39). And being an unclean animal it is, of course, unnamable: Peter's father it is in denial of it and refuses to call it by name despite the material evidence of the otter in Jennifer's nighttime photograph of it. Peter's father calls it a " 'Filthy little mink. . . . We've got to keep in control. Unless you want the garden full of mink' " (96, 7). Furthermore, Char-

lie's sister Zoe (the girl child) attempts to rationalize Peter's (the boy child) peculiar behavior by naming him as a witch and reverts to medieval witch trials when
she throws him bound and gagged into the river to assess his condition and status.

Women's Time

In the water, Peter, in the body of the otter, swims ecstatically in his element, as if
in the amniotic fluid from whence he came and with which he seeks reconnection
and return, "It swam and dived for no obvious reason. Enjoying itself" (118). His
freedom in the water contrasts markedly with the images of entrapment that
define and describe his family home and his life in it. In the water he moves in the
maternal element to the rhythm and gestations of the cyclical time of the seasons,
identified by Kristeva as "Women's Time,"[81] and around which, through Charlie's
camera lens, the narrative is structured: through autumn, winter, and into spring.
Through his camera's-eye view Charlie, too, shares in this rhythmic time with a
newly found hallucinogenic intensity, as if by Peter's biting him he has been
injected into a new dimension of seeing:

> Then he looked up, and the light through the window hit him like a blow in the
> face. . . . and everything on the other side of the window was alive with movement.
> Real and bright as the skin on his fingers, and the marks of Peter's teeth. Holly
> berries flamed scarlet. Cobwebs hung from the dancing bushes like sculptures of
> spun steel. A lingering elder leaf flapped, acid-yellow, over the stripped stalks of a
> cluster of berries. . . . The thickets hummed with different colors, each bush show-
> ing its own distinct shade of red or purple or yellow. . . . Then he began to photo-
> graph what he had seen. (67, 118)

Kristeva reminds us: "It is through color—colors—that the subject escapes its
alienation within a code (representational, ideological, symbolic, and so forth)."[82]
With his newfound vision, the angle, and the object, and the perspective, of Charlie's photography changes; he sees the world through his transformation with
greater detail, and conventional, linear time ceases to exist while he is caught up
in the intensity of snapping his pictures:

> By four o'clock, he had taken two rolls of color film and one of black and white.
> Strange, precise shots, not like anything he'd done before. The thick ribbed bark of
> the willow trees. The empty, spreading seed heads of the cow parsley. The dark arch
> of the railway bridge, with ferns dripping from its underside. Images from another
> world. (68)

In her theorization of return to the mother, Kristeva, in "Women's Time,"[83] has
described just such a space/time dimension as this that Charlie now shares with

Peter in his manifestation as the otter. It harks back to a period when the primary relations were spatial, not temporal, and that she has situated in *the feminine*:

> There are the cycles, gestation, the eternal recurrence of a biological rhythm which conforms to that of nature and imposes a temporality whose stereotyping may shock, but whose regularity and unison with what is experienced as extra-subjective time, cosmic time, occasion vertiginous visions and unnamable *jouissance*.[84]

Semiotizing the Symbolic

Charlie has undergone a process which Kristeva would describe as "semiotization of the Symbolic," induced by "a crisis of representation," expressing and liberating the otherwise unarticulated *jouissance* of the Semiotic, and available, she says, only through transgressive art, religion, and madness. It is a kind of madness that Charlie experiences in his newfound mode of being and that he expresses through his photographic art as a compulsive madness, which like the compulsion of a religion, is all-consuming, and functions in his pictures like another kind of expressive language. It causes him to refuse his family's demands for his attention and to deny their wishes by leaving the Christmas Day family party early and by not joining in his family's igloo-building session. His connection with the Semiotic language of the maternal erupting onto the plane of the Semiotic disturbs his conventional ways of seeing and is bound up with the body as jouissance; "But most of all the body *as* jouissance comes to be seen, as the locus of drive energies in the *chora*."[85]

Body Language

Cixous, like Irigaray, theorizes the maternal in metaphors of water. Her essay, "*Souffles*," ("Breaths") conjectures the mother's role in images of water in her idea of the sea-mother (mother [*mère*] and sea [*mer*]): " 'I enter with the feeling of leaving—of myself leaving myself thus accomplishing a destiny that is always awaiting me.' "[86] It is clear how in this novel water is synonymous with the maternal: the otter swims in it, and Charlie chooses the river as the subject for his photographic essay which liberates him from purely Symbolic constraints. Both Kristeva and Cixous theorize the maternal body in terms of non-verbal language and gesture, "intonations, scansions, and jubilant rhythms,"[87] that connect with primordial, prelapsarian time and is indeed, figuratively and literally, the *myth* of the Mother Tongue that speaks in meanings that are tactile and corporeal as well as conceptual. Cixous refers to "rhythmical breathing," and "lilting flows," in a language that is primarily physical and expressed through holding, touching, caressing, singing, and babbling exchanges between mother and child:[88]

> Listen to me, it is not a captivating, clinging "mother"; it is the equivoice that, touching you, affects you, pushes you away from your breast to come to language, that summons *your* strength; it is the rhythme that laughs you.[89]

Both the otter and Charlie use nonverbal communications that evoke this archaic, maternal language: the otter whistles and sighs, and Charlie uses iconic form. The moment of reconciliation between Peter and is father is realized through the father's watery tears and bodily gestures hitherto unknown and inexperienced as a channel of communication between them, "He reached out for the limp hand that was lying on the edge of the stretcher (194). . . ." Kristeva talks about the "second birth" in puberty in which the subject reactivates the Oedipal experience, which "consequently lets the subject reconnect with his (*sic*) own oral, anal, and phallic stages and to function within the complete gamut of the body, language and the symbolic,"[90] this describes precisely what has happened here. So, although the novel is ostensibly a quest for father/son reconciliation, a reading in *the feminine* reveals it as a story of *maternal* reconciliation expressed in changed relations, and achieved through the resurfacing of the Semiotic in the Symbolic and the newly realized capacity of the male figures to communicate in the language of *le parler femme*, in which the reading subject is also implicated irrespective of gender definitions.

THE TRICKSTERS AND *THE OTHER SIDE OF SILENCE*

Monstrous Mothers

The choices for a feminine subjectivity in psychoanalysis and in the culture of Western patriarchy are contained by their condition of polarization and, from a feminist point of view, are locked in an impossible dualism. Cixous has said that they ("Vous les messieurs psychanalysters")[91] "riveted us between two horrifying myths: between the Medusa and the abyss."[92] For Cixous, the choices for a woman in phallic discourse are between the silence of castration, and the silence of decapitation; either way, she is monstrous.

Even when she speaks, the woman is locked into silence because she speaks with an alien tongue, in a language that is not her own. When she speaks as a woman, Cixous has said, she is not heard because: "Her words fall almost always upon the deaf male ear, which hears in language only that which speaks in the masculine."[93]

The mother is silenced because, in daring to speak, she is the signifier of the desire of the pre-Oedipal, and therefore uncastrated, mother. When she speaks, even though she is able to speak only in the alien tongue, she threatens to destabilize the system of language that would ossify her in the asexual "cult of the mother." This cult is the means by which Symbolic patriarchy has socialized sexual difference and refused the presence in language of the maternal *jouissance*.

When she speaks, she is the phallic mother, the Medusa, the image of whose decapitated, snake-infested head, condenses signification of both externalized female genitals, and many penises, in both castration and the denial of castration.[94] "The phallic mother has possession of our imaginaries because she controls the family, and the imaginary is familial."[95] She undermines, indeed overthrows, the established sexual order of male domination, and the establishment must move to silence her (must cut off her head):

> No language can sing unless it confronts the Phallic Mother. For all that it must not leave her untouched, outside, opposite, against the law, . . . Rather it must swallow her, eat her, dissolve her, set her up like a boundary of the process where 'I' with 'she'—the other, 'the mother'—becomes lost. . . . The Phallic Mother—as blinding pillar of the *polis* and unconscious buttress of the laws of the city—is apprehended, comprehended, and thrust aside.[96]

The mother, in these terms, suffers a triple alienation in language and the Symbolic: first, because she is split between the *je* and the *moi* identified by Lacan as the condition of subjectivity; second, because Symbolic patriarchy has excluded from language not only *the feminine* discourse; but also, third, this; exclusion from *the feminine* necessarily means exclusion from *maternal* discourse. So questions relating to the mother in feminist criticism ask: How can she speak? How can she speak as woman when she is locked into this triple bind of silence? How can she articulate her relationship to her daughter, her experience of *being* a daughter, her relationship to her *own* mother, and to other women, in a phallic economy in which the dominant discourse has excluded the expression of, has repressed, these kinds of relationships, this kind of language? These are the recurring questions that Kristeva, Irigaray, and Cixous, in their different ways, have each addressed and that Irigaray, in particular has attempted to resolve in her conception of *le parler femme*.

We can observe the spectrum of monstrous motherhood being played out in the silent and suffering "good mother" Naomi in *The Tricksters*, in the characters of Annie Rapper and her dark double Miss Credence in *The Other Side of Silence*, and in the trivialized Goldie in Gillian Cross's *Wolf*.

Each in her own way is monstrous. Naomi, the mute and fetishized "mother" of patriarchy who gives *too much* of herself becomes the suffocating mother who, because she is unable to offer her children *language*, offers only food.[97] An even more powerful example is Annie Rapper, who is monstrous because she is the phallic mother who, by subscribing to the alien tongue, has substituted her own nurturing food for the masculine discourses through which she perpetuates the patriarchal economy that has kept women silent:

Her silence as a daughter, her wifely echoing of her man, her professionally 'masculine' adoption of male language would seem to be the only channels open to her as she closes off and drowns out her mother's voice. These two options—speechlessness or fully male speech—structure the whole story of woman's speech.[98]

By speaking in the masculine tongue Annie sustains what Irigaray has described as the male economy of "the same":

Only her father's daughter, she repeats his discourse without much understanding, carries out his law, spreading it everywhere, in the middle of everything; intermediary for all to the point of intrigue, where her charm takes the place of violence.[99]

Words, as the dominant signifiers of the phallic order, are the credo by which Annie Rapper lives and earns her living, ironically, as a researcher of children's language development. "Words," writes the symptomatically and symbolically silent (silenced) hero, Hero, of *The Other Side of Silence*, "had recently swept us to Benallan. And these powerful words were those written down by my mother"(27). Annie Rapper has silenced her own daughters not on an oversupply of her bodily food, as in Irigaray's idea of the suffocating mother who denies her daughter the right to an autonomous subjectivity, but by a suffocation with words, driving Hero's language inward, and silencing her voice.

You have made me something to eat. You bring me something to eat. But you give me yourself too much, as if you wanted to fill me all up with what you bring me. You put yourself into my mouth and I suffocate. Put less of yourself in me and let me look at you. I'd like to see you while you are feeding me. Not to lose my/your sight when I open my mouth to you.[100]

Both of Annie Rapper's girl children have committed acts of violence against themselves as expressions of their rage against their mother. Hero's has been an anorexic response[101] through which she has starved herself of the words her mother would impose upon her, and so she is silent in the face of too many words. It is symptomatic that her mother has failed to give her a language in which to speak in *the feminine* as a daughter, and as a woman. Her symptom is:

A response to her annihilation as active subject, a resistance or refusal to confirm what is expected of her. Not able to take up an active position by will alone (this would mean, at most, acting like a man), she lives out and uses her passivity in an active defiance of her social position. She (psychically) mutilates herself in order to prevent her brutalization at the hands of others.[102]

Ginevra, "the word child," on the other hand, has gorged herself on her mother's words; she has devoured them as a food substitute. But by crashing cars and, in the process, mutilating *her own* body, she is at once both rejecting her *mother's* body, and mourning its loss as the lost (maternal) object. Through these acts of self-mutilation Ginevra is making a symbolically bulimic gesture of vomiting up her mother's phallic words through which she has been denied access to the maternal discourses of the body.[103] Annie Rapper tells Ginevra:

> "You could have been anything you wanted to be." "I have been anything I wanted to be," Ginevra answered indignantly. "I wanted to crash cars." (66)

But in both cases, being whom they wanted to be (to crash cars, and to be silent) falls short of the images imposed by the repressive structures of patriarchy, sustained through and by their mother's professional appropriation of the language of the Father's Law.

In their acts of self-mutilating defiance, these two girl children mirror the self-mutilation by Rinda Credence that are her acts of mute rage against a mother who has starved her, quite literally, of both language and food. Miss Credence is positioned as the negative aspect of Annie Rapper, as an equivalent but inverse image of monstrous motherhood. She is herself a victim daughter of a resented mother and oppressive father.[104] In the drama played out between Miss Credence and her daughter Rinda, we have the "dumb show" of the relations between Hero and her own mother, with Miss Credence as the negative aspect of everything Annie Rapper hides behind with her facade of good mothering: "she is the bad mother who always shuts the daughter in."[105] This is symbolized in the image of Miss Credence as the witch, defining her own identity by subscribing to the words and the sounds of patriarchal symbolization.

Miss Credence has gone through the motions of performing ritual acts of maternal nurturance upon her child but by averting her head and denying Rinda access to the sight of her mother's lips as the organ of both speech and food (and, in Irigaray's description, female sexuality), she has denied her access to both. "Miss Credence fed her, but, even then, I think she always had her face turned a little away" (180). Irigaray, poignantly in this connection, has discussed the need to speak to the child:

> It is also good to speak while feeding a child, so that it does not experience feeding as violent force-feeding, as rape. It is also important to speak while caressing another body. Silence is all the more alive in that speech exists. Let us not be the guardians of silence, of a deadly silence.[106]

Miss Credence attempted to silence her daughter at birth by using a suffocating pillow to blot out the sounds of the screaming. This symbolizes the mothers' attempts to silence the raging screams of all these girl children against their silencing mothers: "Her fury and fear made no sound at all" (150). By variously starving and/or overindulging their children of/in language, Miss Credence and Annie Rapper ironically have failed to enact the Father's Law. Both mothers are archetypal narcissists; both are preoccupied with their own superior intellects, seeking to replace their lost primal narcissism of childhood in their offspring, in which process, "Ideal egos ('Ideal-I') displace the actual ego as targets of self-love."[107] Both mothers are locked in the impossible dualism of trying to define themselves as both "woman" and "mother." Annie Rapper's ideal ego has been sublimated in the pages of her worldfamous book, *Average Wonderful,* for which her own children have acted both as exemplars and poor substitutes. Miss Credence's ideal ego is ossified in the psychotic image of the young Ginevra Rapper (her aspiration of the ideal and idealized "word child") framed as a picture and hanging, significantly, beside the photograph of her father, Professor Credence, on a wall of Credence House. "Miss Credence had invented a daughter for herself, mixed up out of longing and loneliness, and had given her the face of a child who was famous for saying clever things" (118). So too, Annie Rapper has invented, her own daughter, Ginevra, in the image of her Ideal I, her "word child," through the pages of her academic book.

Annie subscribes to the masculine tongue and is positioned in familial structure in opposition to Mike, who, by taking on the maternal role, is ineffectually mute. As the maternal substitute, he is ironically inscribed in the narrative as the "good mother," of the source of a perpetual supply of nurturing food for the family, and as the sop for Annie's reproductive functions. In her role as the Phallic Mother, Annie could have freed herself of the maternal function. But she has exploited it, and she has exploited the children by whom she would be defined as mother. She has attempted to inscribe them, through language, in "The-Name-of-(Law-of)-the-Father," and has used them as commodity products in the academic marketplace, but, nevertheless, they bear their father's name. Irigaray says:

> Their [the mothers'] products are legal tender in that order, moreover, only if they are marked with the name of the father, only if they are recognized within his law: that is, only insofar as they are appropriated by him.[108]

By so doing, Annie abstracts her own body by sublimating her female function into a system of values: forever self-aware of her own body as commodity, and of the exchange value of her bodily functions, she is continuously monitoring her own appearance, and has given birth to her children for the purpose of her own academic experimentations: "'I want to look great, but *accidentally* great . . . as if I've just scrambled into whatever happened to be lying around, and it just happens to be terrific'" (32). Like Christobel in *The Tricksters,* she has the type of self-cultivated "femininity" by which women engage the male gaze, and underwrite the patriarchal Law:

Femininity understands how to seduce, knows how to attract and captivate with the
folds of her garments—a dissimulation which multiplies her. She calculates her
effects, times her blows. . . . Femininity redoubles the burial of the mother with that
of the chorus. In order that Zeus, 'the god of speech,' prevail.[109]

The Maternal feminine

In *The Tricksters*, Naomi is the archetypal "good mother," the fetishized Madonna
mother,[110] with an enigmatic Mona Lisa kind of smile: "a lopsided smile, as if one
half of it were sadder than the other" (29). To her children she is irrefutably
"mother." Harry is shocked and embarrassed to hear her mother describe herself as
"sexy." "I've never had a go at being pretty. Sexy perhaps, but not pretty" (253),
and Christobel confirms the family's regard for Naomi's status as mother, " 'Oh,
you great, old earth-mother you!' cried Christobel. 'Did you remember to put the
milk bottles out?' " (49). As a manifestation of the "Great Mother" aspect of the
many contradictory attributes of Medusa, Naomi has effaced her sexuality in
childbearing, and has accepted her powerlessness. Each time Naomi is mentioned
in the narrative, it is in relation to either: delivering, preparing, or cooking, food;
washing dishes after one of her well–provided family meals; or as intermediary,
uttering maternal words of comfort, peacemaking, or arbitration. She is the whim-
sical watcher of family activities. She arrives alone, bearing the family food, and is
always positioned at the margins of events: in the hammock, in the kitchen, orches-
trating rather than participating, as if to emphasize the maternal body's position at
the margins, at the intersection between, " 'nature' and 'culture', threatening by its
very condition of fluidity, the stability of the paternal and Symbolic Order."[111] It is
a marginality which Naomi unwittingly acknowledges: " 'Perhaps its man and
nature we celebrate,' suggested Naomi. 'At Christmas, I mean' " (93). Like her
biblical namesake, she is the nurturing mother who holds the maternal role to be
her whole existence and, possibly past the age of childbearing herself, she offers to
nurture a child which is not her own,[112] Emma's child, the illegitimate offspring of
her husband Jack's illicit relationship, " 'Naomi just scooped me up—of course I
wanted to be scooped—but then, later, when I was expecting Tibby, she wanted to
scoop her, too. I mean, to adopt her—properly adopt her' " (75).

Irigaray has described the maternal-feminine as the woman, subsumed into
both mother and wife, who has no place or space of her own, who is located as
"the space or place" by and in which man can find a position and locate himself.
She is the place, the "home" of his existence, his "nostalgic place of origin":

> The maternal-feminine remains the place separated from 'her' place, deprived of
> 'his' place. She is or becomes the place of the other who can't separate himself from
> her. Threatening therefore without knowing it or wanting it to be so—with what she
> lacks: a place of 'her own.'[113]

Thus, Jack, having exercised his Oedipal desires by effectively taking his daughter as a sexual partner, is wholly dependent on Naomi as his mother: his home, her womb, his place of origin.

It is not made clear in the narrative whether the Carnival line descends through Jack or Naomi, although it is suggested that Jack's paternity of Tibby is his incestuous perpetuation of the Carnival family line: " 'Isn't it astonishing the way family faces persist?' 'Isn't it just!' Ovid said, idly patting Tibby on the head as she went past him" (66). Naomi is interesting for her role in this familial plot because of the way she is positioned—in monstrous silence—between Jack and Christobel, as the undesiring mother to both of them, and to their potential for incestuous relations with each other. Jack and Naomi's children are in no doubt about the solidity and stability of their parents' role as parents: " 'They've been such terrific parents. They've stayed together and they're really fond of each other,' Christobel burst out at last. 'It seems as if a big lump of virtue like that needs balancing out a little bit, and it's my duty to balance it' " (139).

In "Veiled Lips" Irigaray talks about just such a marriage and the cruelty of its deceits:

> The serenity of marriages blessed by the gods, the sweetest joys of mortals, the bed where fate joins man and woman—the cruelties. The father devouring his children, the departure of the married man for a war among men—the stakes: another woman, the sacrifice of the virgin daughter to gain the victory, the infidelity of the husband, his return accompanied by yet another woman—the anger of the woman, the mother.[114]

It is Naomi's willingness to keep silent about Jack's infidelity which makes her monstrous—her willingness to protect him, not from her own wrath, but from *Cristobel's* wrath; because, in so doing, she becomes, like Medusa, an agent of the incest taboo and colludes in female repression by subscribing to the myth of patriarchy and the affirmation of the male deceit of privilege. It is a maternal position cynically described by Cixous as: "The maternal mistresses to their little pocket signifiers."[115]

In this particular Oedipal drama, Naomi features as the decapitated (silenced) head of the Medusa who is the symbol of both terrifying and desirable female difference. In relation to Christobel as the virgin goddess, Athena; and, in them both, she combines aspects of the good/bad mother. Medusa's petrifying gaze, deflected through the mirror, combines with the Oedipal myth of blindness; but here it is the mother, not Oedipus, who is blinded in a specular economy where, as Irigaray points out, "nothing to be seen becomes nothing to see."[116] Naomi thus has become at once both the invisible woman and the "naturalized" mother, who is both present and absent in the familial Carnival plot.

DANGEROUS SPACES

Speaking the Body

Dangerous Spaces is positioned in *the feminine* as a plot of circularity in which the girl child, Anthea, seeks return and reconciliation with the maternal through a cyclical journey in a regressive space/time called Viridian. It is her quest to go through what is described in the narrative as the "hole in the middle of zero" (76). This is interpreted here as the eternal, maternal space of origins: " 'The hole in the middle of zero. Leo says that's always been there. There and not there, at the same time. Like the horizon' " (117). Through these out-of-time, out-of-body experiences in Viridian, Anthea recovers the lost maternal object and connects with *le parler femme*. Viridian can be viewed as a metaphor for everything Irigaray invokes in her thesis of *le parler femme*: it is a place of illogicality at the center of two polarities, in this case, the polarities of life and death; and it is a place of plurality, other knowledges, and multiple meanings in which the cause-and-effect grammars and syntax of daily life have broken down and been transmuted into a feminine space as described in the narrative in metaphors of fluidity and circularity.

> A rim of a circle of ruined stone. . . . All the angles and lines around her [Anthea] fell into disorder. Some things dwindled; others shot up into the air. The scent of roses came towards her on the playful wind, and broken stone rings became nothing but patches of broken light stretching across the garden and the fields beyond. (76, 78)

In this space Molly emerges as the agent of an aspect of *le parler femme*. Secluded in the patriarchal home, in a monogamous relation with Lionel upon whom she is financially dependent, she is the mother of two children and the adoptive mother to Anthea, because of Antheas' parents' mysterious disappearance and probable death. She is, then, irrefutably a "wife" and "mother," and in every sense a seeming victim of female oppression. But Molly has *chosen* to lead her outback life as earth-mother guardian of the chickens, cats, dogs, pine trees, and children that punctuate her daily living. She says, "I truly want the sort of life I've chosen" (97). It is a life in which she has transcended the circumscription of her social roles, and has realized a subjectivity in which she discursively values her own and her children's corporeal and emotional sensitivities. On this basis she is able to approach her girl children on a subject-to-subject basis of equality and mutual understanding:

> "Anthea, don't stick out your elbows when I hug you," Molly said. "*Now*! Hug me again." "You don't have to hug me," Anthea muttered. Molly still held her. "Anthea, I want *you* to hug me," she said. "*I* want to be the hugged one." So Anthea did the

hugging, and found herself weeping soundlessly on Molly's shoulder, and her tears, pushing their way out through a veil of stone, began dissolving the veil away. (97)

Through this unashamedly tactile discourse Molly liberates Althea's physical and emotional relations with herself and connects bodily with Molly in a newly realized mother/daughter relationship. Molly speaks *le parler femme* because she speaks her body: speaks "woman" irrespectively of her status as wife and mother. In this space both she and Anthea share both speech and pleasure, "This is a space of exchange without debt, without loss, without guilt, a space women can inhabit without giving up part of themselves."[117]

THE CHANGEOVER

The Looking Glass from the Other Side

In *Speculum of the Other Woman*, and in *This Sex Which Is Not One*, Irigaray subverts Lacan's idea of the mirror, which, she says, reflects only an image of the self-reflecting other which is masculine, by using the image of Alice who goes through the looking glass to arrive at a place that symbolizes for Irigaray her accession to *le parler femme* as an alternative language and logic. It is this image of the transition from one state and place to another, an image of metamorphosis implied in Irigaray's use of the term, "the looking glass from the other side,"[118] that is appropriated here to Mahy's *The Changeover*.

The narrative dramatizes a struggle for female liberation from the all-consuming tyranny of male power, in the character of Carmody Braque, and a process of regeneration into a new psychic space where mother, Kate, and daughter, Laura, are able to meet each other as women. They struggle to reconcile their separate experiences of womanhood across the wasting, dying body of the youngest family member, Jacko, whose life is being sapped out of him by the parasitical incubus and demon spirit, Braque. Laura harbors deep resentment against her father for deserting them, and a jealous resentment against her mother's new love relationship with Chris Holly, both of which affect her relationship with, and perceptions of, her mother as mother. Her ambivalence and resentment towards her mother and her father are further complicated by Laura's own first stirrings of a sexual attraction to Sorensen ("Sorry") Carlisle. In turn, Kate is constantly juggling her need to be mother against her desire to be a desirable woman: " 'You actually want to go out with him!' Laura said accusingly. 'Actually I do,' Kate said, 'Oh, Lolly, don't be cross with me. It's over a year since I went out with anyone even vaguely romantic and I enjoyed having my hair done at "Hair Today". . . . 'You've got too much good sense to imagine I'd have arranged to go out if I had known that Jacko was going to be sick' " (44).

The agent of Laura's transmutation is to be the "changeover," a ritual process of initiation through which, "at the other side of the mirror," she will emerge in another psychic and physical state of being. In this changed condition she will connect with what both Irigaray and Cixous have described as the feminine Imaginary[119] and a new corporeal morphology through which to symbolize her sexual difference. She will expel the life–denying male oppression embodied in Carmody Braque and reified in the inert, paralyzed body of Jacko.

Irigaray uses quotations from *Alice Through the Looking Glass* to describe what she perceives to be the condition of female identity:

> "Then it really has happened, after all! And now, who am I? I will remember, if I can! I'm determined to do it!" But being determined didn't help her much, and all she could say, after a great deal of puzzling, was: "L, I know it begins with L."[120]

Irigaray plays upon Alice's inability to recognize herself in the mirror, or to remember her name, and by invoking in the letter *L*, the *elle/elles* as the signifiers, in the French language, of the third person feminine, she indicates that *the feminine* is not fixed and is both singular and plural. This is Irigaray's challenge to the Lacanian thesis of the Mirror Stage, because by insisting on plurality in female identity she challenges Lacan's implication that the specular image of the Mirror is a unified image. It proves to be nothing but illusory when considered in the realm of her alternative discourse of *the feminine* at the other side of the mirror: "We are all written into the text. Once through the looking glass, the unified self is seen as an illusion."[121] "*So either I don't have any 'self' or else I have a multitude of 'selves' appropriated by them, for them, according to their needs or desires.*"[122] Also, by focusing on how Alice fails to recognize herself when she forgets her name, Irigaray exposes how familial names appropriate identity within the Name-of-(Law-of)-the-Father, "*'proper' name, that 'she' is at best 'from wonderland', even if 'she' has no right to a public existence except in the protective custody of the name of Mister X.*"[123]

"L," "Alice," "A-Luce," "An/alyse," Irigaray plays on all of these phonetical variations of Alice's name. Laura too, has a name beginning with the letter *L*, and there are other ways in which she can be compared with Alice as a symbol of female regeneration. Before her "changeover," Laura, like Alice, looks into the mirror and does not recognize herself in the reflection she sees.

> If Laura had been asked how she knew this reflection was not hers she could not have pointed out any alien feature. The hair was hers, the eyes were hers, hedged around with the sooty lashes of which she was particularly proud. However, for all that, the face was not her face for it knew something that she did not. It looked back at her from some mysterious place alive with fears and pleasures she could not entirely recognize. (3–4)

In response to Sorensen Carlisle's question about her knowledge of science, Laura refers to her knowledge of *Through the Looking Glass*.

"I'm not too sure about hypothesis if that's what you're asking, but I know *Through the Looking-Glass*" . . . "We're like scientists," said Sorry. "We compel nature—move it around according to our wishes—but scientists use rules they've worked out through thought, and ours comes through imagination, I suppose." (80, 103)

These differences between scientific and Looking Glass logic are precisely the terms in which Irigaray chooses to describe her idea of the differences between male and female logic, not as polarities but in her term of the "excluded middle." During Laura's changeover she is compared to Alice: "Like Alice she did not think she would ever be small enough to reach the beautiful garden" (150–51). Furthermore, in her transitional journey there are repeated images of, and references to, the looking glass:

She turned Laura slowly so that she looked into the watery depths of the looking-glass where she saw her self, shadowed and delicate, her wrist and ankles as slender as if she had hollow bird bones and could rise up against gravity. (138)

She was in a forest that was all forests, the forest at the heart of fairy tales, the looking-glass forest where names disappeared. . . . Laura now began to feel an ache in her neck and shoulders, as if she were pushing against an intangible resistance, and vaguely thought it might be something like the past, or reality. (145)

And, when her changeover is completed, Laura perceives her changed psychic and physical status through a mirror and, at the same time, connects with the moment of her birth:

He turned her gently to the mirror and by candlelight she saw plainly that she was remade, had brought to life some sleeping part of herself, extending the forest in her head. She was no longer formed simply from warring Stephen and Kate, but through the power of charged imagination, her own and other people, had made herself into a new kind of creature. . . ."Say what you see there." "It's yourself reversed." (152, 3)

The feminine *Imaginary and the Witch*

Mahy chooses witches through which to appropriate *the feminine*, and in so doing she exploits, if not subverts, the construction of the witch at the negative pole of the female spectrum, at the margins of all narratives, and whose repression is necessary to sustain male narratives of supremacy. Here the witches—Sorensen's mother, Miryam, Sorensen's grandmother, Winter, and Laura herself—are at the center of the narrative and are all powerful. Laura has witchy potentialities that are brought to fruition by her changeover. Jacko, as her familiar, is under a spell (overcome by male power) and it is her job to restore him in a ritual of counter-magic, to return the disease to Carmody Braque, and to take possession of her own body.[124] Miryam says, tellingly, " 'It's very much a feminine magic' " (70). She refers to women as " 'imaginary creatures . . . our power flows out of our imagination' " (134). Laura's changeover will complete their long-held desire to make a trio of what they describe as the " 'three female aspects' ": Winter as the old woman, Miryam as the mother, and Laura as the maiden (90). Through this trinity they evoke the triple aspects of the woman as identified in Robert Graves's the White Goddess motif[125] and enshrined in numerous fairy tales.

In the changeover Laura will remake herself into a "woman of the moon" (137), by connecting with the rhythmic time/space dimension of the *the feminine* Imaginary. But, in order to achieve a successful changeover she must be free from the experiences that might tie her to her present life, she must be, in fact, virginal:

> "Tell me, Laura, Chant, are you a virgin?" "Yes," Laura said. "Does it matter?" "It makes some differences," Winter replied. "It makes it easier to change if you aren't too tied to your present state." "We'll get rid of all the world that we can." (129, 135)

Irigaray refers in these terms to the ideologies of patriarchy that keep women from connecting with themselves:

> Our pleasure is trapped in their system, where a virgin is one as yet unmarked by them for them. One who is not yet made woman by and for them. Not yet imprinted with their sex, their language. Not yet penetrated, possessed by them.[126]

In history, women's stories of witchcraft have been described as constituting:

> A powerful fantasy which enabled women to negotiate the fears and anxieties of housekeeping and motherhood. . . . The witch is a fantasy-image of the huge and controlling scattered, polluted, leaky fantasy of the maternal body of the Imaginary.[127]

The story of witchcraft in *The Changeover*, carries similar connotations of motherhood, and is a powerful fantasy of the process of Laura's rebirth. Jacko, is described in fetal images as: "floating in his hospital womb, tied to life by wires and tubes" (141), and Laura herself experiences birthing sensations during her changeover, " 'It's very dark,' Laura said, taking a hesitant step" (140):

> It suddenly occurred to her she was being born again and, as this thought formed, the helix took her as if it had come alive. She was held and expelled, moved in a great vice, believing her intransigent head with its burdens of thoughts, dreams and memory must split open, and she came out somewhere into darkness. Reviving water continued to fall on her face. (151)

The entire process of the changeover is conducted in terms similar to those of the ancient birthing ritual.[128] Historically, the witch, regarded as the antimother, was excluded from the birthing room for fear of bewitching either the mother or the newborn child, and only the women, the "gossips," were admitted to the enclosed room in which the birthing mother was confined before and after giving birth. But, in the changeover ritual, the women admitted to the enclosed chamber are the witches, seeking to assist in the unwitching of a boy child. They perform ritual acts upon Laura similar to those used in the birthing ritual. For example, they give her a warm drink of mulled wine and spices, " 'a sprinkle of cinnamon, an orange stuck with cloves, the blood of grapes, the juice of a girl' " (137), that resembles the "mother's caundle."

> A hot drink containing warmed ale or wine with sugar and spices; this was the mother's drink throughout labor, and the gossips symbolically mothered her by supplying her with this special food.[129]

Diane Purkiss comments in relation to the maternal, female body and witchcraft:

> Magic and its remedies dealt with borders, markers, distinctions, insides and outsides, the limits of bodies and also that which breached those boundaries; bodily fluids, exchanges of objects through bodies and across thresholds. . . . Women's bodies, by virtue of their reproductive capacities, are seen as more open, more grotesque, less autonomous. The identification of the embarrassing and boundless body with the feminine may be one of the constants of Western culture.[130]

Like the birthing ritual, Laura's changeover is a ceremony of containment, demarcating the borders between inside and outside of the body, between self and Other, and between nature and culture.[131] It ritualistically demarcates en passant the territory of the abject that has been described above, " 'You must travel back into yourself Laura. Don't worry! It's only a little nature magic. . . . Your journey is inward, but it will seem outward' " (137, 138).

Discourse of le parler femme

At the end of Laura's journey into psychic and corporeal redefinition, she perceives her body as beautiful. No longer the alien flesh of her former self that she once viewed through the mirror. She loves her body, embraces it, and is freed from the old, patriarchal definition of herself as a jealous and dependent daughter between two warring parents. Her changeover has indeed affected a renewed mother/daughter relation and transcended the old economy of the daughter's separation from the mother. Laura is now in tune with Kate in a new condition of psychic closeness in which her mind is mixed with Kate's in "unconscious support and companionship" (173). But the changeover has also brought with it a new, and unexpected, maternal dimension to Laura's experiences in which, for example, she shares in Kate's memory of Jacko's early breastfeeding as if it were her own: "his nose pressed into her breast. . . . Laura's mind was so mixed with Kate's that the memory seemed entirely her own" (175). She assumes a role of maternal responsibility in which Kate becomes the daughter and she the responsible mother: "She put her arm around Kate as if she were the protecting one" (179). By the end of the narrative, in an astonishing exhibition of mother/daughter role reversal, it is Kate who is jealous of Laura's new love relationship with Sorensen Carlisle and his intrusion into their family life:

> "Come for fish and chips tomorrow," Laura suggested. "Come to tea with F. & C." . . . "Lolly, why on earth did you ask him to come tomorrow? Thursday's our special, family night." "Chris comes," Laura pointed out. (207, 208)

And it is Laura, not Kate, who mothers Jacko while her mother, like a love-struck adolescent, dances to music with Chris Holly in their living room:

> Jacko came over to Laura and leaned against her. "Sorry made a little farm," he whispered. "Yes," Laura agreed. "With little pigs and crocodiles!" said Jacko. He was holding his Ruggie and now began to suck his thumb. "I made the crocodiles," Laura pointed out, and lifted him onto her knee. She could smell the family shampoo in his hair and see his mouth turning up on either side of his thumb as he smiled. (212)

From her new position of heightened perceptions and freedom from patriarchal oppression, won *for* her, and *by* her, through her changeover and subsequently through Jacko's liberation from the constricting powers of Carmody Braque, Laura observes in her mother the folly of patriarchal definitions of love that have kept women enslaved:

> Kate believed in true love which Laura should wait to attain, yet true love had brought Kate unhappiness, and she herself had turned to a man she had known for only two days for consolation and escape. (189)

Irigaray conceives in this definition of heterosexual relations a source of women's entrapment, and of their exclusion from *le parler femme* especially in mother/daughter relations:

> You/I become two, then, for their pleasure. But thus divided in two, one outside, the other inside, you no longer embrace yourself, or me. Outside, you try to conform to an alien order. Exiled from yourself, you fuse with everything you meet. You imitate

whatever comes close. You become whatever touches you. In your eagerness to find yourself again, you move indefinitely far from yourself. From me. Taking one model after another, passing from master to master, changing face, form, and language with each new power that dominates you. You/we sundered; as you allow yourself to be abused, you become an impassive travesty. You no longer return indifferent; you return closed, impenetrable.[132]

Laura is liberated into the a new dimension of womanhood that is plural, autoerotic, and multisensual, in which she speaks her body through her eyes, her lips, her veins, her legs, and her breasts: "She felt totally alive. Each fingernail each hair on her head, seemed to be enjoying something in its own right, not simply as a piece of Laura with no existence apart from hers." (170)

In these manifestations of corporeality, in changed mother/daughter relations, and in the subjects' liberation from the circumscriptions of patriarchal oppressions, the narrative inscribes literary subjectivity in the discourses of *le parler femme.*

These narratives position literary subjectivity in *the feminine* in the many manifestations that have been traced through this chapter, which in its turn liberates new readings, in a reciprocal idea of *l'écriture féminine.*

NOTES TO CHAPTER 3

1. Julia Kristeva, "About Chinese Women," in *Kristeva Reader,* 138–59.
2. Ibid., 151.
3. Ibid., 153.
4. Lacan, *Language of the Self,* 164.
5. Luce Irigaray, "Any Theory of the 'Subject' Has Always Been Appropriated by the 'Masculine,' " in *Speculum,* 133–46; 142.
6. John Lechte, *Art,* 27.
7. Elaine Showalter, "Women's time, women's space," *Tulsa Studies in Women's Literature* 3 (1984): 29–43; 36.
8. Julia Kristeva, *Revolution.* First published as *La Revolution du langage poétique* (Paris: Les Editions du Seuil, 1974). Margaret Waller has translated into English only the theoretical sections of Kristeva's doctoral thesis dealing with the inextricable links between subject and text in her terms of the "Semiotic," "Thetic," and "Symbolic." An abbreviated version of *Revolution in Poetic Language* is published in *Kristeva Reader,* 89–136.
9. Ibid.
10. Julia Kristeva, "The system and the Speaking Subject," in *Kristeva Reader,* 34-33; 28; also Moi, "Revolution," 89–136, 120–3.
11. Grosz, *Sexual Subversions,* 51.
12. Julia Kristeva, "From One Identity to An Other," in *Desire in Language: A Semiotic Approach to Art and Literature,* ed. Leon S. Roudiez, trans. Thomas Gora, Alice Jardine, and Leon S. Roudiez (Oxford: Basil Blackwell, 1982), 124–47; 136.

13. Elizabeth Grosz, *Jacques Lacan: A Feminist Introduction* (London: Routledge, 1990), 152.
14. Kristeva, *Desire*, 136.
15. Ibid., 137.
16. Kristeva, *Revolution*, 80.
17. Kristeva, "Women's Time," in *Kristeva Reader*, 197–213.
18. Ibid., 191.
19. Julia Kristeva, "The Novel as Polylogue," in *Desire*, 159–209; 193–4.
20. See Marianne Hirsch, *The Mother/Daughter Plot: Narrative, Psychoanalysis, Feminism* (Bloomington and Indianapolis: Indiana University Press, 1989), 132.
21. Cixous and Clément, *Newly Born*, 63.
22. Julia Kristeva, *Powers*.
23. Ibid., 2, 5.
24. Ibid.
25. Ibid., 11.
26. Ibid., 13.
27. See, for example, Grosz, *Sexual Subversions*, 63, 65; also Kelly Oliver, ed., *The Portable Kristeva* (New York: Columbia University Press, 1997), 199; Ann E. Kaplan, *Motherhood and Representation: The Mother in Popular Culture and Melodrama* (London: Routledge, 1992), 43–4.
28. In her later work *Black Sun*, Kristeva describes *the feminine* sexuality in the relations between the female infant and the maternal body: "In order to separate from their mother's bodies females must separate from themselves as women; and in order to maintain some identification with the mother as the bodies of women. Females carry around the 'corpse' of their mother's bodies locked in the crypt of their psyches." Julia Kristeva, *Black Sun*, trans. Leon S. Roudiez (New York: Columbia University Press, 1989), 28–9.
29. See for example, Julia Kristeva, "Motherhood According to Giovanni Bellini," in *Desire*, 237–70; "Stabat Mater," in *Kristeva Reader*, 160–86.
30. Grosz, *Sexual Subversions*, 132.
31. Luce Irigaray, 'Etablir un généalogie de femmes', *Maintnant* 12 (May 28, 1979) as cited in Grosz, *Sexual Subversions*, 119–121.
32. Luce Irigaray, "And One Doesn't Stir without the Other," trans. Hélène Vivienne Wenzel, *Signs: Journal of Women in Culture* 7, no. 11 (Autumn 1981): 60–7; 61.
33. Ibid.
34. Luce Irigaray, "When Our Lips Speak Together," in *This Sex*, 205–218; 209.
35. Irigaray, *Speculum*, 11.
36. Irigaray, *Le corps-à-corps avec la mère*, 20, 21.
37. Freud, "Three Essays on the Theory of Sexuality," *The Standard Edition* (London: The Hogarth Press, 1953–74), 7: 130–243.
38. Mary Jacobus, "Judith, Holofernes, and the Phallic Woman," in *Reading Women* (London: Methuen, 1986), 110–36; 111.
39. Marcia Ian, *Remembering the Phallic Mother: Psychoanalysis, Modernism and the Fetish* (Ithaca: Cornell University Press, 1993), 8.
40. Sigmund Freud, "Female Sexuality," *The Standard Edition*, 21: 225–43; 230: "Fetishism, is a substitute for a particular and quite special penis. . . . No male human being is spared the fright of castration at the sight of the female genital."

Jerome Neu, *The Cambridge Companion to Freud* (Cambridge: Cambridge University Press, 1991), 239: "The penis that the mother was once thought to have. All boys struggle with acknowledging female–originally the mother's—castration. Fetishists resolve the struggle by disavowal, or denial, creating a fetish that externally represents the maternal phallus and thus supports such disavowal." In Lacanian theory these fetishized objects are the *objet à* and extend to the entire geography/topology of the female body.

41. Moi, *Sexual Textual*, 58.
42. Kristeva, "The Novel as Polylogue," in *Desire*, 191.
43. Irigaray, *This Sex*, 79
44. Ibid., 79.
45. Luce Irigaray, "Women's Exile," an interview, trans. Couze Venn, *Ideology and Consciousness* 1 (1977): 67; reprinted in *The Feminist Critique of Language: A Reader*, ed. Deborah Cameron (London: Routledge, 1990), 80–96.
46. Irigaray, *This Sex*, 187.
47. Carolyn Burke, "Irigaray Through the Looking Glass," *Feminist Studies* 7, no. 2 (1981): 288–306; 296.
48. Ann Rosalind Jones, "Inscribing femininity: French theories of the feminine," in *Making A Difference: Feminist Literary Criticism*, eds. Gayle Greene and Coppélia Kahn, (London: Routledge, 1985), 80–112; 86. For a stridently negative critique of Irigaray's work on *le parler femme* see Jane Gallop, *Quand Nos Lèvres S'écrivant*: Irigaray's Body Politic," *Romantic Review* 74, no. 1 (1983): 77–83.
49. Burke, "Irigaray Through the Looking Glass," 289.
50. Irigaray, "Woman's Exile," 64.
51. Irigaray, *This Sex*, 101–3.
52. Irigaray, "Women on the Market," 186.
53. Luce Irigaray, *L'Éthique de la différence*, (Paris: Editions Minuit, 1984), 106, quoted in Marianne Hirsch, *The Mother/Daughter Plot: Narrative, Psycho-analysis, Feminism* (Bloomington: Indiana University Press, 1989), 13. See also Cixous, "Laugh of the Medusa," 67: "Too bad for them if they fall apart upon discovering that women aren't men, or that the mother doesn't have one. But isn't this fear convenient for them? Wouldn't the worst be, isn't the worst, in truth, that women aren't castrated, that they have only to stop listening to the Sirens (for the Sirens were men) for history to change its meaning. You have only to look at Medusa straight on to see her. And she's not deadly. She's beautiful and she's laughing . . . Castration? Let others toy with it. What's a desire originating from lack? A pretty meager desire."
54. Irigaray, "And One Doesn't Stir."
55. Irigaray, *Speculum*, 40.
56. Irigaray, "And One Doesn't Stir," 67.
57. Irigaray, *Speculum*, 33.
58. Irigaray, "When Our Lips Speak," 205–17.
59. Freud, "Family Romances," *The Standard Edition*, 9: 237–41.
60. Kristeva, *Powers*, 165.
61. Cixous, "Castration or Decapitation?"
62. Cixous, "Laugh of the Medusa."

63. Margaret Homans, *Bearing the Word: Language and Experience in Nineteenth-Century Women's Writing* (Chicago: University of Chicago Press, 1986), 4. See also, Margaret Homans, " 'Her Very Own Howl': The Ambiguities of Representation in Recent Women's Fiction," *Signs* 9, no. 2 (1986): 163–8.

64. Luce Irigaray, *L'Ethique de la difference sexuelle* (Paris: Minuit, 1984), 106, quoted in Marianne Hirsch, *The Mother/Daughter Plot*, 43.

65. Gilles Deleuze and Félix Guattari, *Anti-Oedipus: Capitalism and Schizophrenia*, trans. Robert Hurley, et al., (Minneapolis: University of Minnesota Press 1983).

66. See Adrienne Rich, *Of Woman Born: Motherhood as Experience and Institution* (London: Virago, 1977).

67. Kristeva, *Powers*, 10.

68. Ibid., 2.

69. Ibid., 3.

70. Ibid., 15.

71. Ibid.

72. Kristeva, *Revolution*, 48.

73. In an extension to the categories of the Thetic as "two heterogeneous realms," Kristeva has cited it as the basis of all theses and antitheses, of all oppositions: for example, as the precondition of the difference between signifier and signified, denotation and connotation, language and referent. The Thetic, Kristeva points out, is the precondition of the subject of *énonciation*; see Kristeva, *Revolution*, 43–50; *Desire*, 131–2; and *Polylogue* (Paris: Editions du Seuil, 1981), 107–8.

74. Kristeva, *Powers*, 2.

75. Ibid., 80.

76. Ibid., 8.

77. Ibid., 1–31.

78. Ibid., 77.

79. See J. Saler, "Leviticus: A Purity of Place, A Purity of Speech," "Semiotique de la nourriture dans la Bible," *Annales*, (July-August 1973): 93 ff, quoted in Julia Kristeva, *Powers* 113.

80. Gross, "The Body of Signification," 91.

81. Kristeva, "Women's Time," 187–213.

82. Kristeva, "Giotto's Joy" in *Desire*, 210–36; 221.

83. Kristeva, "Women's Time."

84. Ibid., 191.

85. John Lechte; *Julia Kristeva* (London: Routledge, 1990), 128; also Kristeva, *Revolution*, 25: "The *chora* is a mobile and extremely provisional articulation constituted by movements and their ephemeral stases."

86. Cixous, *Souffles*, 8.

87. Kristeva, "The Novel as Polylogue," 195.

88. Sellers, *Cixous Reader*, 8.

89. Cixous and Clément, *Newly Born*, 93.

90. Ibid., 95–6.

91. Luce Irigaray, "La Misére de la psychanalyse," *Critique* 33, no. 363 (1977): 879–903.

92. Cixous, "Laugh of the Medusa," 885.

93. Cixous, "Castration or Decapitation?," 49.

94. Jeremy Neu, *The Cambridge Companion to Freud*, 239: "Fetishists resolve the struggle by disavowal, or denial, creating a fetish that externally represents the maternal phallus and thus supports such disavowal. Disavowal also enters the realm of mythology, as the snakes of 'Medusa's Head' condense signification on the one hand of the mature female external genitals and on the other of many penises, which in turn stand both for castration (because the one has been lost) and denial of castration (there are many penises). See Sigmund Freud, "The Medusa's Head," *The Standard Edition*, 23: 7–137.

95. Kristeva, "The Word as Polylogue," 191.

96. Ibid., 191, 192.

97. Irigaray, "And One Doesn't Stir," 11.

98. Juliet Flower MacCannell, "Things To Come: A Hysteric's guide to the Future Female Subject," in *Supposing the Subject*, ed. Joan Copjec (London: Verso, 1994), 106–32; 107.

99. Luce Irigaray, "Veiled Lips," *Mississippi Review* 11, no. 3 (1983): 93–131; 99.

100. Irigaray, "And One Doesn't Stir," 11.

101. See note 103 below.

102. Grosz, *Sexual Subversions*, 138.

103. Eating disorders have been described as the modern form of hysteria. Elizabeth Grosz has indicated that anorexia and bulimia: "seem most interestingly interpreted in terms of a mourning or nostalgia for the lost (maternal) object, and either an attempt to devour or consume it (bulimia) or to harden oneself against its loss (in anorexia)." Gross, *Sexual Subversions*, 242, n. 15.

104. See Naomi Segal, "Patrilinear and Matrilinear," in *The Body and the Text: Hélène Cixous, Reading and Teaching*, eds. Helen Wilcox et al., (Hertfordshire: Harvester Wheatsheaf, 1990), 131–46.

105. Cixous, "Castration or Decapitation?," 43.

106. Whitford, *Irigaray Reader*, 44.

107. Susan E. Gustafson, *Absent Mothers and Orphaned Fathers* (Detroit: Wayne State University Press, 1995).

108. Irigaray, "Women on the Market," 185.

109. Irigaray, "Veiled Lips," 99.

110. See, Mary Jacobus, "*Dora,* and the Pregnant Madonna," in *Reading Woman: Essays in Feminist Criticism* (London: Methuen, 1986), 137–93.

111. Ibid., 140.

112. Naomi Segal, "Patrilinear and Matrilinear," 139.

113. Irigaray, *L'Éthique*, 18.

114. Irigaray, "Veiled Lips," 101–2.

115. Cixous, "Laugh of the Medusa," 890.

116. Irigaray, *Speculum*, 48.

117. Grosz, *Sexual Subversions*, 126.

118. Luce Irigaray, "The Looking Glass from the Other Side," in *This Sex*, 9–22.

119. Luce Irigaray, *Parler n'est pas jamais neuter*, quoted in Margaret Whitford, "Re-reading Irigaray," 5–6; also Cixous, "Castration or Decapitation?," 52.

120. Irigaray, *This Sex*, 9.

121. Burke, "Irigaray Through the Looking Glass," 299.
122. Irigaray, *This Sex*, 17.
123. Ibid.
124. See, Diane Purkiss, "The Body of the Witch," in *The Witch in History: Early Modern and Twentieth-Century Representations* (London: Routledge 1996), 119–44.
125. Robert Graves, *The White Goddess*.
126. Irigaray, *This Sex*, 211–2.
127. Purkiss, "The House, the Body, the Child," *The Witch in History*, 93–119.
128. Ibid., 91–118.
129. Ibid., 101.
130. Ibid., 102.
131. Ibid., 97.
132. Irigaray, "When Our Lips Speak," 210.

4

The feminine Postmodern Subject in Children's Literature

THEORETICAL INTRODUCTION TO THE CHAPTER

Questions about subjectivity have been central to post-structuralist theories. Subjectivity is deeply bound up with notions of identity, but in post-structuralism questions of human identity move away from pre-structuralist concepts of an immutable, stable "self," and a liberal paradigm of individualism, to a consideration of a human subject that does not occupy the center ground of knowledge and agency. Rather, it is diffused and fractured across the spectrum of discourses. Conceptions of the subject like these would appear to be anathema to children's literature, which is, at least in its realist manifestation, generically and historically dependent on the kind of premodernist, centered, and stable subject (usually a *child* subject who is also often the agent of focalization); a subject who is, in fact, knowable and predictable within the discursive framework. Few, if any, children's writers have veered away from this characteristic paradigm of the subject, not even those whose writing may be classified as the most obviously "experimental," among whom we might rank Robert Cormier, Paul Zindel, Alan Garner, Robert Swindells, Aidan Chambers, and Berlie Doherty.[1] These writers, even while they are overtly and radically challenging realist modes and structures, cling on to an idea of a quasi-humanist subject both of and in the text. This paradoxical mixture of realist and postmodern forms is being proposed here as the essence of *the feminine* postmodern, and is characteristically present in children's fiction.

There is a question about what postmodernism is exactly, but to have an understanding of the idea of *the feminine* postmodern in children's literature it may be useful first to have a context in which to appreciate its digression from versions of postmodernism per se. The voluminous and partisan writings and criticism debating the postmodern have not resolved it as either a style, a mood, a periodizing concept, or an aesthetic practice; neither can it reliably be described as a disruption to, exhaustion and repudiation of, or radical break from modernism, or a continuation and addition to it. Neither has the critical establishment established whether, indeed, such a category as the postmodern exists. So the idea of the postmodern continues to be a slippery and sliding category with a plurality of meanings: from a paradoxical cultural paradigm and condition of late modernity, to an aesthetics of impersonality and objectivism. The refusal of definition is symptomatic of the problem, and is the source of fascination. However, there is some sort of consensus in the critical discourses that debate the postmodern, that the essentialist, centralist, Romantic and monadic subject of humanism has given way to the loss of personal identity and agency, and the loss of belief in any essentialist self preceding its social construction.

In the postmodern aesthetic, as with the psycho-dynamics of textual relations in psychoanalysis as it is defined here, the subject is constituted and subsumed in language and *all* is text: the subject is subsumed in text, and postmodernism assumes that there is nothing outside the text. Victor Burgin points out that,

> The postmodern subject must live with the fact that not only are its languages arbitrary, but it is itself an "effect" of language, a precipitate of the very symbolic order of which the humanist subject supposed itself to be the master.[2]

As such, even while in principle we should acknowledge that the discourses of postmodernism in literature would deconstruct and delegitimize such a "grand and totalizing narrative" as the Lacanian theory of the Symbolic Order, it is also the case that the subjects of both the Lacanian Symbolic and the subject of postmodernism are both the "effect" of language. Language is the moment of intersection between the world, the reading subject, and the literary text and is the locus where literary subjectivity is fabricated in the act of reading; it annexes literary subjectivity to the wider discursive field. McHale proposes "*intertextual space*"[3] as the network of codes (or literature as a field), whose nodes are the actual texts of literature.[4] "The intertextual space is constituted whenever we recognize the relations (at whatever fictional level) among two or more texts, or between texts and larger categories such as genre, or school."[5] The issue for literary subjectivity in the framework of postmodernism is, then, very much about "what the reading subject brings to the text"; but now the reading subject and the literary text have a psycho-social dimension and the concept of text is manifold, intersubjective, and intertextual. In these conceptions of postmodernism, the literary object is no longer a "work" (which implies the agency of authorship) but "text" as a "multi-dimensional space in which a variety of writings, none of them original, blend and clash."[6]

Both postmodernism and Lacanian versions of psychoanalysis celebrate the dissolution of the sign into the unstable signifier precipitating the release of an infinite play of signifieds. The literary subject of postmodernism has itself been dissolved into a series of signs in what Jameson has described as consumer capitalism's system of commodity exchange. In such a system, the assumption of a coherent spatiality and temporality of language and experience break down into the condition he calls "schizophrenia." The "schizophrenic" subject of postmodernity will experience language not as the interrelationship of words producing global meanings but as "isolated, disconnected, discontinuous, material signifiers which fail to link up into a coherent sequence,"[7] and, in Lyotard's definition, as a series of "language games" with an emphasis on "performance" not "truth."[8]

For Jameson, postmodernism is not just a style, or an aesthetics, it is also a periodizing concept[9] in which he perceives the condition of schizophrenia as the cultural and stylistic logic of late, consumer capitalism.[10] Jameson has correlated postmodernism's formal features of discontinuity and disintegration with the emergence of a new economic order, what he has called "the new moment of capitalism," dating from the postwar late 1940s/early 1950s boom in the United States and late 1950s France, and culminating in the 1960s as the key transitional period of the new international order of neo-colonialism, the Green Revolution, computerization, and electronic information.[11] In such a condition, Jameson says, the humanist depth models of interiority, self-realization, and unshaken belief in transcendental individualism that pervaded the postwar period have given way to a late-century culture and aesthetics of surface, plurality, heterogeneity, pastiche, and paranoia. This, in turn, has given rise in literature to discursive practices of fragmentation, effacement, and a literature of surfaces. This is the site upon which the ego of the contemporary subject must be de facto inscribed if we accept Jameson's theorization, and Lacan's theory of a socially constructed *moi*, given that language (the Symbolic) cannot exist outside its social and cultural context.

In postmodernism, humanist assumptions of and beliefs in ideas of "truth," "the real," "knowledge," and its relationships to "experience,"[12] have been subsumed in a Baudrillardian panoply of simulacra and "hyperreality." Hyperreality is the transformation of reality into images in which traditional boundaries between the real and the fabricated have been irreconcilably dissolved (as in fantastic narratives, for example); it represents a move from the logic of centrality to peripherality, a move away from an emphasis on temporality to an emphasis on spatiality. The emphasis on the past and history has given way, in the Jamesonian condition of schizophrenia, to "historical amnesia," where *time* is experienced as a kaleidoscope of perpetual presents, and where the collective notion of "pastness" has been colonized by a series of pseudo-historical images and signs in the "nostalgia mode" bearing little relation to a lived, historical period. On the other hand, Jameson shares with Patricia Waugh[13] and Linda Hutcheon,[14] a belief that the "radical-break from modernism" theory of postmodernism, breaks down under scrutiny because many of the features that are present in the postmodern aesthetic also were present in modernism (and for Waugh they were present also in Romanticism and the pre-Enlightenment.) The difference is that features that were then subordinate have now become dominant, and those that had been dominant have become secondary.[15] Postmodernism, Waugh points out:

> Is nearly always parodic, acknowledging its implication in a pre-existing textuality, creating through decreation, displacing that secure perspective of a stable vantage point from outside (Romantic Vision or Enlightenment transcendental ego as pure reason).[16]

Waugh, Jameson, and McHale claim that what we have lost in postmodernism is a faith in the historical structures and moral conditions that allowed and sustained the idea of a unified subject. We also have lost a belief in history as an ordered, representative narrative of human experience. These are just two of the problems of postmodernism for children's literature because children's literature assumes, and is premised on, an understanding of a historical self that is infinitely knowable, and on history as a coherent and continuous narrative. However, in the postmodern consciousness as it is being interpreted and defined here, history itself is transposed into a plurality of "islands of discourse," and as "a series of metaphors which cannot be detached from the various institutionally produced languages which we bring to bear upon it."[17] In the words of Christine Brooke-Rose:

> The society they refer to is no longer there, in the sense that there is no fixed or certain belief in it. Serious writers have lost their material. Rather, the material has gone elsewhere: back to the novelist's original sources in documentary, journalism, chronicles, letter writing—but in their modern forms such as the media and the human sciences.[18]

This kind of observation is what allows McHale to make his distinction between modernist narratives as epistemological, and postmodern narratives as ontological: he says, the questions are no longer, "Who am I?" and "How can I interpret the world of which I am a part?" but rather, "Which world is this?" and "Which of my selves is to do it?"[19]

And, contrary to received theories of the postmodern as anti-mimetic, McHale claims that postmodernist narratives continue to hold a mirror up to everyday life, but now the world is a plural ontology, and reality is: "pervaded by the 'miniature escape fantasies' of television and the movies. . . . Mimesis clearly is alive and well in postmodernism."[20] McHale uses well-worn terminologies, borrowed from Genette and from Foucault to describe the ontological strata of (postmodern) fictions, such as Genette's various kinds of "diegeses"[21] as an indicator of narrative levels, and Foucault's use of "homotopia" and/or "heterotopia,"[22] to describe relations between singular and/or plural fictional worlds. Foucault suggests in relation to the postmodern, that we should, "prefer what is positive and multiple, difference over uniformity, flows over unities, mobile arrangements over systems,"[23] and he has consigned late century existence to an experience of "heterotopia."[24]

As has already been suggested, we may glean from such panoply of debate and argument that postmodernism, as a category, seemingly is immediately at odds and incommensurate with the essentialist notions of the subject of both children's literature and psychoanalysis. Whereas postmodernism is premised on the *dissolution* of any notion of a subject that is not a product of the practices and discourses of the culture in which it finds itself, both children's literature and psychoanalysis are premised on the very idea of discrete and identifiable subject. Nevertheless, as is suggested above, even while it preaches a "depth model" of the subject in its theories of the conscious and unconscious, desire, and primary processes, psychoanalysis maintains a model of the subject that is *decentered* and plural but not *dissolved.* It is being suggested here, therefore, that this *decentered* but not dissolved subject is a characteristic of what is named here as *the feminine* postmodern and that it is especially evident in children's literature.

Feminist theorists, particularly of the Anglo-American school such as Patricia Waugh, Linda Nicholson, and Jane Flax, have been keen to add their voices to the discourses of postmodernism. They have perceived these discourses to be otherwise wholly masculinist, and usually male, with no mention, in postmodern criticism from these male sources, of gender relations, or any evidence of engagement with or concern for feminist thought. So, the idea of *the feminine* postmodern in this chapter is a move to theorize the way that paradigms of the postmodern have been appropriated in children's literature. It is here claimed that this can best be done by partially borrowing from the discourses of feminist criticism that have challenged the masculinist centrality and questioned "universal" notions of postmodernism's dissolution of the subject.

In principle, postmodernist and feminist criticism have a great deal in common: both are concerned with positions of marginality, both have questioned and sought to destabilize the master narratives mediating received notions of subjectivity, both have been founded in crises of identity, both have questioned power relations and received forms of knowledge. In addition, both postmodernism and feminism have mediated these concerns through literary narratives which efface boundaries, are self-referential, and self-reflexive, and they both use and abuse fictional conventions to challenge and subvert; they are meta-discursive; and they celebrate liminality, use fantasy, the fantastic, utopias, and parody and pastiche as disruptive techniques. Feminist postmodern criticism has recognized the female condition in the fragmented, decentered, and alienated subject of poststructuralism, but it has resisted the idea of a *dissolved* subject, and the manifestations of impersonality in postmodernism. Instead, it has craved "essence," human relationship, and human agency, which is why it is more appropriate to theorize the postmodern of children's literature in relation to the discourses of postmodern feminist criticism, (irrespectively of the authorial gender of individual texts) than in the discourses of postmodernist criticism per se. Waugh points out that fictions written by many contemporary women writers:

> Articulate the processes of fictionality as functions of human desire and imagination rather than as an impersonal, intertextual play of signification. They express optimism about the possibility of human relationship and human agency, which rarely is articulated in "classic" postmodern texts.[25]

So, it is in a space analogous to *feminist* appropriations of postmodernism in literature, that literary subjectivity is inscribed in these paradigm texts of children's literature.[26] It resides in an alternative liminal place that is not wholly humanist, nor entirely conceptually poststructuralist; and it uses and incorporates the narrative ramifications of postmodernism but with none of its nihilistic dissolutions of the subject. Waugh has described it thus:

> Such writing constructs a new subject, one who is necessarily "dispersed" but who is also an effective agent, neither the old liberal subject nor the contemporary poststructuralist site of the play of signification. This subject is positioned in a fictional world, too, where morality has neither been relativized out of the window nor been seen simply as the reflection of an 'essential' human condition.[27]

Crucially, Waugh, in what she described as the "grand and totalizing narrative" of her paper on women's writing and the postmodern[28] (which could be just as easily appropriated to writing for children) has suggested that impersonality, "is not a mode with which women can easily identify," and that, "Feminism must posit some belief in the notion of effective human agency."[29] In opposition to the poststructuralist/postmodernist appeal to separation and objectivity as the markers of identity, Waugh suggests that the female aesthetic (which is analogous to what is here called *the feminine*) should instead valorize "relationship" and "connection," and the centrality of *"primary* affectional relations," which, she says, need not be pathological.[30] Similarly, Cixous, in her essays on women's writing, believes that "the feminine" text valorizes feeling over meaning, "perhaps because there's something in them that's freely given, perhaps because they don't rush into meaning, but are straightway at the threshold of feeling."[31] Following through her idea that the feminine text is not gender specific she says,

> To be signed with a woman's name, . . . doesn't necessarily make a piece of writing feminine. It could quite well be masculine writing, and conversely, the fact that a piece of writing is signed with a man's name does not in itself exclude femininity.[32]

Jane Flax has considered the limitations of postmodernist constructions of subjectivity and she says there is a need for what she has called a "core self" as a predicate to an experience of decenteredness in the subject:

> Only when a core self begins to cohere can one enter into or use the transitional space in which differences and boundaries between self and other, inner and outer, and reality and illusion are bracketed or elided. . . . It is grandiose and misleading to claim that no other space exists or that this one alone is sufficient.[33]

She goes on to suggest that feminist theorists have a special interest in constructing concepts of the self that do justice to the "full complexity of subjectivity." These notions of centrality predicating decenteredness are controversial and problematic and, like the "chicken-and-egg" dilemma, are insoluble. But it is clear from these arguments, that late twentieth century/early twenty first century feminist literary criticism, like children's literature criticism, is in pursuit of a language with which to describe the condition of subjectivity. This desired language is not entirely the decentered subject of post-structuralism, nor the dissolved subject of postmodernism, but is rather one which draws upon both, while also, paradoxically, sustaining and confronting centeredness and agency. These are the ideas which speak to and are attractive to a theorization of the subject in children's literature criticism that move us closer to a theorization of the postmodern in children's literature as *the feminine* postmodern.

SUMMARY

This chapter shows how and why these focus texts act as paradigms of *the feminine* postmodern in children's literature. They feature, and *imply*, decentered, fragmented subjectivities but they resist dissolution of the subject. They exhibit tensions between unity and disunity, between interiority and exteriority, and between discursive structures and fictional worlds that open up a proto-postmodern text/reading-subject contract. However, unlike the features of classic postmodern novels, which often disrupt the linguistic surface of the narrative, these narratives appropriate postmodern techniques *inter-diegetically*, that is, at the level of *story* and *fictional* worlds—in the mode of McHale's fictional "zones."[34] At the same time and, it would seem, paradoxically in relation to definitions of classic postmodern literature, they exhibit strongly humanist qualities in their discursive representations of the subject and subjective relations. In short, they exhibit postmodern narrative techniques and the kinds of decentered subjectivities, which accord with Lacanian psychoanalytic descriptions of the subject; still, their predisposition to resist the classic postmodern dissolution and objectification of psycho-textual identity distinguishes them as texts of *the feminine* postmodern.

In these ways, they resemble the literature of many contemporary women writers identified by Waugh in her work on the female postmodern,[35] and other recent
women writers who, though ideologically different, share in their writing the common characteristic of proto-postmodernist narrative techniques while at the same
time maintaining a sense of subjective agency. Waugh has described the way in
which certain canonical contemporary women writers adopt many of the narrative
techniques of the masculinist postmodern fictions that have defined postmodern
writing, but, she claims, although these novels feature decentered and fragmented
subjectivities (and, presumably, by extension, imply and inscribe an equally decentered and fragmented reading subject), they do not *dissolve* the subject in quite the
way that has become synonymous with the postmodernist definition.[36] So, in summary, *the feminine* postmodern of children's fiction in the terms as it is defined here,
suggests the maintenance of the seemingly paradoxical notion of *agency* in the literary subject both *in* and *of* the fictions that is more sympathetically theorized through
feminist-postmodernist criticism in different models of literary subjectivity and literary texts than the purely phallocentric versions that are generically dominant.

The section "*the feminine* Postmodern Landscapes," shows how the psychical,
material, and textual landscapes in *Memory* and *Wolf* relate to postmodern discourses
of fragmentation, dissolution, and marginality. In these fictions, subjectivities are
dispersed across a kaleidoscope of refracted surfaces that confound pre-modernist
conceptions of interiority, depth, and transcendental individualism, even while sustaining paradoxical notions of centeredness, truth, and reality. They exhibit the kinds
of classic postmodern features described above, particularly in their expression of
the past as a "plurality of islands of experience" in the lives of their central characters—Sophie, Jonny, and Cassy. Simultaneously, their elliptical plot structures rely
on the motivation of human agency and intersubjective relations that are characteristic of *the feminine* postmodern textuality. The possibility of the reader's move to
ascribe monadic subjectivity to these characters is contained by the texture of the
narrative as characters move back and forth, in and out of time and place, and by discursive discontinuity that disrupts conventional temporality and simultaneously fragments subjectivity. In these kinds of techniques, the reading subject is interpolated in
the narrative through a range of complex textualities that are belied by straightforwardly realist and humanist seeming plot and characterization that are the common
characteristics of children's literature texts of *the feminine* postmodern.

The subject position, and the narrative and discursive structures in, and of,
Memory and *Wolf* as paradigm texts of *the feminine* postmodern, thus, are analogous to the works of many contemporary women writers. They exhibit many of
the techniques and literary devices associated with the classic postmodern novel,
but are distinguished by their insistence on agency, and by their refusal to dissolve
the subject or, in psycho-semiotic terms, to reduce the subject to a nominal linguistic signifier that is symptomatic of classic (usually, male) postmodern narratives. Like many of the works of contemporary women writers, and unlike classic
(male) postmodernist narratives, these paradigm texts employ their postmodern

techniques inter-diegetically, that is, at the level of the story and restrict their disruptive techniques to the topographical and typographical features of the narrative. They bear sophisticated narrative codings in which meanings between text and reading subject are inscribed in an interplay of typographical signifiers that are more than the mere words on the page. *Wolf*, and *Memory*, carry all the hallmarks of postmodern narratives, but they are positioned in the mode of *the feminine* postmodern by maintaining a single center of focus through the agency of their main characters. The literary subjectivity of *the feminine* postmodern resides here, in and through the experience of these particular literary exchanges.

MEMORY

The feminine *Postmodern Landscapes*

Lacanian psychoanalytic theory, founded in structural linguistics, inscribes subjectivity in the signifying chain of language where ego formation is constituted in, and is the consequence of, the gaze of the Other in the form of objects of desire (*objet a*). It is in this conjunction between language as a chain of signifiers and the Lacanian psychoanalytic concept of the fragmented subject, and between Lacanian psychoanalysis and the sociocultural scene, that the idea of *the feminine* postmodern landscape is pursued here in the sense that they relate to both physical and psychic topologies.[37]

Neville Wakefield has pointed out how Lacan's work on language is related to the postmodern condition:

> Lacan offers a route to understanding some of the pathologies that have become associated with, and representative of, our present postmodern condition. . . . The breakdown of the signifying chain can, accordingly, no longer be distinguished from the emergence of a correspondingly "broken down" or disjunctive subjectivity.[38]

In *Memory*, the enigmatic mingling of memory as fiction, the fictions of memory, and representations of the fictive neuroses of character, position the narrative on the cusp of the real and imaginary in that ambiguous space described in chapter 1 as the place of the fantastic, because, as has been identified there, fantastic narratives share many features in common with narratives of the postmodern, conceived in both cases here as manifestations of *the feminine*. Jonny Dark is a loner in this narrative. He is on a personal quest to track down Bonnie Benedicta, who is the only person who will be able to rid him of the memory of his sister's death. He finds himself in the early hours of the morning, and after a night of drunken stupor, at the scene of his childhood. This is the point at which he encounters old Sophie, a widow who lives alone, and wanders alone through the early morning streets in an equally mindless state as Jonny, but because she suffers from dementia. The events of the narrative are structured round Jonny Dark's movement between the inside and outside of Sophie's house. The narrative configurations between the inside and outside of her house structurally and symbolically inscribe Jonny respectively in psychic interiority (the unconscious) and material exteriority (consciousness and the Other) and are part of the process of Jonny's working through the memories of the events of his past life.

The different temporalities of memory and actuality in *Memory* are indicated topographically by the use of roman and italic type-sets, in a double movement of the narrative that pushes the reading inexorably forward but is caught in a countercurrent that drags the reading subject back through Jonny's guilt, hauntings, and the anxiety of lost origins.[39] In these senses the narrative structure replicates the characters' (and, by extension, the reading subject's) experience of fragmentation. Therefore, the experience of reading *Memory* is not only the movement in time between the past, the present, and future projections of an otherwise seemingly linear (realist) narrative, it is also a spatial movement between interiority and exteriority and the movement between the signifiers of conscious contents and the repressed signifieds of the unconscious. These narrative configurations of interiority and exteriority are a way that texts of *the feminine* postmodern give the illusion of behaving in a straightforwardly classic realist mode while at the same time embedding characteristically postmodern narrative techniques and simulating a correspondingly postmodern literary experience in the reading subject.

In their work, *The Postmodern Scene*, Arthur Kroker and David Cook have adopted an especially bleak view of postmodernism that seems aptly to describe the especially bleak geographical and psychic landscapes of *Memory* and *Wolf*. Postmodernism, in Kroker's and Cook's definition, is a catastrophe that has already happened.[40] In an age when, "computers reify memory," postmodernism, they say, has condemned the human subject to, "a dead space," marked by increasingly random outbursts of political violence and schizoid behaviors.[41] The implosion of all signs of communication has reduced history to a Baudrillardian scene of a "smooth and transparent surface" of "hypercommunication,"[42] that describes the condition where media messages—like Baudrillard's idea of the image being more real than the real in his conjecturings on "hyperreality"[43]—imitate and reproduce themselves in an endless circulation of nonmessages. This condition of media saturation reduces TV messages, the electronic sound track, rock music, and other mediums of mass communication, to what they describe as "panic noise": "A hologram providing a veneer of coherency for the reality of an imploding culture," in which the social mass vanishes into a fictive world of media hypercommunication.[44] The self-liquidation of value itself, and the cancellation of the referent, has reduced consumption to symbolic exchange, and money to an endless circulation of electronic displays of the computer monitor. The postmodern self, according to Kroker and Cook, is a refracted subject who lives on the edge between violence and seduction, between ecstasy and decay, and is simultaneously predator and parasite: in short, is an empty sign across which run "indifferent rivulets of experience neither fully localized nor fully mediated."[45]

It is from just such a scene that Kroker and Cook describe that Jonny emerges in *Memory* in his personal quest to reconcile memory and imagination. He is in pursuit of ultimate meanings; but it is a futile pursuit, confounded and reified by his drunken stupor of incoherence. His experiences are a bleak and ironic parody of Kroker and Cook's vision of the postmodern scene. Both predator and parasite in Sophie's life, Jonny appears in the narrative, like Sophie, as a marginal figure on the margins of society. But, whereas Sophie is presented as a social casualty suffering from brain damage induced by aging, Jonny is presented as bruised and battered from a recent round of pub fighting. He is a casualty and victim of physical violence, and is suffering from the kinds of random violent outbursts that characterize Kroker and Cook's postmodern scene and that are the consequence and condition of the age. Jonny's head vibrates to interminable snippets of rock-band songs issuing from the headphones of his Walkman; words from songs which, like the fragments of his memories, intrude onto the surface texture of the narrative by being topologically marked in bold upper-case typescript, " 'DREAM CITY, DREAM STREET,' sang the band" (74); " 'WHEN THE WORLD EXPLODES WE'LL BE DANCING IN THE DUST,' sang the band" (77); " 'SILENCE IS GOLDEN—WORDS FALL LIKE STONES,' the band sang to him" (117–8). They serve a double narrative function of, on the one hand, ironic comments upon Jonny's movements and experiences and, on the other, as so much noise in Jonny's life that blots out the panic that threatens to engulf him in the brief moments of silence when he is not attached to his Walkman: "in case the silence got too much for him" (18).

Against a backdrop of broadcasting messages from national radio and TV reporting the progress of political protests in the cause of "Maori Land Rights" marches, Jonny moves through empty city streets that are in every sense the image of postmodernism's post-catastrophic "dead space."[46] These streets are variously described in the narrative as "a sterile plain," a "stone desert" of "decaying," "mean," "empty," shops with broken glass and boarded up windows, with "loading bays, fences of steel pipe, and wire mesh" (23, 27). There are factory fences warning that the buildings are, "protected by electronic devices, security services, or guard dogs" (26), all of which descriptions collectively paint a picture of the landscape of *Memory* as bleak, forbidding, and impersonal. In this desolate, early-morning cityscape there are neither cars nor people to provide identity: "A beach or a hillside might be deserted and still seem completely itself, but an industrial street depended on cars and people" (27). Graffiti messages, advertisements, and flashing neon signs, "Alpha," "Cogito Systems," and "Plastic Fabrications" (27–32), bear satirical but indifferent witness to postmodernism's exteriorization, commodification, and expendability of the subject. In such a landscape, Jonny senses the powerlessness and inconsequence of his postmodern condition, feeling "small and strange and desolate" (26).

Sophie, too, exemplifies the postmodern condition. While Jonny continuously relives his past in the present, Sophie is permanently imprisoned in a timeless past that is her perpetual present. She is described as suffering from dementia, but as an aspect of the postmodernist landscape of language and memory, she is seen, at least metaphorically, as a quasi-postmodern figure embodying all the postmodern ennui that saturates the material and psychic landscape of this narrative. She shares many of the postmodern symptoms of dislocation, amnesia, and the breakdown of language and temporality that Fredric Jameson described as symptomatic of the postmodern condition.[47] Her fragmented memory is reflected in the broken pieces of her language, and in the chaotic interior of her house that, in turn, evokes, metonymically, and as ironic parody, the commodity cityscape outside. The life and material environment that Sophie moves in are comparable to the descriptions of anarchy that pervade the postmodern critique of subjectivity and the social order. All the commodity icons that symptomize late capitalism's postmodern landscape are inside Sophie's house: radio, television, an abundance of consumer goods, and an accumulation of money. But, they signify the negative inverse of consumer capitalism, acting as signs, not of accumulation and wealth, but of the ultimate detritus of postmodern entropy inducing in the reader the kind of cognitive dissonance that is synonymous with the experience of reading postmodern narratives, per se. The radio and TV have become the conduits and signs of postmodernism's hypercommunication, and hyperreality, and are described as "old," and "light and trashy" (76, 112). Baudrillard described how TV images are absolved in what he called "the whirlpool and kaleidoscope of radical semiurgy" and as a "mediascape" within which images fly by with such rapidity that they lose any signifying function and no longer have any discernible effect.[48]

It is with some sense of irony that the images emitting from Sophie's TV screen are equally without discernible effects by being, "shortened and crushed both up and down into an invisible horizon that ran across the middle of the screen" (91). Her consumer goods are described as "decaying," or "full of holes" (76, 106). Kroker and Cook described how the postmodern economy has rendered money worthless by "velocity circulation" and that it has become the "spent fuel of an overheated reactor. Nobody knows what to do with it, yet all know it must be expended."[49] There is money in abundance inside Sophie's house, real money, in dollar notes that for Sophie, as an ironic comment on consumerism, has lost all sense of its value. She does not know what to do with the money except to know that she must accumulate it, using it as so much worthless paper for lining the shelves of her kitchen cupboards, and for stuffing in her underwear, "There was about six hundred dollars, some of it damp and rotting, stuck to the wooden slats under Sophie's sink" (76).

As a parody of the archetypal postmodern subject, Sophie's life has imploded into disjointed, disconnected, and discontinuous fragments and is lacking in depth and temporality. She is a subject of refracted surfaces, and bits and pieces of experience are all she now knows of her life; a life that has typically failed to connect into any kind of homogeneity or coherence. She lives *in* and *for* the moment, acting as a metaphor for Fredric Jameson's definition of the post-modern subject who lives in a perpetual present of "isolated and sovereign moments."[50] Like Baudrillard, who suggested that the information age has made the subject into a simulating machine for filtering the meaningless messages of mass-communication,[51] Sophie's language (like Jonny's hallucinogenic addiction to the sounds of his Walkman) functions in this postmodern description as "panic noise" without referent and meaning.[52] Her world has collapsed into a flat, one-dimensional wasteland of superficial sounds and images; and her language is a collection of meaningless clichés and quotations that could be related to sound bites because of their meaninglessness. She speaks by repeating unconnected phrases, broken fragments of newspaper articles that are quotations from a once coherent life of fallen gentility, and accompanies these nonsensical utterances with endlessly futile acts of repetition: for example, she incessantly makes tea: " 'I'll have a cup of tea for you in next to no time' " (42, 44, 59, 127, 183, 223); endlessly buys cookies: " 'I like to have something in the house because you never know who's going to pop in from nowhere' " (55, 56, 72, 190); continually tidies up: " 'I'll have to straighten things up' " (161); and repeatedly draws money from her post-office savings account (61, 66). She continually displaces material objects into ever-more bizarre and surreal contexts, arranging them, unwittingly, by metonymic association. And by being so displaced, they draw attention to themselves in ways that echo the displacement of signs in Magritte paintings:[53] cakes of soap in the refrigerator (41); yellow cheese in the soap dish (101); a dead blackbird in a pie dish in the refrigerator (55); her money-lined shelves (76); tea towels used as antimacassars (86). The changing array of objects in the pigeonholes of her desk are imbued with grotesque significance by being so displaced from their everyday context and use: a banana skin, a roll of lavatory paper (43); a dish mop, a saltcellar, a pair of glasses with one missing lens (86); a grubby hairbrush, a tin of dried cat food, two pencils, and a cake of soap (128).

These are the outward signs of a life in which memory has broken down, where words and actions have been severed from their meanings, where signifiers have been severed from signifieds, and where signs have been split from their referents.[54] Fredric Jameson's definition of the postmodern discourse could accurately describe Sophie's condition, as a language disorder in which syntactical time has broken down leaving a succession of empty signifiers and absolute moments of perpetual presence.[55] In such a condition, language becomes an infinite play of signifiers without origin or connection:

> The sign separates itself from the referent liberating the signifier from the signified, or from meaning proper . . . This play is no longer of a realm of signs, but of pure or literal signifiers freed from the ballast of their signifieds; it is the realm of the autonomous play of signs when the ultimate final referent to which the balloon of the mind was moored is now definitively cut.[56]

This kind of breakdown of language gives rise to the kind of "absolutely fragmented and anarchic reality" that has become Sophie's life. Jameson has linked the breakdown of language to the breakdown of memory and defined the postmodern replay of memory as the desire to reinvent the past in the nostalgia mode[57] by association with historical objects. Quoting Lacan's psychoanalytic work on language, he describes the postmodern subject's experience of the breakdown and disintegration of temporality as a kind of schizophrenia embedded in language:

> For Lacan, the experience of temporality, human time, past, present, memory, and the persistence of personal identity over months and years—this existential or experiential feeling of time itself—is also an effect of language. It is because language has a past and a future, because the sentence moves in time, that we can have what seems to us a concrete or lived experience of time.[58]

Neville Wakefield attempts to define the postmodern subject in the nostalgia mode, the subject looks to the past for signs of moments of stability in the chaotic and contradictory violence of the present, "Nostalgia assumes that there was once a stable exchange between meaning and the real, when both had their designated place in the order of things.[59] In her broken bits of language, Sophie continuously refers to her past: " 'Do you remember the good old days?' " (45, 52, 184). However, her past is nostalgia without desire, provoked by metonymic association with objects that are frozen in time and long-term memory is collapsed into the short-term that is always "just now." For example, when Jonny suggests sausages for dinner (158), and when Sophie offers Jonny a cookie to eat with his tea (183), she makes a connection to a newspaper article from five years earlier that Jonny subsequently finds, old and yellowed by age, pinned up on the notice board in her kitchen: " 'You know I was reading something the other day—it must have been in the paper—and it said that refined sugar is not good for you' " (183). Jonny's striped jacket is seemingly just like a jacket once worn by Sophie's cousin Alva, and by association in her shattered memory and mind, Sophie makes Jonny into Alva, whom clearly she loved, raising the ghosts of her past temptations and sobrieties played out, once again, as if in the present, by sexual innuendo, in her naked attempts to seduce Jonny, and in the hollow pathos by which she replays the ghosts of the feelings she once knew: " 'It breaks my heart,' she wept, naked and shivering. 'Oh, my darling . . . ' . . . 'I'm not him,' Jonny said. 'I'm just Jonny Dark—you know—the one who looks after you' " (163).

    Both Sophie and Jonny act as agents of plot in this narrative, as they would in any humanist definition. But this reading is exemplary of the *the feminine* postmodern in the terms it has been described, because of the way it demonstrates how, through the agency of character, centrality, centeredness, and emotion, it simultaneously manifests classic postmodern narrative features of decentered subjectivities, plurality, temporal fragmentation, and narrative discontinuities between story and discourse. This is also the case in the reading of *Wolf* that follows.

WOLF

Fragmented Subjectivity

The narrative and psychic manifestations of fragmentation in *Wolf* indicate that the main character, Cassy, is encoded in the narrative as the archetypal, fragmented subject of postmodernism in Jameson's definition of postmodernism as the breakdown in relationship between signifiers.[60] This section will show how these psychic structures are reflected and inscribed in the textual and architectural landscape of the novel.

Wolf is positioned, topologically, in an urban landscape of brute reality where nature, as conjured in the multiple images and tropes of the wolf, is red in tooth and claw: bleak, threatening, and portentously savage. This singularly unnatural landscape—much like the landscape depicted in *Memory*—is manifested in terms of urban debris and decay symbolizing the detritus of capitalism's promise of riches and good living. In *the feminine* postmodern, these expressions of the breakdown and disintegration of the material landscape are symptomatic of the breakdown of the language function in the Symbolic and the emergence of *the feminine* and the psychic landscape in which the characters operate.

Cassy is the single center of consciousness in this narrative. She has been sent away from her grandmother's house to stay with her mother Goldie. Cassy calls her grandmother "Nan." Nan's son, Mick Phelan—who is Cassy's father—is an IRA terrorist whom Nan is protecting. Goldie is living a bohemian and bizarre life with her lover, Lyall, and his teenage son Robert, in a South London squat. They earn a hand-to-mouth living as a team of itinerant performers of the "Moongazer Show" in local schools, aided by their psychedelically-painted "Moongazer" van. They accommodate their material bodily presence in the narrative between contradictory conditions of austerity and self-indulgence. The story is told in the alternating pattern of Cassy's dreaming and waking, represented in the narrative by italicized and roman type. In this reading of the novel, Cassy struggles through an Oedipal drama to reconcile herself with her deserting mother by working through her Oedipal attachments to her estranged father. This kind of Oedipal struggle is a feature of three of the novels featured here (Gillian Cross's *Pictures in the Dark* of the preceeding chapter is the third example). These novels are symptomatic of the way in which *the feminine* struggles for expression in the Symbolic Order of patriarchy. The conflict occurs between the body of the primordial mother, as described in chapter 3, and the language and Law-of-the-Father, which is pursued in more detail in the discussion of *Pictures in the Dark* in chapter 3.

The chaos and squalor of Goldie's squat, and the destruction of all the material signifiers of late capitalism's commodity culture, give a glimpse of life being lived on the very margins of society, suggesting the quality of peripherality that characterizes the postmodern condition. The manifest absence of any ambition in Goldie, Lyall, and Robert to transcend the material circumstances in which they live is symptomatic of their position of powerlessness. They display the kind of inertia that David Harvey in *The Condition of Postmodernity* has identified as the subject's unquestioning submission to the very conditions by which it is identified and defined, ephemerality, fragmentation, and discontinuity: "Postmodernism swims, even wallows, in the fragmentary and the chaotic currents of change as if that is all there is.[61]

Cultural Nostalgia

Goldie and Lyall's squat is a signifier of a breakdown in linear temporality and of the referential codes which had formerly conferred (the illusion of) stable meanings and coherence on Cassy's life. In the squat, all the old, secure meanings have been swept away; for example, her bed is no longer a "proper" bed. It is a characteristic motif of children's literature that she can no longer rely on adults to be responsible; what Lyall, Goldie and Robert perceive to be work, Cassy perceives to be play. The ordered, seemingly stable life she once knew with Nan is now fragmented into a series of unconnected moments that are the discursive manifestation of her psychic fragmentation. These experiences of fragmentation and temporal discontinuity are symptomatic of the schizophrenic, postmodern condition in which the subject, Jameson says, is condemned to live in a perpetual present with little connection between the various moments of past and present and future—an experience of isolated, disconnected, discontinuous material signifiers that fail to link up into a coherent sequence.[62]

Cassy senses these discontinuities between her past and future when she tries to make contact with Nan as her only link with her past, and when she reconciles herself to the potential loss of her future by recognizing that she might be condemned to stay in the squat forever because Nan had wanted her out of the way (71). She is enmeshed in a network of unconnected material signifiers that define Lyall and Goldie's life and comprises a succession of vacuous moments of heightened, hallucinogenic intensity in which the past and future collapse into a series of perpetual "nows": impromptu and instantaneous meals at unpredictable times, spontaneous and continuously changing decisions—about what they should or should not eat, or should or should not do, when or when not to rehearse, and, out of the blue, Lyall's (from Cassy's point of view) irrational decision to make a dawn trip to the zoo.

The squat that Cassy must now call "home" is a perversion of late modernity's gentrification of the inner cities by which, as Sharon Zukin has pointed out, once-derelict lofts and low-income housing have been restored and culturally reappropriated as desirable spaces."[63] The squat is the perverse symbol of Jameson's idea of postmodern "nostalgia"; it is the kind of cultural oscillation where, as Patrick Wright identifies, people continuously reinvent the past in the present, they "pursue the authenticity of the past in newly fabricated replicas of eighteenth-century plumbing fixtures."[64] In a postmodern game of playful irony *Wolf* makes cultural comment by presenting the plumbing fixtures in Goldie's squat not as eighteenth century originals but as tellingly authentic examples of old and defunct plumbing now primitively reclaimed as a standpipe in the ruined kitchen and, "a toilet down the hall that almost works" (17).

The Hyperreal

While, on the one hand, *Wolf* occupies a landscape of brute reality, it also hovers in a space of unreality. In its feminine postmodern mode, *Wolf* juxtaposes Cassy's absolute and unquestioned notions of truth and the real in multiple textual references to these terms that undermine any pretension to the stability that the words themselves imply. This reduces their status to a pair of elusive and unstable signifiers that match entirely Baudrillard's description of the hyperreal and "hyperspace."[65] In the hyperspace of the squat, a mirage of images simulate and substitute for the real in a circuit of unreality, and the boundaries between the imaginary and the real are effaced in a phantasmic play of illusion. For example, we cannot be sure that Michael Phelan exists—Cassy has only a photograph (an image) of him, and the truth about Goldie's supposed sightings of him are constantly undermined by both Lyall, and the voice of Nan: "*You don't want to take any notice of Goldie. She's always telling fairy stories*" (75); meanwhile, everyone doubts the authenticity of the note Cassy allegedly receives from him. We only know for certain that Michael Phelan is real when, in the closing pages of the book, his story about the big bad wolf with a gun comes true as a perversion of the best of fairy stories, and annexes *Wolf* to the intertextual space to which its title and contents allude.

Elements of Cassy's dreams impinge on her waking life as shapeless, half remembered and disconnected fragments that may or may not have originated in her dreams: the yellow winter aconites, the knock on the door (was it her own knocking on the door of her dream, or the unremembered trace of the knock on Nan's door?), the padding feet and yellow eyes: Did they belong to the wolf of her dreams? Or to the loping, leering, Lyall of her waking, as the embodiment of the lost image of her father? The silent, primal scream of Cassy's dreaming, "*the clearing was like a shout, raucous and shocking*" (18)—evokes another intertextual allusion to the image of Edvard Munch's screaming mouth, which is identified by Jameson as the quintessential image of the alienated subject of modernity, that erupts eventually onto the surface of her waking life, "*curving, murderous teeth and blackness, that came rushing rushing rushing, no time, no time and no defense and nothing to do except scream and scream and screamandscreamand-SCREAM . . . ANDSCREAMANDSCREAM*" (127–8). Eventually, the dream itself becomes a fiction; a forgotten memory of childhood: "Nan closed the book and leaned over the cot to give Cassy a brisk kiss" (140).

Wolf plays throughout, and at many levels, with recognizably postmodern narrative devices of ludic space, the dissolution between inner and outer realities, inversions, and the slippage between actuality and illusion. Sharon Zukin described the postmodern urban landscape in terms that reflect and imply the narrative spaces of *Wolf*. It is, in her view, "a stage set, a shared private fantasy and a liminal space that mediates between nature and artifice, market and place."[66] Zukin claims that Disney World is the prototype utopian postmodern dreamscape:

> Disney World develops on the basis of commercializing a shared private fantasy (originating in fairy tales, dreams of adventure and frontier, and Disney Studio products). . . . It abstracts an image of desire and childhood pleasure from the vernacular, and projects it through the landscape of an amusement park. . . . the pasteboard stage props of his Magic Kingdom evokes a continuity between childhood fantasies and new construction. This is a landscape for the eye of the child in the mind of an adult.[67]

If we replace Zukin's description of Disney World with the Moongazer Show, it exemplifies the Moongazer world of Goldie and Lyall, not as Disney's utopian dreamscape, but as a dystopic nightmare: a place where landscape impinges on mindscape in a commercialized play on, not private childhood pleasures, but private childhood fears, made manifest in the stage props of comically grotesque and exaggerated images of the wolf, the most feared of fairytale characters. Successful delivery of the Moongazer show depends on how far the players can blur boundaries between artifice and nature, ensured by Robert's encyclopedic self-education about the world of wolves and the show's incipient mixing of fiction and fact. The entire lives of Goldie and Lyall are lived at the interface between story, storytelling, and actuality, against which Cassy acts as the reactionary voice of the adult in another example of inversion: "Play-acting, thought Cassy. She ought to have guessed that Goldie wouldn't be doing real work" (30). Moreover, Cassy's dream is an indicator of the luring, seductive, psychic games circulating round images of the wolf as multiple manifestations of her father: "*Shall I show you the path? We could play a little game*" (34).

Goldie's mirror-room, with its candlelights and drapes, is like a stage set that, "had no limits" (14), as is the psychedelically painted Moongazer van, and the school hall, transformed for purposes of the show into a hyperreal setting by a fabrication of effects and information overload. This is the world of postmodern surfaces where essence is continually elided behind appearance: characters wear literal and metaphorical masks that distort identity, we can never be certain, for example, about the "true" identity of Lyall—as clown, or wolf man, or caring adult, and we can never be sure when Goldie is play-acting and when she is not, or, indeed, whether there is any stable center that we might call Goldie. Cassy's delusions of a once stable self of her life with Nan have exploded into a cataclysm of pieces, and her struggle for identity, between an inadequate mother and an absent father, is worked out through her dreams.

By use of these sinister mixings and inversions of codes, in the promiscuous slippages between mirage and meanings and the dissolution of illusion and actuality, *Wolf* typographically and stylistically effaces boundaries at many levels of textuality: between reading subject, text, and textualized characters. In addition, it denies access to stable points of reference, and collapses distinctions between art and everyday life.

At the level of narrative reality—Cassy's waking life—there is an *implied* conventional narrative closure that mimics a fairytale ending " 'And all we have to do is live happily ever after?' Cassy said" (140). However, this is not a statement but a question suggesting a degree of irony. The ending in fact is a series of temporal shifts. The story first reverts to a memory of Cassy's childhood at the point when Nan comes to the end of her reading to Cassy of (what could only have been) the tale of "Little Red Riding Hood." Then it returns to the narrative present in Cassy's waking life; at this point, the promise of an ending gives way to a parodic postmodern flourish in the direction of an open-ended narrative. In Cassy's psychic life there apparently has been no closure because she has failed to reconcile herself with her estranged father, so too, in its lack of closure, the narrative finishes with a gesture toward *the feminine* postmodern, but it does so much more significantly by its finishing with an incomplete sentence, *"Dear Wolf, Don't vanish into the dark forest again. I still need to know about you. Perhaps I can come and visit you, or . . . or . . .* (140). This utterance however is inscribed in the italicized print that has signified the dream-contents throughout the narrative, but is now displaced into the narrative of Cassy's waking life. The dream has surfaced into consciousness, and with it comes the promise of a peaceful sleep (and the suggestion of reconciliation). Also with it comes another paradox: that of an open-ended closure. This is a further symptom of the novel's generic definition in *the feminine* postmodern: "Slowly her eyelids drooped. She knew that she wouldn't finish the letter in this dream, but she wasn't worried. She would write it when she woke up" (140).

NOTES TO CHAPTER 4

1. The overtly "experimental" texts in mind here are Robert Cormier's *After the First Death* (New York: Panthcon Books, 1979); *Fade* (New York: Delacorte Press, 1988); Alan Garner's *Red Shift* (London: Collins, 1973); Paul Zindel's *My Darling My Hamburger* (London: The Bodley Head, 1970); Robert Swindells *Stone Cold* (London: Penguin Books, 1993); Aidan Chambers's *Breaktime* (London: The Bodley Head, 1978); *Dance on my Grave* (London: The Bodley Head, 1982); Berlie Doherty's *Dear Nobody* (London: Hamish Hamilton (1992).

2. Victor Burgin, *The End of Art Theory: Aestheticism and Postmodernism* (London: Macmillan, 1986).

3. McHale has added another category to his spatial considerations of the literary text, which is the physical space of the material book, in particular the two-dimensional space of the *page*. This latter is particularly relevant to children's

literature because the genre of the children's picture book has pioneered a particularly unique form of disruption to the spatial zone of the material book and the page: it plays metafictionally with the book as artifact and the book as fictional world. These are the proliferation of interactive books, such as, most famously, Janet and Alan Ahlberg's *The Jolly Postman, or Other People's Letters*, (London: Heinemann, 1986), and books that can be transformed into material objects such as Christmas Cribs, Edwardian houses and fairy castles. I have explored these ideas in my chapter, "Intertextuality," in *The Routledge International Companion Encyclopedia of Children's Literature*, 131–7; 133.

4.   Ibid., 133–7.
5.   McHale, *Postmodernist Fiction*, 56–7.
6.   Roland Barthes, "The Death of the Author," in *Image Music Text*, trans. Stephen Heath (London: Fontana, 1977), 142–8; 146.
7.   Fredric Jameson, "Postmodernism and Consumer Society," in *Postmodern Culture*, ed. Hal Foster (London: Pluto Press, 1985), 111–25; 119.
8.   Jean-Francois Lyotard, *The Postmodern Condition* (Manchester: Manchester University Press, 1985).
9.   Jameson, "Postmodernism," 113.
10. Jameson's idea of time in postmodernity as a discontinuity and loss of memory: as a "waning" of time, is critiqued by Peter Nicholls in Peter Nicholls, "Divergences: Modernism, Postmodernism, Jameson and Lyotard," *Critical Quarterly* 33, no. 3 (Autumn 1991): 1–18.
11. Fredric Jameson, "Postmodernism," 113.
12. Jean Baudrillard, "The Evil Demon of Images and The Precession of Simulacra," in *Postmodernism: A Reader*, ed. Thomas Docherty, (London: Harvester Wheatsheaf, 1993), 194–9.
13. Patricia Waugh, *Practising Postmodernism, Reading Modernism*. (London: Edward Arnold), 1992.
14. Linda Hutcheon, *A Poetics of Postmodernism, History Theory, Fiction* (London: Routledge, 1989).
15. Jameson, "Postmodernism," 123; Waugh, *Practising*, passim; Hutcheon, *Poetics*, 49. The idea of "the dominant" originated in Russian Formalism; see Roman Jakobson, "The Dominant," in *Readings in Russian Poetics: Formalist and Structuralist Views*, eds. Ladislav Matejka and Krystyna Pomorska (Cambridge, Massachusetts: MIT Press, 1971), 105–10.
16. Waugh, *Practising*, 11.
17. Ibid., 5.
18. Christine Brooke-Rose, "The Dissolution of Character in the Novel," in *Reconstructing Individualism: Autonomy, Individuality and the Self in Western Thought*, ed. Thomas C. Heller et al, (Stanford: Stanford University Press, 1986), 185–221.
19. McHale, *Postmodernist, Fictions*, 9–10.
20. Ibid., 55, 128.
21. See Gennette, *Narrative Discourse*.
22. Michel Foucault, *The Order of Things: An Archaeology of Human Sciences* (New York: Pantheon, 1970), *xviii*: "Heterotopias are disturbing, probably

because they secretly undermine language, because they make it impossible to name this *and* that, because they destroy "syntax" in advance, and not only the syntax with which we construct sentences but also that less apparent syntax which causes words and things (next to and also opposite to one another) to 'hold together.' "

23. Michel Foucault, *The Foucault Reader*, ed Paul Rabinow (Harmondsworth: Penguin, 1984).
24. Ibid.
25. Patricia Waugh, *Feminine Fictions: Revisiting the Postmodern*, (London: Routledge, 1989), 169.
26. I have explored more fully the historical similarities between children's literature and women's literature in my journal article, "The Dilemma of Children's Literature and its Criticism," *File: A Literary Journal* 6, no. 3: 1–7.
27. Waugh, *Feminine Fictions*, 169.
28. Patricia Waugh. "Reassessing Subjectivity: Modernity Postmodernity and Feminism in Theory and Aesthetic Practice," *Bete Noir* 8–9 (1989): 64–77.
29. Ibid.
30. Ibid.
31. Cixous, "Castration or Decapitation?," 54.
32. Ibid., 52.
33. Flax, *Thinking Fragments*, 218.
34. See chapter 1, "Introduction."
35. Waugh, "Stalemates? Feminists, Postmodernists and Unfinished Issues," in *Modern Literary Theory: A Reader*, eds. Philip Rice And Patricia Waugh (London: Edward Arnold, 1992), 352: "It is evident that many women writers are using postmodern aesthetic strategies of disruption to re-imagine the world in which we live, while resisting the nihilistic implications of the theory. Certainly one can see the writing of Angela Carter, Jeanette Winterson, Margaret Atwood, Maggie Gee, Fay Weldon, to name but a few, in this way."
36. Waugh, *Feminine Fictions*, 1–33.
37. A version of parts of this chapter and chapter 5 have been published in "Body Language: Speaking the *Féminine* in Young Adult Fiction," *Children's Literature Association Quarterly* 25, no. 2 (2000): 76–87.
38. Neville Wakefield, *Postmodernism: The Twilight of the Real* (Winchester: Pluto Press, 1990), 79–80.
39. Williams, *Critical Desire*, 127.
40. Arthur Kroker and David Cook, *The Postmodern Scene: Excremental Culture and Hyper-Aesthetics* (Basingstoke: Macmillan, 1988), i–vii.
41. Ibid., i.
42. Ibid., vii.
43. Jean Baudrillard, "The Ecstasy of Communication," in *Postmodern Culture*, ed. Hal Foster (London: Pluto Press, 1985), 126–133.
44. Kroker and Cook, *Postmodern Scene*, v.
45. Ibid., vii.
46. Ibid., i–vii.
47. Anika Lemaire, "Metaphor as Symptom," in *Jacques Lacan*, 206–7.

48. Jean Baudrillard, *Simulations*, trans. Paul Foss, Paul Patton, and Philip Beitchman (New York: Semiotext(e), 1983), 194–213, quoted in Douglas Kellner, "Constructing Postmodern Identities," 141–77; 147, *Modernity and Identity*, ed Scott Lash and Jonathan Friedman (Oxford: Blackwell, 1992).

49. Kroker and Cook, iv.

50. Jameson, "Postmodernism," 111–125.

51. Jean Baudrillard, *Simulations*.

52. Kroker and Cook, v.

53. See, for example, René Magritte, *"La durée Poignardée"*(1939); *"La Jeunesse Illustrée"* (1935); *"Golconde"* (1953).

54. See, also, in this connection, René Magritte, *"Ceci n'est pas une pomme"* (1964); and *"Ceci n'est pas un pipe"*(1929).

55. Fredric Jameson, "Periodizing the Sixties," in *The Sixties Without Apology*, ed. S. Saynes, et al., (Minneapolis: The University of Minnesota Press, 1984), 178–218: reproduced in *Modern Literary Theory, A Reader*, 309–40; 328, 332.

56. Ibid.

57. Patricia Waugh, "Stalemates?," 341–60; 347: Patricia Waugh has defined nostalgia as: "the desire to recover the past as *Paradise*, as the myth of origins."

58. Wakefield, *Postmodernism*, 69.

59. Jameson, "Postmodernism," 119.

60. Ibid., 119.

61. Harvey, *Postmodern Condition*, 44.

62. Jameson, "Postmodernism," 119.

63. Sharon Zukin, "Postmodern Urban Landscapes: Mapping Culture and Power," in *Modernity and Identity*, eds. Scott Lash and Jonathan Friedman (Oxford: Basil Blackwell, 1992), 212–45; 231.

64. Patrick Wright, "The Ghosting of the Inner City," in *On Living in an Old Country* (London: Verso, 1985),228–9.

65. Jean Baudrillard, "Simulacra and Simulations," in *Jean Baudrillard Selected Writings*, ed. Mark Poster, (Stanford: Stanford University Press, 1988) 166–84; Jean Baudrillard, "The Evil Demon of Images and the Precession of Simulacra," in *Postmodernism: A Reader*, ed. Thomas Docherty (London: Harvester Wheatsheaf, 1993), 194–213; Jameson, *Postmodernism*, 43–4, 115–18.

66. Zukin, "Postmodern," 232.

67. Ibid., 232–3.

5

The feminine Textual Unconscious in Children's Literature

THEORETICAL INTRODUCTION TO THE CHAPTER

Freud formulated his model of the psyche around the conscious, the preconscious, and unconscious. These terminologies were superseded in his later works by his now more familiar triadic model of the Id, Ego, and Superego. In the "dream-work" described by Freud[1] and reinterpreted by Lacan's psycho-linguistic model, the language of the conscious and preconscious become linked to the repressed signifiers in the unconscious. This is a process that Freud described as "condensation" and "displacement," and that involves substitution on the paradigmatic axis. In Freud's account of dreams, the dream-work lies in the transformation of latent contents of the dream into manifest contents. They are represented as visual images through what Freud called "representability," which is closely related to, but different from, displacement. Kristeva describes this process as the "specific articulation of the semiotic and the thetic for a sign-system;"[2] and some of the less coherent elements of the raw material of the dream are rationalized through a (secondary) process Freud called "intelligibility." They are necessarily an abridgement of the latent contents (hence Freud's version of *condensation*), and are the representations of associative chains. Freud described dreaming as "another kind of remembering,"[3] deriving from mnemic traces, the system preconscious,[4] and the unconscious, as stimulated by four main sources: external, internal (sensory), internal somatic, or purely psychical.[5] Material from all sources can influence the "manifest content of the dream," but Freud maintained that the motivating source is always an infantile, repressed wish, impulse, or experience:[6]

> The present state of our knowledge leads us to conclude that the essential factor in the construction of dreams is an unconscious wish [in the dynamic sense]—as a rule

141

an infantile wish, now repressed—which can come to expression in this somatic or psychical material . . . The dream is in every case a fulfillment of *this* [dynamically] unconscious wish, whatever else it may contain.[7]

Freud's theories of dreaming share a great deal with his psychoanalytic theories of repressed memories explored in his case of the "Wolf-Man."[8] He interpreted the Wolf-Man's dreaming through analysis of the Wolf-Man's childhood dream about wolves, and his wolf phobia, recollected fifteen years after the event; and he found the key to the Wolf-Man's childhood neurosis in a repressed memory of a childhood seduction, (actual or imagined). The latent material of the dream is transposed into the "manifest contents" of his dream through the processes of representability and intelligibility into wolves, trees, and fairytale images (what he called "dream-images"), and through the dream-work mechanisms of condensation, displacement, distortion, and reversal.

In his idea of "repetition compulsion" Freud identified the tendency in the human unconscious to try to recover, without any apparent resolution, an irretrievable "lost object," which may have been a primary fantasy ("psychoneuroses") or actual experience, past or present, such as trauma ("actual neuroses").[9] The recovery is achieved by some kind of (painful) repetition of the experience of the loss either through fantasies, or displaced activities. We see these phenomena being played out in the story ("case") of the Wolf-Man's replaying of his dream, and, indeed, in Freud's own need to replay through his writings, the experience of his unsuccessful counter-transference in the case of "Little Dora" by his repeatedly returning to rewrite the narrative but never concluding it.[10] Freud's idea of "deferral" is closely related to repetition compulsion, but here the memory of the earlier event is triggered by a later experience. The term *Nachträglichkeit* is used to refer to this phenomena, which also means "afterwardness" or "belatedness" and is linked to the idea of repetition compulsion by the same notion of latent or repressed memory as is expressed in the case of The Wolf-Man. But, unlike repetition compulsion, where the trauma is replayed several times, *Nachträglichkeit* describes a complex temporality which separates two events and involves the revision of the past in the present:[11] "The event remains latent in the subject."[12] In addition, "Deferred action, or belatedness, is, then, a product of the excessive character of the first event which requires a second event to release its traumatic force."[13] And, in the Freudian definition, the memory of the event has less to do with the recollection of it than the repetition of the structure.[14]

This theory postulates that nothing can be inscribed in the human unconscious except in relation to at least two events which are separated from one another in time by a moment of maturation that allows the subject to react in two ways to an initial experience or to the memory of that experience.[15]

Lacan's famous "return to Freud" was through Freud's earlier works that included *The Interpretation of Dreams*. The dream, for Lacan, thus becomes significant in *language* through the mechanisms of condensation, displacement, distortion, and reversal, and through the tropes of metaphor and metonymy, and their distorting effects:

> Lacan's uncompromising equation of "condensation" and "displacement" with metaphor and metonymy, his reading of *trans-fer* as *meta-phorien, and* as a language *act*, gets at the radically primary status of trope or figure, and the *dis*figurative character precisely of the figural dimension of language.[16]

It is possible, therefore, in Lacan's linguistic model of the dream to "distinguish between a metaphor and a metonymy according to whether the displacing terms are related by contiguity (metonymy) or comparability (metaphor) to the terms they displace."[17] And the capacity for plural interpretation and the appropriation of signification to the dream or the memory, lies in the slippage between the sign (word) and the meaning (signified). It is in this sense that the subject is caught up in the causal chain of language and can never be any more than its effect.

In his much discussed, much criticized, "Seminar on 'The Purloined Letter,' "[18] Lacan demonstrated how he viewed Freud's idea of the repetition compulsion as being any repetition of the story, and the circulation of signs in the literary text (which is, in the case of the purloined letter, both literally and metaphorically *a letter*) and as a manifestation of the subject's need to rework in the Symbolic earlier memory traces of the Oedipal trauma experienced on entry into language. For Lacan objects in the text function as signs that are both metonymic and metaphoric, displacements and substitutions, for the thing they represent:

> For Lacan the letter (signifier) functions in the story [of 'The Purloined Letter'] . . . because of its position between people, the role in producing certain interpersonal effects and subjective responses.[19]

As it is with objects, which are interesting as metonymic/metaphoric indicators of unconscious contents and for the concept of repetition compulsion, so too, for Lacan, it is with subjects: Lacan is not interested in the subject-identity of, and in, the discourse but in the Symbolic structural drama that identifies where the subject is positioned in the signifying chain. In other words, a purely Lacanian psycho-*literary* analysis, based on his own reading of this single text, reduces the subject to a signifier, to a linguistic cipher, and is interested only in Symbolic contents—is interested only in the play of signifiers and their formal functioning in the text. David Carroll, for example, pointed out that:

> The questions Lacan raises about the signifier, are, by and large, the same as those raised by a majority of literary critics today . . . their goal is to analyze the signifier, the formal functioning of the text, rather than the signified, its sense. . . . Lacan accords to the Symbolic an absolute, transcendent status, for it ultimately determines everything else—all subject, actions, desires etc.,—but he cannot defend its status except in terms of its opposition to the Imaginary.[20]

Lacan's version of literary subjectivity in this reading evokes the same kind of depersonalized and objectified subjectivity that is present in classic postmodern narratives in which, as Patricia Waugh has indicated, the very idea of subjectivity breaks down into a play of differences in a system of linguistic structures; " 'Identity' is simply the illusion produced through the manipulation of irreconcilable and contradictory language games . . . 'narrators,' 'characters,' and implied 'readers' dissolve into categorizations of grammar,"[21] all of which is anathema to an understanding of *the feminine* subjectivity as agency as it has been described and defined in chapter 4. So, while in principle we have in Lacanian psychoanalysis the potential for the textualized nature of both texts and reading subjects in all the richness of his psycho-dynamics of the subject that are incorporated into the idea of the textualized subject and literary Transference as they are described in chapter 1, it appears on the evidence available from Lacan's own reading of "The Purloined Letter," that he reduces the subject of, and in, the literary text to a schematized actant in the chain of signifiers.[22] This is just one of the points at which feminist criticism has intervened in classical psychoanalytical criticism, and in the criticism of the postmodern, to shift the balance and reinstate the sense of agency through character in literature in texts of *the feminine*.

It is, however, clear from his reading of "The Purloined Letter" that Lacan was interested in the whole concept of loss, and how the circulation of the lost object (the phallus) is a replaying of the loss effected by the Oedipal drama. For Lacan, the emphasis is on the realization of the loss of the phallus that is subsequently regained in the Symbolic and displaced into *objet a*. But in feminist reworkings of the theory, the loss equally is the traumatic loss of the "desire of the mother" experienced in the child's separation from the mother in its transition from the Imaginary relations to the Mirror Phase, and the Symbolic Order and displaced into *objet a* that symbolically evoke the lost objects of the mother's body such as we have seen being played out here in the theorization of the mother through the narratives featured in chapter 3. Feminist criticism has insisted that the subject cannot be reduced to a mere signifier in what has been perceived to be the masculinist, phallocentric economy of the Symbolic. So in these senses a strictly orthodox Lacanian analysis of text/reader relations is ultimately unsustainable within *the feminine* frame of reference. We are able to take from it, however, Lacan's theory of the repetition compulsion as the subject's need to replay in the Symbolic early memory traces (whether these be maternal or paternal in their origin and manifestation); and also his idea of objects (and subjects) in the text functioning as signs that are both metonymic and metaphoric, displacements and substitutions, for the thing they represent, the (irretrievable) lost object.

The transformational processes between latent and manifest contents in dreams as described by Freud and reinterpreted by Lacan could be made analogous to the process of transferring the unconscious of the literary work into finished product through the act of writing,[23] where unconscious contents are displaced and codified in the text into metaphor, metonymy, objects of desire (*objet a*), and textual motifs. In the process of literary Transference, and countertransference, it is the job of the reading subject as analysand to interpret the codified textual messages of the textual unconscious, just as the text itself works simultaneously upon the unconscious of the reading subject to access latent desires, and to produce meanings through those same processes of transformation that operate in the dream-work. Dreams, by their distinguishing features of fluidity, mobility, their indifference to the laws of logic in signification, their inability to speak *about* themselves,[24] and the fact of their locus in the unconscious, are very close to the characteristics of *the feminine* Imaginary. These are the reasons why it is appropriate here to relate the idea of dreaming, and memory as a related phenomena and theorization, to a reading of these paradigm texts of *the feminine* textual unconscious.

Memory, Wolf, and *Dangerous Spaces* are being read in this chapter as paradigm narratives that lay bare in their textuality Freud's and Lacan's theories of dreaming and the closely related phenomena of memory, to show how the textual unconscious that is recovered by Transference *in* the story, between characters, mirrors the Transferential process between reading subject and text, and the recovery of the unconscious of the reader during the act of reading. The recovery of a textual unconscious is the locus of individual meanings (indeterminacy) and is the reason why meanings in readings are multiple. As "dream texts" these focus texts also lend themselves to a metacritical account of the workings of the idea of *the feminine* textual unconscious in the act of reading and its related process of literary Transference, for the qualities of fluidity, mobility, and the like that are described above as being closely akin to the idea of *the feminine* Imaginary. In practice, *any* literary work offers the possibility for this kind of Transferential process, but these texts are especially interesting because the dreaming subjects in the narratives, Cassy and Anthea in *Wolf* and *Dangerous Spaces* respectively, for example, occupy a position analogous to the analysand in analysis, and through their dreaming they effect a transition in the Transference of latent unconscious contents that is their moment of cure. This happens because dream and Transference work on the same processes of substitution, displacement, condensation, and contiguous referentiality.[25] Through their acts of dreaming, the narratives themselves subscribe to the structures of the dream as described by Freud and inscribe Cassy and Anthea as not only the decentered subject of conscious and unconscious contents, but also as subjects whose psychic processes of Transference are both precipitated by and reified in their movements. In the case of *Wolf*, Cassy's movement between Nan's flat and Goldie's squat, and in the case of *Dangerous Spaces*, the shift from home to the dream space of Veridian. Their dreaming acts as metaphor for that process insofar as it demonstrates the workings of the unconscious contents surfacing, through dream-work, in symbolic form. They are exemplary of the way, in literary Transference, the unconscious works as a structure we may call a text, and how the text contributes to the already formed unconscious of the reading subject. The Oedipal dramas worked out in Cassy's relation to her mother and her father and Anthea's quest to reconcile herself to the trauma of her parents' death, operates as the process of recovery of unconscious contents, just as the narrative drive generated by textual desire[26] works to uncover the textual unconscious during the act of reading.

These, then, are the conditions in which the reading subject is inscribed in the role of analyst and is caught up in a process of Transference and counter-Transference in which the workings of the textual unconscious, in a dialectics of reading, are mirrored in Cassy and Anthea's working through the contents of their dream. The personal responses to *Wolf* that follow in this chapter, and, indeed to the other novels which feature in this book, therefore, by definition, are an analytic process of *interpretation* in which the "I" who reads as the subject/analyst produces meanings through a dialectical process in which the textual unconscious engages the unconscious of the reading subject in a process, if not an experience, equivalent to dreaming. "Transference is the dream process itself, in that an unconscious idea enters the preconscious by establishing a connection with an idea that already belongs to the preconscious, by transferring its intensity on to it and by getting itself 'covered' by it."[27] And, "Transference does not arise out of some mysterious property of affectivity, and even if it does betray itself in the form of agitation, the latter is only meaningful as a function of the dialectical movement within which it occurs."[28]

The reading subject in the act of interpretation, in this context, does not seek to recover meaning but *signification*.[29] Shoshana Felman pointed out that:

> Seeing is always reading, deciphering, *interpreting*, it is because reading is also transferring: just as a dream is a transference of energy from the 'day's residue' and the unconscious wish, so does the act of reading invest the conscious daylight signifiers with an unconscious energy, transfer on recent materials the intensity of an archaic sleep (*sic*). Seeing, thus, is always in some manner sleeping, that is, looking with the very eyes of the unconscious—through the fabric of a dream, reading not literally but rhetorically.[30]

The textual revelations which surface in literary Transference, then, are not directly equivalent to the analyst's attempts to uncover the contents of the unconscious in the "constituting," the "speaking," subject of analysis, because the text itself behaves as analyst in this relationship just as it did for the writer in the process of producing it. In both cases the writer and reader are in process of uncovering from the text what Peter Brooks has described as "previously unperceived networks of relation and significance finding confirmation in the extension of the narrative and the semantic web."[31] Language, Lacan says "is the *condition* of the unconscious"; but it is also, and importantly, the *expression* of the unconscious.[32] When the text being analyzed is a dream-text, there is a *special* responsibility on the role of interpretation because the dream, of its nature, is imagistic and sensory and because, unlike poetic imagery, it has no intrinsic metaphorical or metonymical operations. The dream-text, therefore, relies entirely on the agency of interpretation for its explanation and explication:

> In a dream the metaphorical operation loses its entire foundation in resemblance: nothing is *like* anything in a dream, and this is what makes the dream's irresponsibility possible.[33]

There is the dynamism between two sets of conscious and unconscious systems in this process which are, on the one hand, the workings of the conscious and unconscious and, on the other hand, the conscious and unconscious workings of the text converging in a dialectical and dialogical exchange. The process is essentially *intertextual* and *mutable* not only in the sense of its being allusive, but also for its participation in the network of codes as infinite semiosis;[34] it is, more precisely, the textual meeting ground between two "constituting," "speaking" subjects (*je*), and two "constituted," "spoken" egos (*moi*) because, as Ragland-Sullivan pointed out, the literary text is "an allegory of the psyche's fundamental structure."[35] The I and the ego are never fully correlated and are always in process because the subject, like the literary text, is never completely knowable. These dynamic systems have their textual parallels discursively in what is *said*, and *not said*, in the text. At the level of story in *Wolf, Dangerous Spaces,* and *Memory*, they surface in symbolic form and manifest themselves as *symptoms* of anxiety in, for example, Cassy's and Anthea's struggles between the (Imaginary) contents of their dreams and the Symbolic (spoken) utterances of their waking, or, for Jonny, in his continuous need to search for Bonny Benedicta as the outward expression of his guilt and the repressed memory of Janine's fall to her death. This process mirrors and is mirrored at the level of the discursive exchange between text and the reading subject, as the dynamic interplay of textual structures releases signification.

Metacritical responses such as these are an act of analytic *intervention*, which is the essence of Transference. Interpreting, Lacan says, is *not* the literary text: interpretation is not directed at recovering *a meaning* so much as *a signification*; and, as Lacan points out, is aimed "towards reducing the non-meaning of the signifiers."[36] So, "meaning" in literary Transference is transmuted into "signification," but they are, like all meanings, multiple and indeterminate in every exchange. The reading subject, therefore, is in pursuit not of meaning but signification, and in the process "works over" the text, as in the manifest content of the dream, through a web of modifications that are, as has already been indicated: distortion (censorship), displacement (disfiguration, metonymy, contiguity), and condensation (metaphor—described by Lyotard as: " 'compression' of the primary text; . . . 'crumpling it up'; to squeeze signifiers and signifieds together").[37]

Lacan said that the function of the analyst is to listen and to intervene. As, John Forrester pointed out in relation to Lacan's work on Transference that, "In teaching analysts, as Lacan did from the late 1940s in his weekly seminars, one must teach how to *listen* and how to *intervene*: how to say the right things at the right moment."[38] In *literary* terms, then, these acts of "listening" and "intervention" are transposed into "reading" and "responding." It follows, then, that the objectives of literary Transference are achieved through the agency of *reading* and *responding*. The reading subject's Transferential relation to the text implies also counter-Transference because "the text finds in the reading subject what the reading subject finds in the text."[39] The text operates by exercising the kind of magnetic pull upon the reading subject that was described so graphically by Ragland-Sullivan.[40] So, in the role of analyst-cum-analysand, the reading subject is forced into interpretation through Transference, and is plunged into what Freud has described as "the analysis of the minutest details of the text, in which process the textual unconscious is uncovered."[41]

The recovery of the textual unconscious is simultaneously the recovery of the reading subject's own unconscious. What is selected for interpretation is the working of *textual* Transference on the reading subject which surfaces through the textual utterances. Conversely, what is *not* selected, by definition, is repressed. These are the textual silences that are equally significant in Transferential processes. These are the reasons why a reading can never be final or absolute and because, as Ragland-Sullivan pointed out,

> No interpretation of a literary text can ever arrive at the fullest (or final) meaning; not just because of the nature of language, but also because of the complexity and representational specificity of the representations that condition languages.[42]

David Harvey, in quite a different context, unwittingly describes something of this process when he says,

> Whatever is written conveys meanings we do not or could not possibly intend, and our words cannot say what we mean. . . . because the perpetual interweaving of texts and meanings is beyond our control. Language works through us.[43]

In this one-to-one relationship between the reading subject and the literary texts featured in this chapter, the textualized and structural nature of the psyche is exercised and the textual unconscious is laid bare. The critical responses in the paragraphs that follow are, then, the realization of this process, and are, of course, another text: an intertext that is, in its turn, a candidate for literary Transference, ad infinitum.

SUMMARY

The texts in this chapter are identified as "dream texts" and they represent a significant body of children's literature in which dreaming is a recurring trope. The term "dream text" is used psychoanalytically to refer to the *account* of the dream and it is being used here because it effectively describes the characteristic and tenor of the narratives that recount the experiences of their dreaming subjects. Memory and dreaming are closely linked psychoanalytically in the theories of both Freud and Lacan, so it is appropriate to position *Memory*, (that doesn't actually figure dreaming) as a dream text here, because memory in this narrative, like the dream contents, relate to latent unconscious contents brought to consciousness through a process analogous to the dream-work. These dream texts also lend themselves more readily to the explication of the process of recovering what is here being called *the feminine* textual unconscious through an act of literary Transference in the act of reading, because dreaming and the Transferential experience share in the same elements of substitution, displacement, condensation, representability, and intelligibility. Signification is the dominant mode of analysis in both, and the features of fluidity and mobility that characterize the dream are also characteristic of aspects of *the feminine* Imaginary.

The section on "Metaphor, Metonymy, and Memory" focuses on Mahy's *Memory*, and uses Freud's and Lacan's work to show how tropes of memory are metaphor and metonymy, and their relationship to language inscribes fragmented subjectivities. This section also analyses the subjective behaviors that motivate the particular manifestations of *the feminine* plots that figure in all these narratives. In particular, it shows how *the feminine* is latently present in the psychic contents of the male subject of the narrative, Jonny Dark, and how it is worked out through a series of narrative events and personal encounters precipitated by the repressed memories that are at the core of his narrative. Lacan's work on guilt, condensation, and repression, and Freud's theory of *Nachträglichkeit* meaning "deferral" or "belatedness" explain the events which trigger the replay of the earlier, repressed memory.

The section on "Dreaming the Wolf" shows how the central narrative subject, Cassy, in Gillian Cross's *Wolf*, resolves her unconscious Oedipal conflicts through the agency of dreaming the wolf, and also how these dream contents surface in Cassy's waking life in a chain of metaphoric substitutions and metonymic images in the course of the narrative, as she makes her psychic shift from the Other of masculinist signification in the Symbolic, to the Semiotic (m)other. Freud has described one aspect of the dream as "a substitute for an infantile scene modified by being transferred on to a recent experience,"[44] and Lacan has said that the Oedipal structures are already inscribed in language and the Symbolic, and precede the child's entry into them: In these senses both *Memory* and *Wolf* raise questions of psychic and social identity as a given, set against the individual struggle to shift the balance of masculinist signification and inscription.

Mahy's *Dangerous Spaces* also is a text about dreaming, analyzed here in the light of Freud's idea of the "uncanny" as a space of return and ambiguity by being simultaneously frightening and reassuring, alien and familiar. The place called Viridian in this narrative is positioned as an occluded dream-space where projected conscious and unconscious desires and fears are worked over and the whole is positioned as another exemplification of *the feminine* narrative of circularity and return, in this case, from death through mourning to the reconstitution of subjectivity in *the feminine*.

MEMORY

Metaphor, Metonymy, and Memory

Memory is structured round Jonny Dark's movement between the inside and the outside of Sophie's house and it signifies his psychic movements between interiority and exteriority that are his process of "working over"[45] the events of his past. This is his process of Transference and his working through repressed unconscious contents while the story of his life is played out in and through the narrative.

Jonny is on a quest to track down Bonny Benedicta as the only objective witness to his sister, Janine's, cliff top fall to her death. As such, is it also his quest to rid himself of the repressed guilt he has carried inside ever since his sister's death, a form of repression that has thus been semiotically defined in Lacan's linguistic theory of memory:

> Repression ensures a more-or-less fixed connection between a repressed content (a signifier acting in the position of the signified) and the conscious symptomatic behavior it engenders (the dream or symptom as signifier of the unconscious signified). . . . Repression places key infantile signifiers into the position of more or less permanent signifieds by casting them into the unconscious where their relations are no longer governed by the basic principles of arbitrariness, double articulation and pure difference.[46]

Jonny's repressed guilt would be described in Lacanian terms as a metaphoric process (the substitution of one term for another, related to Freud's use of the term "displacement"). His guilt is the signified that, by being repressed in the unconscious, becomes the "lost object," and is here displaced into his quest to track down Bonny. In these terms, his repressed guilt, as the lost object, has been replaced in his conscious mind by a different signifier which becomes the *symptom* of his repression, realized metaphorically in his seemingly endless and futile searching:

> The symptom is a formation of the unconscious in the sense that in it, the true speech of the unconscious is translated into enigmatic signifiers. But they also tell us that the process whereby the symptom becomes fixed is that of metaphor: the substitution in a signifier-signified relation of signifier S for another signifier S. The symptom is, in effect, a substitutive sign for a traumatic experience. . . . [t]he link uniting the mnemic symbol and the traumatic experience may be individual or may on the other hand be of the order of symbolization. In the latter case the symptoms express the traumatic experience in their very configuration and present an immediate relationship of analogy to that experience.[47]

Lacan's idea of memory, then, is closely bound up with repression which precipitates the search for the "lost object," and relates to Freud's idea of memory as:

> An interpretative elaboration or working-through whose role is to weave around a rememorated element an entire network of meaningful relations that integrate it into the subject's explicit apprehension of himself.[48]

So when Jonny finds himself on the threshold of Sophie's house, it is the symbolic and literal marker of his journey into his past, and into his memory of Janine's death:

> Saturated as he was with memory, it seemed he must make his way home through a memory-desert which might drain some of the burden from him. (126)

During his days of exile in the out-of-time experiences of old Sophie's house, Jonny exorcises the ghosts of his childhood selves that have haunted his recurrent memories of Janine's death: in this process he transits from a state of psychic homelessness in his past life in his parents' house, to a psychic homecoming of self-determination, autonomy, and intersubjectivity, worked out through patterns of memory, repetition, and his mental replays of the trauma. In his need, belatedly to come to terms with the trauma of Janine's death, it is more than a little significant, then, that Jonny's sense of himself has been tied up with naming himself as the "Wolfman" (37, 38, 77, 190, 206) with all that is implied in Freudian analysis to the case of the Wolf-Man and to the Freudian idea of *Nachträglichkeit* as the triggering of an earlier repressed memory of an event through a later experience:

> In the game with Janine and Bonny he demanded to be known as the Wolfman.
> " *'Look' she said. 'The moon! That means he can be the Wolfman. He can have a forest of his own. / In which to wander, howl and groan.'* " (25, 26)

These events are both effected and symbolized, first when Jonny actually leaves his family home and comes to live with Sophie and, second, and most significantly, at the site of Jonny's replay of the initial trauma when he leaps from the rain-drenched balcony of Sophie's house to confront his literal childhood enemy in the character of Nev Fowler. Nev Fowler embodies all the evils and threats to his identity that Jonny has carried inside himself. Jonny had been jealous of Janine, and resented her success: " 'You'll never catch me up,' she had cried, challenging him, and had vanished before his very eyes" (166). When Janine had fallen off the cliff and died, Jonny believed there had been a mistake, that *"he should be the one to be lying below among the serpents of foam"* (50). And the thought had pursued him even into his adulthood, "the tension of that unfulfilled jump was still coiled up in him, and some day, on some other occasion he might set it free" (50).

The significance of the balcony as the site of Jonny's replay of the trauma is prefigured early in the narrative as the metaphorical site for a cliff top fall into the sea:

> The shells on the window-sill, turned to show their linings of pearl and opal, suggested all over again that the rise and fall of the sound on the other side of the window might be the sea, that stepping out on to the balcony he might breathe in the scents of salt and seaweed. (53)

Jonny's eventual, and seemingly unpremeditated, leap from the balcony can be explained, then, in the terms of Freud's thesis, as the psychic necessity to replay the memory of his sister's death by water and, through it, he brings to consciousness what hitherto he has been unable to assimilate into his conscious mind. In the process he assuages not so much the memory of the fall, nor the grief of her death, as his repressed *guilt* at *wanting* her to die, and his belief that his secret thought might actually have caused her death; that figuratively, or even perhaps literally, he might have pushed her over the edge of the cliff. " 'I *thought of it,*' " he utters after his violent confrontation with Nev Fowler, " 'I was actually thinking of grabbing her when she said that about me never catching her up. . . . I knew I must have done something to make it happen . . . well, not *knew* but *believed* I had' " (215). But he has been unable to speak these thoughts until after the moment when the "second fall" had released them to consciousness: "He cried out in the very echo of Janine's single cry. The saved energy of the leap he had not taken five years earlier filled him, and he leaped now as if he might fly" (211).

It is clear from the narrative repetitions that subjectively and discursively replay the memory that Jonny is unable to mourn the death of Janine because he is locked in what Freudian psychoanalysis would describe as a post-traumatic state of "incorporation." Incorporation stands in opposition to "introjection" in the process of mourning that perpetuates the existence of the dead person; it keeps the dead person's existence alive as a presence within the self, reconstituted from the memories of words, images, and feelings that give rise to a topography known as the "crypt":

> Grief that cannot be expressed builds a *secret vault* within the subject. In this crypt reposes—alive, reconstituted from the memories of words, images, and feelings— the objective counterpart of the loss, as a complete person with his own topography, as well as the traumatic incidents—real or imagined—that had made introjection impossible.[49]

The crypt is a part of the Freudian theory of the "split ego" that roughly approximates to Lacan's linguistically based distinction between *je* and *moi*. When Jonny finds Bonny living in the house next door to Sophie, he begins his attempted assimilation of the event, significantly imaged in references to Bonny's room of books as a "grotto" (143), and "the cave" (154), and by his relating the story of his past to the faceless mannequin on Bonny's balcony as the projection of his split ego: " 'What's that?' Jonny asked the dummy. 'You have a dark past? So have I! You show me yours and I'll show you mine.' And he began to tell it his story" (151).

Sexual Subjectivity

Memory is distinguished from the other Mahy novels featured in this book by its focus on a male subject. But questions of sexual subjectivity that have characterized the novels featuring female subjects equally are present in *Memory*. This time, how- ever, we see a male central character struggling to retain, at one level of conscious- ness, his inscription in "rationality," and "autonomy" as the code of masculinity against, at another level of his unconscious, "emotionality" and "attachment" asso- ciated with femininity and culturally projected onto Western women.[50] Jonny's anx- ieties about his sexual identity are tied up with memories of Janine's death, recollections of his childhood in relation to her and Bonny, and to the whole busi- ness of ambiguous sexuality implied in his tap dancing, TV-ad performances as the "Chicken-bits boy" with bleached blonde hair who chirped "*Chick-chick-chick chicken*" (34, 82). These words, which had made him famous, and had also been used to taunt him, echo in his head as an antithetical image threatening his ambition for macho sexuality.[51] His serendipitous return to the scenes of his childhood in Colville is a replay of the gender-related tensions that haunted his early life there, and continue to haunt him, recalled by the psychic showdown in the public bar between himself and the bully of his Colville school days, Nev Fowler.

The scene is played out as Jonny's macho fantasy in the style of an old-fashioned Western movie, ("Peter drew low and fired, Pow! Struck by the amber shaft Demon Thirst fell, mortally wounded. No one faster on the draw than Beer-gun Pete!" [111]), with Jonny as the icon of his own sense of masculinity in the role of swashbuckling hero, facing down the enemy, playing it cool, eyeball-to-eyeball with Nev Fowler in a battle for macho domination. This macho fantasy is contrasted with the reality of the tellingly bathetic image of his swilling down pints of lemonade as manifestation and symbol of the not-so macho aspect of his psyche that he knows and fears.

In this barroom showdown, Jonny is the quintessentially postmodern male subject, playing the identity game, "trying out" different sorts of selves constructed in, and influenced by, the media images of maleness that surround him, which focus on looks, appearance, and style.[52] He implicitly recognizes that subjective identity is not fixed, or given, but is potentially multiple and unfixed, borne out by his willingness to experiment with different selves that are culturally, as well as psychically, determined, and can be undone. When he finds bundles of Sophie's money hidden in her underwear, and rows of fifty-dollar notes lining the shelves of her kitchen cupboards, he hovers between the image of himself as the "bad guy" who steals it and the "good guy" who leaves it. In this scene, he comes face-to-face with the idea that the carefully constructed moral boundaries that have supported a sense of his own integrity might at any moment dissolve. He reacts with surprising naiveté, then, when he learns that Bonny's sister Samantha has reconstructed her Maori identity and coincidentally reaffirmed the value of her mother's heritage by reverting to her natural mother's name. She is now known nationally as the activist Hinerangi Hotene, " 'Gosh,' said Jonny feebly. 'All those lessons in ballet and reading *Winnie the Pooh* and she's gone back to the *marae*. All that culture for nothing' " (150). His awakening awareness that subjectivity is both constructed and tenuously fragile not only affronts his masculinist notion of himself as fixed and immutable, it also means that he is caught in the trap of "schizoid dichotomy," the sense of fearing that somehow or other one *becomes* the roles that one plays.[53]

These dichotomous tensions pervading Jonny's struggle for a male identity are founded on the myth of unitary selfhood and, in the context of a post-structuralist, feminist reading, they foreground the patriarchal and liberal principles which contradict the ideas of plurality and fluidity in the postmodern subject. They manifest themselves in the narrative as the anxieties that Jonny moves between: on the one hand, his desire for macho maleness, and, on the other hand, the inescapable knowledge of his feminization through dancing. This feminization is underscored by personality traits associated with "femaleness" that he despises in himself, "Whether he liked it or not, something fair, even kind, in him made it difficult to walk off and leave her lost in her own kitchen" (57); "He did not want to turn into the sort of man who worried over wet mattresses, baths and breakfasts; he hated the heavy harassed feeling that possessed him" (105). At the same time he is confused by his wish to possess the kind of female power he had perceived in Janine and Bonny:

> Jonny had yearned to be like Janine and Bonny, to have another secret self, some-thing fierce and wild and full of uncontrollable power, as different as possible from the way he was in real life. (25)

Jonny, at nineteen years of age, and still struggling with the feminine in himself, takes comfort from the way he has distilled into the macho achievements of his recent past a desire to be powerful, "He liked to think he had learned to be tough, able to give and take blows" (70); "Over the past year and half he had developed the reputation, among his parents' friends, of being 'bad, mad, and dangerous to know' and he was 'often surprised when people acted as if they believed it' " (105). He continually revises and reinvents his past and even harbors an old, famil-iar, but facile, self-deception that, like a story, Janine's death had been a sort of fic-tion that, by finding Bonny, he might *uninvent*, even while knowing rationally that the fact of Janine's fall was not the sort of thing that it is possible to uninvent.

He realizes too that, as in a story, he is the unreliable narrator of his own past: that Janine, who had overshadowed him and in whose shadow he had danced as a child, and who had been the cause of his jealous childhood resent-ment of her, had known all along that *he* was the true dancer: " 'You were the true dancer. Everyone knew that, even Janine' . . . 'So we were both jealous of you!' " (147, 8) Bonny had been the "Story-and-word girl. . . . Jonny had never quite escaped the suspicion that things happened because Bonny invented them or fore-told them" (20). " 'Might is right,' Bonny joked in his head. 'Might is write. It's all a story in a book.' She had always been a reader" (54).

By beating up Nev Fowler he simultaneously delivers himself from his need to use physical strength as an agent of male power, and purges the ghosts of the enemies of both his actual and psychic history. But more importantly, he resolves the conflicts that have been the source of his anxieties by recognizing that the boundaries between cultural constructions and the separations of "maleness" and "femaleness" are as mutable as the several constructions of self. By coming to live in Sophie's house he has demonstrated to himself that he recognizes not only the intersubjective nature of subjectivity that is a feminist aspiration for postmod-ern subjectivity, but also the constructedness of identity that gives him freedom to *choose* and to *change* his subject positions without privileging any one of them, in which process he is the unquestionable agent.

Fictional Time and Memory

Time and memory are the two markers of the narrative in which Jonny lives and relives his past in the present through the latent presence of "this memory which never left him" (21). Memory is intrinsically linked to time but, paradoxically, an idea of temporality only comes into play when the unconscious memory is brought to consciousness.[54] Jonny's history, like the narrative temporality it is related to, is directed back as much as it is projected forward, as he moves repeatedly between his memory of the fall and his anticipation of finding Bonny. Peter Brooks points out in relation to repetition and oscillation in narrative time that "We cannot say whether this is a . . . return to its origins or a return of the repressed. Repetition . . . appears to subject it to an indeterminate shuttling or oscillation which binds different moments together as a middle which might turn forward or back."[55] This notion of fluidity is one of the markers of *the feminine* plot structure in *Memory* and it raises the intriguing issue of the simultaneous power and the ephemeral characteristic of *the feminine* narrative.

These temporal complexities operate equally in the reading subject, and are reflected in plot structure as they each negotiate the retrospective and anticipatory movements of the narrative in a process of recovering both the repressed textual unconscious and the psychic unconscious of the subject through the character of Jonny. When Jonny finds Bonny, he begins the slow process of realizing the fictive nature of memory, and the deceits and discontinuity of history. Bonny is not the magical "Pythoness" of his memory, which image of her he had carried with him for these five years:

> When he tried to remember the Pythoness he found she no longer existed. All he had was a memory of his own invention and nothing more. . . . He had invested the memory of their embrace by the danger-sign with significance so secret he was only aware of it. (169, 159)

Through all of these self-revisions the narrative appears to sum up an entire psychoanalytic thesis on memory while seizing another opportunity for another, typical of Mahy, postmodernist metafictional flourish: "Though memories were often regarded as careful files in a catalogue, Jonny now believed they could just as easily be wild stories, always in process of being revised, updated, or having different endings written on to them" (171). And Jonny himself, as the agent of plot and narrative theme, recognizes that the past is never entirely past, that through memory everything and nothing is forgotten, "There's no such thing as the past really. That's what I've worked out. It's always hanging around waiting for its chance to get going again . . ." (184).

Such complex narrative temporalities as these, which are also present in *Wolf* and *Dangerous Spaces*, mirror the promiscuous behavior of memory and dream, which are characteristically neither stable nor linear, and to which the reading subject assigns signification through Transference, are the quintessence of the "dream text."

WOLF

Dreaming the Wolf

Freud's case of the Wolf-Man acts as an illustration of the way the "latent content" of Cassy's unconscious is transformed into the "manifest contents" of her dream[56] through fairytale images and sensory images (smell, touch, and sight), and through the agency of narrative functioning in the role of dream-work:

> The sweet smell of pine trees was all around her and the ground under feet was soft with needles. Layer upon layer upon layer. (18)
> The sugary freshness of the pine trees was all around but under that, half-hidden and confusing, was another, wilder smell. Strong and animal. (50)

Several parallels can be drawn between Freud's case of the Wolf-Man and Gillian Cross's *Wolf* beyond the fact that they both inscribe the subjectivity of a dreaming subject. There is at least a superficial intertextual similarity between the illustrations on the dust jackets of the Puffin first edition of *Wolf* and the Pelican edition of *The Wolf-Man and Sigmund Freud*[57] that suggests an intentional association by the dust jacket illustrator of *Wolf*. More significantly, the Wolf-Man's childhood caregiver is called "Nanya" and is the person on whom he displaces his childhood fears of his father in an act that condenses the roles of father and caregiver. In *Wolf*, Cassy's childhood caregiver is similarly named "Nan," and, as in the case of the Wolf-Man, Nan is conflated with Cassy's father and so becomes synonymous with the father in the Lacanian, Symbolic Law-of-the-Father. The Wolf-Man's account of his dream and Cassy's dawn visit to the zoo resemble each other in that both accounts feature winter trees and wolf imagery:

> I know it was winter when I had my dream . . . Suddenly the window opened of its own accord and I was terrified to see that some white wolves were sitting on the big walnut tree in front of the window. . . . they had their ears pricked like dogs when they pay attention to something.[58]

And in *Wolf*,

> Bare brown winter trees clustered round, like the ghost of a forest. And, on top of the hillock huddled four shapes with pricked ears. (45)

In both cases of dreaming, these manifest contents feature as transpositions of latent material that is the dreamers' fear of their fathers, metaphorically and metonymically transposed through the dream-work. Freud explained that in the case of the Wolf-Man "both his father and his mother became wolves. His mother took the part of the castrated wolf, which let the others climb upon it; his father took the part of the wolf that climbed."[59] In *Wolf*, both Goldie and Cassy's father, Mick Phelan, are insinuated in these respectively passive and predatory positions: Goldie is acted upon by both Lyall and Mick Phelan in her role as the already silenced (castrated) female of Freudian and Lacanian theories of the woman, and in Cassy's reported sightings of her father he is always in the role of predator.

The Wolf-Man's dream is derived from fairy tales, particularly the stories of "Little Red Riding-Hood," and the "The Wolf and the Seven Little Goats." Freud explores this originary material through his work, "The Occurrence in Dreams of Material from Fairy Tales."[60] Both these tales involve both an eating-up and a cutting open of the belly to remove people. These actions are, according to Freud, the transposition of the fantasy of incorporation,[61] and the wish for copulation with the father. In both the tales recollected by Freud's Wolf-Man, the wolf finally perishes. Freud concluded from his interpretation of the Wolf-Man's dream that the wolf was the Wolf-Man's father:

> If in my patient's case the wolf was merely a first father-surrogate, the question arises whether the hidden content in the fairy tales of the wolf that ate up the little goats and of 'Little Red Riding-Hood' may not simply be infantile fear of the father. Moreover my patient's father had the characteristic, shown by so many people in relation to their children, of indulging in 'affectionate abuse'; and it is possible that during the patient's earlier years his father . . . may more than once, as he caressed the little boy or played with him, have threatened in fun to 'gobble him up.'[62]

Like Freud's Wolf-Man, Cassy also dreams the tale of "Little Red Riding Hood":

> There was no path through the forest. She turned slowly, gazing down alleys of trees. The lower branches barred her way, and the higher ones shut out the light. . . . She stood with her back to a tree, in that stillness which makes movement impossible in dreams. *Where are you going? Can I show you the way?* (18, 34)

By dreaming the wolf, Cassy replays her Oedipal, sexual relations with her father, which is and *was* her struggle for subjectivity through language and the Law. When she finally meets her father, it is the sight of his wolf-like teeth that triggers the repressed childhood memory of him. And, as in the story of the fairy-tale wolf that finally perishes, her father is whisked off to perish in a prison.

As has been already indicated, Lacan, in the wake of Freud's work on dreaming, pointed out with respect to the relation of the unconscious to the social Other, which includes the Symbolic Father and the Law, that Oedipal structures are *already* inscribed in language and the Symbolic and, therefore, *precede* the child's entry into them. Cassy's guilt at her dream of primary return is not her own individual or childhood guilt but an inheritance from her father:

> Oedipus is first the idea of an adult paranoiac, before it is the childhood feeling of a neurotic. . . . The first error of psychoanalysis is in acting as if things began with the child.[63]

This observation is not incompatible with Lacan's claim that the unconscious is laid down *through*, and because of, the child's entry into the Symbolic Order; and, because of it, Lacan was able to make his claim that "the unconscious is structured as a language."[64]

In Cassy's waking hours the dream-time wolf is metonymically evoked as a shifting signifier in polysemic imagery, not only of the wolf, and wolf masks, surrounding her, but also the character of Lyall as a father surrogate described tropologically as "leering" and "loping." The narrative movement between Cassy's sleeping and waking is signaled by the spatial arrangement of the page and by the use of roman and italicized print. These textual inscriptions of dreaming and waking are the manifest contents of Cassy's conscious and unconscious systems through which the reading subject seeks, through Cassy as textual agent, to uncover the textual unconscious. Cassy's waking life is contiguous with the dream where images and tropes, as objects of the other (mother) and the Other (the Symbolic, Father, the Law, and interdiction), surface in the chain of metaphoric substitution and metonymic images, as episodes of ever-more bizarre, unconnected, and unpredictable fragments embedded in the daily events of her waking life. For example: there is metaphoric substitution in her exchanges with Lyall when he attempts to define the essence of the Wolf show, and in Goldie's picture-representation of the wolf as a black circle surrounded with jagged triangular shapes pointing inward and outward:

> "What we're doing is—Wolves." *Wolves—and winter aconite.* . . . "Not *Wolves*" Lyall said impatiently. "That sounds like some kind of nature talk. It's *Wolf*, boy. That's what we're doing." (32, 33)
>
> The triangles had been drawn so fiercely that, in one or two places, the pen had gone right through the paper. "I must be stupid. I can't even see what it's meant to be." "Wolf, of course." "But it's nothing like a wolf." "Not *a* wolf," Robert said patiently. "We've got lots of photographs of those. This is something quite different. Lyall said 'Wolf'—and then he got people to draw the picture that came into their head." (37)

There is also metonymic contiguity with the dream in the images that surface in Cassy's conscious mind during numerous moments of her waking:

> She tried to make some kind of picture in her mind, but the image slid about shape-
> lessly, splitting into disconnected fragments. A gaping, murderous mouth. Long yel-
> low fangs. Sharp ears, lifted or laid back. . . . She couldn't drive the pictures out of her
> head. Grey shapes, moving like water under dark trees . . . Tireless feet, padding on
> and on across the snow . . . Yellow eyes, gleaming beyond the camp fire. . . . (33, 49)

Cassy's eventual, and reluctant, involvement in the "Wolf show," is, in terms of the dream and in Lacanian terms of the structural nature of the unconscious, her process of *"acting out"* that is the second order of Transference culminating in her eventual psychic and physical breakdown during her first public performance (127–8). This is the crucial moment of her Transference when she is liberated from the constraining effects of her unconscious wish. Until this moment she has been the passive victim: acted upon rather than acting. After this moment, which also is the moment of her "cure," she is released from the evil demons of her unconscious and proactively assumes control of her own actions by making a clear decision to return to the house of Nan:

> Cassy felt the terror fall away from her. . . . there was a cool, empty space in the
> middle of her mind. . . . The terror had gone now, and her mind was perfectly clear
> and alert. . . . And, sitting there in the back of the van, she understood what was
> needed. (129–30)

This is also a crucial moment of *textual* Transference, signified by the dream-time narrative erupting onto the surface of the waking narrative: it physically crosses the page and emerges in the waking narrative as the conscious realization of Cassy's primordial scream.

By dreaming her father in the image of the wolf, Cassy's unconscious memory surfaces in her preconscious (in the Freudian model of the psyche), and finally comes to consciousness when she meets him after years of separation, a meeting that, significantly for the symbolic (and Symbolic) relations between Nan and her father, takes place in Nan's flat. This meeting, in turn, provokes, metonymically, Cassy's memory of her dream-time wolf and is another example of contiguity between her dreaming and waking:

> His face was very close to hers. She could see the separate hairs of his stubbly beard
> and the drops of sweat on his nose. The smell of his body was all around her,
> strong—and unfamiliar. . . . "What are you putting on me?" It triggered a memory
> she didn't know she had of herself as a two year old child in a high chair, eating
> jelly. (135–136)

She has an image of Nan's "neat, white false teeth" mingling in her memory with another set of teeth: her father's, "stained, irregular teeth. Real teeth. *Oh Grand-mother, what big teeth. . . .*" (136)

The incident has been prefigured in Cassy's third dream (50–1): a sensory dream in which there had been no pictures, and it is one that carries unequivocally sexual connotations: "Everything came through her other senses." She smells a wild smell: "Strong and animal!" She feels "the smooth handle of the basket," a sensory image that connects directly with the phallic imagery of her second dream in which she had observed the "long, smooth rod of the bottle's neck" as a phallic image that eventually surfaces in her waking life as her father's wielding the barrel of a gun at her. There are connotations of pubic hair—her father's pubic hair: "under her left hand was thick hair, springy and strange. It was so deep that she could run her fingers through it." (50). In this dream Cassy conjectures and confronts her projected sexual relations with her father and is lured by his invitation to seduce her: " '*Shall I show you the path? We could play a little game....*' " (34).

Cassy is presented unsubtly as a late-twentieth-century "Little Red Riding Hood" figure. In the Perrault and Grimms versions of the tale, "Little Red Riding Hood" was confronted by a real wolf, but Cassy must wrestle with the fictive wolf of her dreams and the wolf's multiple manifestations in the metaphorical, metonymic, and literal forms of both her dreaming and waking life. In classic versions of the tale[65] the red-hooded cape carries sexual symbolism, described in Cixous's feminist analysis as "a little clitoris,"[66] and is satirized graphically in Angela Carter's "The Company of Wolves," as the young girl's adolescent menses:

> But this one, so pretty and the youngest of her family, a little late-comer, had been indulged by her mother and the grandmother who'd knitted her red shawl that, today, has the ominous if brilliant look of blood on snow. . . . She has just started her woman's bleeding, the clock inside her that will strike, henceforward, once a month.[67]

In *Wolf*, the red-hooded cloak has been replaced by a blue mac metaphorically inscribed as a child's "comfort blanket"—Cassy's *objet a*, which she puts on, takes off, and wraps around herself in moments of heightened anxiety, or when she experiences extreme cold; this is, after all, the story of Cassy's symbolic replay of infancy in which, through dream, she dramatizes her pre-Symbolic relations with her mother and her Oedipal relations with her father.

From Other to (M)other

In classic versions of the tale of "Little Red Riding Hood," the little girl is sent by her mother to the home of her grandmother, but in *Wolf* she is sent by her *grandmother* to the home of her *mother*, bearing not a basket of newly baked cakes but—in a bleak image of late-twentieth-century lifestyle and social disintegration—a bag of prepacked food and a quantity of Semtex. She moves between two houses that conjure contrasting views of the mother. She is the "Little Red Riding Hood" who leaves home, "not to go into the big wide world but to go from one house to another by the shortest route possible. . . . between two houses, between two beds."[68] Between her grandmother and her mother, Cassy moves from Other of Symbolic to her (m)other.

Questions of parenting and parent/child relations that are central to traditional versions of the story of "Little Red Riding Hood" are central, too, to the tale of Cassy as a Red Riding Hood figure. Traditionally, parents are rational and the children are the fantasists. But in *Wolf* (as in so many other examples of children's literature that ascribe precedence to the child) the female parent and the father surrogate behave like children, and the children, Robert and Cassy, are rational, "talking to Goldie was like arguing with a nagging child" (28), "Lyall and Goldie were like children after a party" (59) and, "that was Goldie's voice, giggly and excited" (14).

Nan is presented as the responsible female parent in contrast to Goldie who is an infantilized, irresponsible, inadequate, itinerant, and abandoning mother. Goldie is far from the image of the caring mother "who makes everything all right, who nourishes and who stands up against separation."[69] Between them, Goldie and Nan are presented as feminist criticism's definition of the angel and monster polarity of women and are closely aligned, in the context of the all-pervasive allusions to the tale of "Little Red Riding Hood," with inverse images of the mother and stepmother figures of children's fairy tales.

Nan's "sensible" voice (the voice of the Father by proxy) echoes in Cassy's head throughout her day as the internalized voice of the Law and is seemingly the only regulator of stability in her newly rootless and chaotic life. Nan's voice echoes the prescriptive, interdictory voice of "Little Red Riding Hood's" mother in the Grimms' version of the tale, (who also is the voice of the Father's Law of prohibition) " 'Don't dally around now. Go straight there,' " (9), denying Cassy the pleasure of straying off the path to experience the sexual pleasures of her pubescent journey "through her own forest."[70] In the absence of Cassy's father, Nan has been the figure of the Oedipal father and her voice is the voice of Symbolic patriarchy which has kept Cassy docile, submissive, and innocent. Nan embodies, then, the roles of the father and the patriarchal "good mother," but, in Cixous's definition, she is also the "bad mother," who has effectively "shut the daughter in" by shutting her out from answers to her questions about her father, and her questions to her mother:

> She had always known, ever since she was very small, that it was forbidden. *We won't talk about him now, Cassy. And don't you go asking your mother, either. She knows she's not to tell you. It'll be time enough when you're grown up.* (47)

Cassy dreams in Goldie's house like she has never dreamed before ("She never dreamed. Never, never. But she knew, as she sat there with her heart thumping, that she had dreamed every night in that house" [52]), because it is here, in Goldie's squat, the home (the womb) of her mother, from whom she has been separated since early childhood, that she finds the necessary *space* to replay this Oedipal drama of her struggle for subjectivity. It is in Goldie's squat that Cassy inhabits that space that Lacan described as the *gap* between the experiential self and the Other, between the Imaginary and the regulatory laws of Symbolic patriarchy in which the subject is constantly recreated and reformed in the play of differences between the *moi* and the *je*. It is here that her specular (Mirror Phase, pre-Oedipal) experiences erupt into the Symbolic to disturb the balance of rationality bestowed by language and the Law.

In this paradoxically homely space[71] suspended in a nowhere between anarchy and the Law, between her *waking* life and her *dreaming*, on the brink of her adolescence, and at the conclusion of that period that Freud described as the "latency period,"[72] Cassy reexperiences her Mirror Phase relations with her mother symbolized in the refracted images of the "magic forest" of mirrors where she first found Goldie in the "mirror room":

> The room had no limits. . . . Slowly she realized that she was looking at reflections. The only real lights were two candles, standing in bottles in the middle of the floor. Their flames were reflected backwards and forwards, over and over, up and down, in a hundred fragments of mirror. (14)

The untold story of the Oedipal drama is that, for girl children, the process is as much about the desire to reexperience primary narcissism with the *mother* and, conversely, the mother's desire for the girl, as the struggle to expiate her sexual relations with her father. Cassy finally achieves this at the end of the narrative when Michael Phelan is removed from the Oedipal scene, and she is reconciled with her mother: "Goldie sobbed as she hugged Cassy tighter and tighter: 'I thought I was going to be too late! They were all so slow! I couldn't bear it!' " (139).

Imaginary Pleasure/Symbolic Law

The profligate collapse of "civilized" social norms and the pervasive stench of debris and dereliction in Goldie's squat can be interpreted, in terms of psychoanalytic textuality, as the material manifestations of the dissolution of the Symbolic Law. Goldie and Lyall behave like children because the squat is their retreat into the Imaginary where the laws of the Symbolic are suspended, and, in it, all life becomes a game of fantasy and Imaginary pleasure. Goldie's squat is, as has already been indicated, a symbolic return to infancy providing Cassy with the material environment conducive to her experiencing the Oedipal, nighttime dream. The narrative movements between waking and dreaming, and the tensions between cleanliness and squalor, inscribe the subjective pull between the "primitivism" of the Imaginary, imaged in narrative allusions to animality, and the orderliness of "culture" in the Symbolic, manifested in Cassy's initial need to impose order and cleanliness on the chaos and squalor that engulf her in the squat. She mimics Nan's housekeeping routines and is disgusted when Lyall and Robert suggest that she should eat her Indian take out from the carton and with her fingers. At narrative moments such as these Cassy hovers in the liminal space between her fear of the primal fantasy associated with primitivism and animality, and the regulatory pull of culture in the Symbolic:

> "Eat with our *fingers?*" Cassy was horrified. "But that's—" "Wild?" Lyall said mockingly. "Savage?" "What's the matter Cassy? Will civilization be destroyed if we don't use a knife and fork? Shall we drop down on to all fours and tear the food with our teeth?" (63–4)

Cassy's move from one bed in Nan's flat to another bed on the bare boards of Goldie's run-down squat has precipitated her being able to dream the repressed dream-contents she has been hitherto unable to admit to consciousness in the prohibitive confines of the domain of the patriarchal Law in Nan's flat. The text of *Wolf* is, in this sense, a material manifestation of the process of Transference where textual unconscious contents surface through the tropological signifiers identified in a single act of reading. And the text that has been thus produced, is effectively another dream text that is subject, in its turn, to another process of literary Transference, ad infinitum.

DANGEROUS SPACES

Dual Ontology

Dangerous Spaces is another text about dreaming. But here the dream is both a psychic space *and* a fully articulated parallel world: "Viridian" is constructed as a disturbing, metaphysical, space between the zones of life and death through which the literary subjects of the narrative, Anthea and Flora, reconstruct and reconcile their relative and contrasting conditions of subjectivity. Anthea's parents have gone missing and are presumed drowned, after a boat trip. Her former life as the only daughter of her parents had been secure, orderly and affluent and is the narrative present she is working hard to adjust to the relative chaos and squalor of her new life in the house of her cousin Flora, her aunt Molly, and her uncle Lionel, a smelly, crying baby, a pregnant dog, various cats and small holding hens. The house in which Anthea and Flora spend their waking and sleeping lives is haunted by the spirit of old Lionel and his dead son Henry. Old Lionel built the house, lived and died in it, but his legacy lives on in the decor and landscaping that still inhabit and surround the house. Once again, as she did in *The Tricksters*, Mahy has chosen a haunted, ancestral home as the site of subjective transformation.

Viridian is populated by the specters of both dead Henry and old Lionel whose spectral names, Griff and Leo, conjure mythical images in a mythical, unreal, space. Viridian is recovered as three-dimensional space from the collapsed images on stereoscope cards that Anthea finds in dead Henry's box. In the sense of Anthea's opening up a two-dimensional space, Viridian is positioned, semiotically, as that space that prizes open the signifier (as dominant) and signified, and operates between signs and their meanings, to disturb and disrupt everyday significations. It is the kind of space described by Lacan as the space in which subjectivity is constituted.[73] Viridian is affected by what Freud, in his topoi of the dream, called "the day's residues," "the operation in which the silt of daily experience (the day's residues) come to cover over archaic desire. But this desire carries within itself its primary repression."[74]

Dangerous Spaces, as well as being a dream text, also is a paradigm narrative of the fantastic in which the act of dreaming serves, not as the usual site of a contested boundary, but as a *conduit* to what McHale described as a "dual ontology"[75] between, in this case, the supernatural world of the dream, and the normal, everyday world of Anthea and Flora's waking. In these senses the narrative is positioned in the borderland of the human psyche, in that place where "the actual and the imaginary intermingle."[76] These two worlds encroach upon each other through an act of dreaming that ultimately is shared by Anthea and Flora. In this "uncanny" space, the paradigms of fantastic subjectivity as described in Freud's seminal essay on "The 'Uncanny' "[77] are made manifest and "worked over" in themes of "doubling," "transformation," "alienation," "homecoming," and "death," all of which are the manifestation and locus of *the feminine* narrative.[78] This occluded, interstitial space is, in Freud's terminology, the place of projected, unconscious desires and fears: "those qualities, feelings, wishes, objects which the subject refuses to recognize or rejects in himself [and that] are expelled from the self and located in another person or thing."[79] Anthea has longed for Viridian as the private space in which to *be* in her efforts to escape what she perceives to be the life-denying and suffocating squalor of Molly and Lionel's country house:

> It [Viridian] was dangerous—she knew that now—but still it was something of her own in a house where there was so little space for her, so little space that everything private was precious and had to be guarded. (79)

At the same time, Viridian was a place, "which felt more and more like home" (38). As a space of the uncanny, Viridian is, then, the ambivalent space evoking the two semantic meanings of the uncanny. The uncanny can be related precisely to the "dangerous space" named in the narrative as "the secret land of Viridian," a limitless space of death and desire, which is here inscribed in *the feminine* as a place of homecoming:

> A space so small it could be carried in a tin box, yet so big it could hold halls with doorways like keyholes and even whole ranges of mountains; could hold a wind that could be heard but not felt, together with a road, and the promise of an ocean with an island in the middle of it. (41)

Viridian, like the illogical, atemporal space of the dream, has its own distinctive climate, and is timeless. It has a statue weeping tears behind a stone veil that is a projected image of Anthea's petrified self, mourning, but unable to mourn, her parents' death. The rocky landscape is marked out by a series of arrows containing eyes, and keyhole-shaped doors, and suggests a new vision and unlocked spaces leading, and pointing the way, to the center of the Viridian universe: an inverted land/seascape where an island floats on an inland sea housing "the hole in the middle of the zero." This is the inevitable and final point of death toward which dead Henry leads Anthea, inexorably, in the chain of signifiers as the execution of her "death wish," across the rocky terrain of Viridian.

The Vel *of Alienation*

Anthea's dream of Viridian is the space of Desire born of the experience of lack. She seeks reunification, in death, with her dead parents, to fill the space that has been opened up in her lack-of-being, her loss of love effected by their loss, especially the loss through death of the primal object, her mother. Lacan says:

> It is this ex-istence (Entstellung) of desire in the dream that explains how the significance of the dream masks the desire that is present in it, whereas its motive vanishes by being simply problematic.[80]

In his essay on "Desire in Hamlet," Lacan points out that: "The navel of the dream to which Freud refers is perhaps nothing but the psychological counterpart of this lack."[81] Anthea exists in a psychic state of alienation and fragmentation described in the narrative as:

> A thousand almost-thoughts. For they were more like pieces of broken pictures mixed together and slowly boiling around mind-soup made up of scraps that rose and sank and turned over and over. One piece came to the surface and then vanished as another replaces it . . . (95)

This experience of flux describes the condition Lacan referred to as "the *vel of alienation*."[82] It is positioned at the intersection between being and meaning/ object and Other in the place of non-meaning and is significant for Anthea's interstitial position between two states of being:

If we choose being, the subject disappears, it eludes us, it falls into non-meaning. If we choose meaning that is, strictly speaking that which constitutes in realization of the subject, the unconscious. In other words, it is of the nature of this meaning, as it emerges in the field of the Other, to be in a large part of its field, eclipsed by the disappearance of being, induced by the very function of the signifier.[83]

Ultimately, Anthea's process of subjectivity in the Symbolic economy will demand that she makes an either/or choice between being and meaning against which the not-chosen element, in Lacan's terminology, is *"aphanisis"* or "the *fading* of the subject."[84] Anthea's journey through Viridian follows what Lacan has called the "patterning of the structure of metonymy," which represents the "desire of the Other":

In this interval intersecting the signifiers, which forms part of the very structure of the signifier, is the locus of what, in other registers of my exposition, I have called metonymy. It is there that what we call desire crawls, slips escapes, like the ferret.[85]

The Other is constituted in Viridian, as Anthea traverses the signifiers of its landscape towards her ultimate desire for the other that is her condition of inorganicism, her Nirvana, her zero point of non-being that is paradoxically the point of her recovery:

"She *wanted* to go," he said. "But he'll take her to the island and there's no way back. You have to go through." "Through what?" Flora asked. "The hole in the middle of the zero," said the ghost beside her. . . . "But then you go *inwards* . . . into the centre, the smallest point. It's so tiny you couldn't even see it through a microscope, but it's there, and you go *through* it, you *squeeze* through." (76, 117)

Lacan describes the metonymic structure as:

The incessant movement of the human subjectivity to fill the gap between signifier and signifier in that 'reference back' to that always posited (but never grasped) original signifier of being.[86]

Griff tells Anthea that, " 'There's no way back.' " But, in Viridian, the journey is not linear as in Lacan's metonymic structure, it is circular: it is *feminine*. Because the end contains the beginning, and Anthea's desire for reconciliation with her parents is in the ultimate place of non-meaning, that is, death, it is also her return to the womb, her longed-for homecoming. It can be seen as the primal, original *Heim* of Freud's *Das Heimliche*:

> The gap of non-meaning thus becomes a hole [which is] the opening onto the unsymbolized real. [it] may well be the opening of subjectivity back into the body, the place where the *objet a* and its metonyms and the symptom-as metaphor gain their entry to discourse.[87]
> Home is finally the place from which one comes—the mother or, more specifically the woman's genitals, and the 'home' or origin of the inorganic.[88]

"Remembering, repeating, working through": these are the components of Transference. They have been played out in Anthea's experiences of Viridian and are the way that textual unconscious is recovered. Molly acts as the Transferential agent in the process for Anthea; it is she who listens to Anthea's retelling (repeating) the events of her quarrel with Flora; it is she who listens to Anthea's remembering and retelling (the "repetition" of) the story of her life with her mother and father. It is Molly's Transferential love that ultimately saves Anthea from the jaws of death in Viridian: " 'Anthea, I want *you* to hug *me*' she said. '*I* want to be the hugged one' " (97). This is the climactic moment of the narrative in which Anthea's stone veil (*vel*) of tears, imaged in the stone statue of Viridian, dissolves, "and the tears, pushing their way out through a veil of stone, began dissolving the veil away" (97).

As much as it is a narrative of the restructuring of subjectivity, *Dangerous Spaces* is a narrative about the return to the mother in the figure of Molly as surrogate. It is Anthea's memory of her hugging Molly that sustains her during the critical moments of her transformational Viridian experiences:

> The chain held, and she, not being entirely part of Viridian, and shielded in some way by the memory of Molly hugging her on the other side of sleep, was less affected by the explosion. (102)

In Freud's formulation of the death-drive,[89] "home is also where we return *to*. Death is a woman's—the mother's—body.[90]

Revenant

The entire narrative of *Dangerous Spaces* is thus structured around the concept of *return* in a circular movement from death through mourning (worked out in the dream of Viridian), and the reconstitution of subjectivity. In the sense of its being a circular narrative, it subscribes to definitions of the female plot structure as implicated in Kristeva's idea of "Women's Time,"[91] and feminist definitions of female narratives. More especially, it conforms to Freud's idea of *revenant* relating exclusively to the return of a ghost; of an ancestral return from the dead:

The spirits of deceased parents . . . The attitude of awe and fear in respect of dream visitors from the dead has been thought to be one of the main sources of ancestor-worship.[92]

All the narrative subjects in *Dangerous Spaces* are inscribed and circumscribed by the presence of *revenant*, especially Anthea who awaits the return of her dead parents, and through her longing to return to them in death, she actualizes Viridian. Moreover, the entire household is haunted by the return of the ghost of Old Lionel and is paralyzed by his spiritual presence: Flora meets him as a young boy in the hall of the house, and she constructs a perception of herself as the feckless victim of his house and routines; Lionel suffers an all-pervading ennui, is unable to act to finish the job of transforming the house because of the eternal return of the presence and spirit of Old Lionel. All of the family's fights and discomfitures ensue from the single issue of the house's unruliness, described in terms that are significantly evocative of the ghost of Old Lionel, as their living, "inside a sort of skeleton, skin gone, and bones, nerves and blood vessels revealed" (5–6).

Flora is structured as Anthea's obverse double: freckled, short, round, and mousy-haired; she is in direct opposition to Anthea's slender translucence and flowing "raw silk" hair—she is Cinderella to Anthea's (Sleeping) Beauty. Their differences are reflected and signified in the contrastingly poised and downtrodden demeanors of their respective cats, Glorious, and Taffeta. One of the objectives of the narrative is to reconcile their conflicting selves into a harmonious accord, effected in the doubling of dreams experienced by both girls through the agency of Viridian, reconciled in the double image of Anthea in the weeping statue, and liberated by Flora's mythical and heroic quest through Viridian, like Boudicca, to rescue Anthea by pulling her back from the margins of beyond. This is Flora's chance "to fly" ("She might be as wide as a door and covered in freckles but at least she could hope to fly, one way or another" [2]), her moment of *revenant*, when she shrugs off her commodity-based identity and reconciles herself, in Anthea, through the signifiers of the dream.

By choosing meaning over being, which, Lacan insists, is the necessary condition of decentered subjectivity, Anthea finally reconciles herself to a place in Flora's household. It is a subjective transformation that is graphically realized in a displacement of signifiers: the honey-pot with the silver bee on it has been linked throughout the narrative (like Anthea's beautiful, pin-tucked night-dress), to the chain of objects which connect Anthea to her past life with her parents, and is one of the defining objects of her subjectivity (her *objet a*). Through Anthea's transformation it is metaphorically transposed for a more utilitarian usage into "plum-jam pot" for Molly's homemade jam bearing, not a honeybee, but what they shall now refer to as a wasp: " 'What a pretty pot,' people would say. 'I love the bee on it.' And she, and possibly her children too, would cry, 'It's a wasp!' "

(129). This seemingly insignificant detail of the transposition from "bee" to "wasp" is symptomatic of the changing psychic state of Anthea as she moves from her attachment to her past life with her parents to an integrated life in the household of her "adoptive" family, and is indicative of the way in which the positioning of the object in the Symbolic inscribes subjectivity in language:

> In this place, the subject rises as what can be stood in for; it is represented there; it is nothing but this representation, and this representation must do for all subjects. Language creates the place where subjects find each other.[93]

Viridian has thus acted in the place of the "dream-work" in this text. In it the dreaming subject through a system of significations analogous to the workings, structures and function of language has worked out her unconscious desires, though here they have been shown to be the workings of *the feminine* Imaginary, and the reconciliation between Symbolic displacement and Semiotic "homecoming."

NOTES TO CHAPTER 5

1. Sigmund Freud, *The Interpretation of Dreams*, vols. 4–5 of *The Standard Edition*, 633–87.
2. Kristeva, "Revolution," 112.
3. Sigmund Freud, "From the History of an Infantile Neurosis," *The Standard Edition*, 17: 51.
4. Richard Jones has described Freud's theory of the system Preconscious thus: "The system Preconscious is used in two quite different ways (1) as a kind of storage bin for thoughts and memories which are not, but could become, conscious; and (2) as a kind of converter, ceaselessly engaged in transforming old thoughts, memories and perceptions into new symbolic forms." Richard M. Jones, *The New Psychology of Dreaming* (Harmondsworth: Penguin Books, 1970), 126. In Lacanian theory the preconscious and the unconscious are conflated. It is also worth bearing in mind that the Freudian unconscious is prelingual and the Lacanian unconscious is postlingual and that the latter comes into being only as a consequence of the Oedipal experiences upon the child's entry into the Symbolic.
5. Freud, *Interpretation of Dreams*, 22, 191, 553, 561.
6. Ibid.
7. Sigmund Freud, "An Evidential Dream," *The Standard Edition*, 12: 267–77; 273.
8. Sigmund Freud, "The 'Wolf-Man'," in "From the History of an Infantile Neurosis," *The Standard Edition*, 17: 7–122.
9. See Laplanche and Pontalis, *Language*, 10.
10. See Steven Marcus, "Freud and Dora: Story, History, Case History," *In Dora's Case: Freud—Hysteria—Feminism*, eds. Charles Bernheimer and Claire Kahane

(New York: Columbia University Press, 1985), 56–91; 90; also quoted in Williams, *Critical Desire*, 147.

11. Peter Nicholls, "The Belated Postmodern: History, Phantoms and Toni Morrison," in *Psychoanalytic Criticism: A Reader*, ed. Sue Vice (Cambridge: Polity Press, 1996), 50–74; 53.

12. Lacan, *Écrits*, 48.

13. Nicholls, "Belated," 53. See also Laplanche and Pontalis, *Language*, 113.

14. Jean Laplanche and Serge Leclaire, "The Unconscious: A Psychoanalytic Study," *Yale French Studies* 48 (1972): 118–79; 128.

15. Jean Laplanche, *New Foundations for Psychoanalysis*, trans. David Macey (Oxford: Blackwell, 1989), 112.

16. Cynthia Chase, " 'Transference' as trope and persuasion," in *Discourse in Psychoanalysis and Literature*, ed. Shlomith Rimmon-Kenan (London: Methuen, 1987), 211–29; 214.

17. Ibid., 216.

18. Jacques Lacan, "Seminar on 'The Purloined Letter,' " *Yale French Studies* 48 (1972): 38–72.

19. Williams, *Critical Desire*, 53. For an excellent critique of Lacan's "Seminar on 'The Purloined Letter' " and Derrida's reading of Lacan's reading of Poe, ("The Purveyor of Truth"), see Barbara Johnson, "The frame of reference: Poe, Lacan, Derrida," *Yale French Studies: Literature and Psychoanalysis* 55, no. 6 (1977): 457–505; 464.

20. Carroll, *The Subject*, 34, 47.

21. For examples of these types of postmodern fictions, see Waugh, *Feminine Fictions*, 1–7.

22. Johnson, "The Frame of Reference," 459: Johnson points out that Lacan's reading, which reduces the "The Purloined Letter" to a triangular structure, can only be achieved by the elimination of the narrator. This is, she claims: "A blatant and highly revealing result of the way 'psychoanalysis' does violence to literature in order to find its own schemes. What psychoanalysis sees as a triangle is therefore really a quadrangle, and the fourth side is the point at which literature problemetizes the very possibility of a triangle."

23. This idea was first raised in Marie Bonaparte, *The Life and Works of Edgar Allan Poe: A Psycho-Analytic Interpretation*, trans John Rodker (London: Imago, 1949), 641.

24. See Margaret Whitford, *Luce Irigaray: Philosophy in the Feminine* (London: Routledge, 1991), 35.

25. See Ragland-Sullivan, "Magnetism," 318, 383.

26. See Mellard, *Using Lacan*, 147, 175.

27. Lemaire, *Jacques Lacan*, 220.

28. Lacan, *Écrits*, 14.

29. Jean-Francois Lyotard, "The Dream-Work Does Not Think," *Oxford Literary Review* 6 (1983): 3–34; 4: "No doubt that is why Freud believes that an interpretation (something quite different from pure invention on the interpreter's part) is possible, because such an interpretation does not have to recover a meaning (*sens*), but a *signification* just as that which pertains to 'normal' discourse."

30. Felman, "Turning the Screw," 137.
31. Peter Brooks, "Idea," 346.
32. Lacan, *Écrits*, xiii.
33. Bert O. States, *The Rhetoric of Dreams* (Ithaca and London: Cornell University Press, 1988), 135.
34. In his critique of Peter Brooks' work on "The Idea of a Psychoanalytical Literary Criticism," James Mellard emphasizes how he believes Brooks elides the essential textuality of knowledge: "What is at stake is in fact the relationship between several different 'texts', and it may simply be moot to wonder which has authority over the other. The fact is, all that we 'know' these days is regarded by structuralists, post-structuralists, and deconstructionists as some sort of text. Understanding and knowledge are textual, both generated by the relations among texts and textualities." James M. Mellard, *Using Lacan, Reading Fiction*, 39.
35. Ragland-Sullivan, "Magnetism," 381.
36. Lacan, *The Four Fundamental Concepts*, 212.
37. Lyotard, "Dream-Work," 7, 8.
38. John Forrester, *The Seductions of Psychoanalysis: Freud, Lacan and Derrida* (Cambridge: Cambridge University Press, 1990), 148.
39. Mellard, *Using Lacan*, 5.
40. Ibid.
41. Freud, *Interpretation of Dreams*, 106, 6. This invocation to uncover the textual unconscious is also the role demanded of the reader by Freud in his account of Irma's dream: "And now I must ask the reader to make my interests his own for quite a while, and to plunge, along with me, into the minutest details of my life; for a transference of this kind is peremptorily demanded by our interests in the hidden meaning of dreams."
42. Ragland-Sullivan, "Magnetism," 388.
43. David Harvey, *The Condition of Postmodernity: An Enquiry into the Origins of Cultural Change* (Oxford: Basil Blackwell, 1990), 50–1.
44. Freud, *Interpretation of Dreams*, 546.
45. Laplanche and Pontalis, *Language*, 114.
46. Grosz, *Jacques Lacan*, 100.
47. Lemaire, "Metaphor as Symptom," 206–7.
48. Jean Laplanche and Serge Leclaire, "The Unconscious: A Psychoanalytic Study," *Yale French Studies* 48 (1972): 118–78; 128.
49. Nicolas Abraham and Maria Torok, "Introjection—Incorporation: *Mourning or Melancholia*," in *Psychoanalysis in France*, eds. S. Lebovici and D. Widlocker (New York: International University Press, 1980), 8. See also, Laplanche and Pontalis, *Language*, 211: "Freud uses 'incorporation' to describe the process whereby the subject, more or less on the level of phantasy, has an object penetrate his body and keeps it 'inside' his body"; also, Nicolas Abraham and Maria Torok, *The Wolf Man's Magic Word: A Cryptonymy*, trans. Nicholas Rand (Minneapolis: University of Minnesota Press, 1986), xvi–xvii; Sigmund Freud, "Mourning and Melancholia," The *Standard Edition*, 14: 243–58.
50. Waugh, "Stalemates?," 347.

51. Kellner, "Constructing Postmodern Identities," 141–77: Kellner points out that TV ads aim to associate their products with positive images and desirable gender role models; also, Roland Barthes has said that advertising provides models of identity, and lays down codes of social behavior that have the contemporary function of myth, Roland Barthes, *Mythologies* (New York: Hill and Wang, 1972). Passim.

52. See Kellner, "Constructing Postmodern Identities," 153.

53. Ibid.

54. Sigmund Freud, "Beyond the Pleasure Principle," *The Standard Edition*, 18: 7–64.

55. Brooks, "Freud's Masterplot," 288.

56. See the introduction to this chapter.

57. Muriel Gardiner, *The Wolf-Man and Sigmund Freud* (Harmondsworth: Penguin, 1973).

58. Ibid., 192.

59. Ibid., 210.

60. Sigmund Freud, "The Occurrence in Dreams of Material from Fairy Tales," *The Standard Edition*, 12: 281–7.

61. See for example, the variants formulated by Susan Isaacs, 'The Nature and Function of Phantasy," *International Journal of Psycho-Analysis* 29, (1948): "I want to eat her all up," "I want to keep her inside me," "I want to tear her to bits," "I want to throw her out of me," "I want to bring her back," "I must have her now," etc., quoted in Jean Laplanche and Jean-Baptiste Pontalis, "Fantasy and the Origins of Sexuality," *The International Journal of Psycho-Analysis* 49, no. 1 (1968): 1–18; 14 n.33.

62. Freud, "Infantile Neurosis," 7–112.

63. Gilles Deleuze and Félix Guattari, *Anti-Oedipus* (London: Viking Press, 1977), 274–5.

64. See Lemaire, *Jacques Lacan*, 3: "The unconscious is composed of signifiers and is itself structured in the sense that, although distinctive and summable, the elements are still articulated in categories and sub-sets in accordance with precise laws of arrangements. In this sense, the structure of the unconscious is identical with that of language."

65. I am referring here to the versions of the tale by Charles Perrault in seventeenth century France and by the Brothers Grimm in nineteenth century Germany.

66. Cixous, "Castration or Decapitation?," 43.

67. Angela Carter, "The Company of Wolves," in *The Bloody Chamber* (London: Vintage, 1995), 10–118; 113.

68. Cixous, "Castration or Decapitation?," 44.

69. Cixous, "Laugh of the Medusa," 882.

70. Ibid.

71. See, in this connection, later in this chapter in relation to Freud's "*das Heimliche*" and "*das 'Unheimliche.*'"

72. Christopher Badcock, *Essential Freud* (Oxford: Basil Blackwell, 1992), 105: "During the so-called 'latency period,' the child's preconscious infantile sexuality appeared to lessen and, indeed, to undergo some degree of repression."

73. Lacan, *Four Fundamental Concepts*, 206.
74. Lyotard, "The Dream-Work," 9; see also: Sigmund Freud, "On Dreams," of *The Standard Edition*, 5: 633–87; 667.
75. McHale, *Postmodernist Fictions*, 73.
76. Ibid., 49.
77. Freud, "Uncanny."
78. As has already been indicated in relation to *The Tricksters*, Freud uses the terms "*Das Heimliche*" and "*Das Unheimliche*" to describe the "uncanny," which is at once both "homely" and "unhomely": *das Unheimliche* "uncanny" he says, is "undoubtedly related to what is frightening—to what arouses dread and horror," to what is "dangerous and unsafe." *Das Heimlich* "uncanny" simultaneously signifies, "all that is familiar, friendly cheerful comfortable, intimate," and means also "that which is concealed from others: all that is hidden, secreted, obscured." See Jackson, *Fantasy*, 64: 219.
79. Laplanche and Pontalis, *Language*, 349.
80. See Lacan, *Écrits*, 263–4.
81. Jacques Lacan, "Desire and Interpretation of Desire in Hamlet," *Yale French Studies* 55–6 (1977): 11–52; 40.
82. Lemaire, *Jacques Lacan*, 76.
83. Lacan, *The Four Fundamental Concepts*, 210.
84. Ibid.
85. Ibid., 214.
86. Mellard, *Using Lacan*, 25. See also: Lacan, *Écrits*, 164–6.
87. Mellard, *Using Lacan*, 23.
88. Williams, *Critical Desire*, 178.
89. Freud, "Beyond the Pleasure Principle," 7–64.
90. Williams, *Critical Desire*, 178.
91. Kristeva, "Women's Time," 187–213.
92. Ernest Jones, *On the Nightmare* (London: Hogarth Press, 1931), 63, quoted in Williams, *Critical Desire*, 179.
93. Thomas A. Hanzo, "Paternity and the Subject in *Bleak House*," in *The Fictional Father*, ed. Robert Con Davis (Amherst: The University of Massachusetts Press, 1981), 44.

Conclusion

UNE LECTURE FÉMININE

It has been possible to show through these close readings of just seven paradigm texts how *the feminine* can be read in certain, diverse, but generically specific texts of children's literature. Readers will wish to bring their own personal bibliographies to bear upon such readings. But it is also suggested that readings in *the feminine* may reside in these other texts: David Almond's *Skellig*, Natalie Babbitt's *Tuck Everlasting*, Tim Bowler's *River Boy*, Berlie Doherty's *Dear Nobody*, Zibby Oneal's *A Formal Feeling*, Katherine Paterson's *Bridge to Terabithia*, Catherine Storr's *Marianne Dreams*, and, perhaps also in many of the works of the Australian writer Patricia Wrightson. (Can the Aboriginal "Dreamtime" topology, for example, be theorized in the terminologies and concepts appropriated to *the feminine*?) At the levels of both story and discourse, these fictions manifest many of the features of Cixous's *l'écriture féminine*, Irigaray's *le parler femme*, and Kristeva's Semiotic that have been described here because of the way that they connect with the other—which is the place of *the feminine* Imaginary—in their features of self-referential and transformational writing, their fantastical, out of space time characterizations, through their discursive patternings of circularity and return, metaphors of transformation and rebirth, and in their representations of subjectivities that are heterogeneous, unfixed, and in continuous process of becoming.

The reading of Gillian Cross's *Wolf*, and Margaret Mahy's *Memory*, show the possibilities for *the feminine* postmodern in children's literature in that these narratives undermine the masculinist definition of postmodern fictions because they occupy a space described as the center ground—Irigaray's "excluded middle," in their simultaneous and paradoxical inscriptions of fragmentation and centrality, unconnectedness and coherence, powerlessness and agency. Through their circular and elliptical plot structures, and in their rhythmic linguistic gesturing, which are the embodiments in language of corporeal experiences, these fictions of *the feminine* variously dramatize the child's reconnection to the pre-Oedipal relations with the mother. As is evident from such readings, the language of *the feminine* is primarily a physical mode of communication. In *the feminine*, transformation demonstrably is achieved through the mode of the fantastic, and in the imagery of four primal elements, especially water.

Through representations of dreaming and memory, through repression and displacement manifested in tropes of metaphor and metonymy in, and the transmutation of, mother and daughter relations through the discourses of *le parler femme*, such as those we have seen in *The Changeover* and *Dangerous Spaces*, these fictions depict new, spatial, relations that both symbolize and realize Cixous's, Irigaray's, and Kristeva's, repositioning of female relations to their origins. These are the kinds of narrative features that are, in Cixous's definition, the exceptional expression in language of the woman's sex-specific experiences of childbirth, nourishment, and love. In *The Newly Born Woman*, Cixous perceives these transformational, spatial relationships as a "bond" with the "other" that, she says, "Comes through in the metaphor of bringing into the world . . . her *jouissance*, the feminine Imaginary—and her way of self-constituting a subjectivity that splits apart without regret."[2] These are expressions of the "fundamental language"[3] of the body that Kristeva, Cixous, and Irigaray have, in their various ways, perceived the eruption of *the feminine* Imaginary in the Symbolic, and are the alternative signifying practices across which *the feminine* moves and in which it is constituted.

The feminine literary subjectivity has been defined as the psychic space and place of the reading subject during an act of reading, and is described as analogous to Transference in psychoanalysis. So, in this sense, these readings in *the feminine* describe also a theory of reading that, it is claimed, is available equally to all levels and experiences of literary engagement, including those of the historical child reader. The features that mark it as an especially *feminine* experience in relation to the paradigm texts reside in the way that their particularities of discursive and manifest contents predispose reading subjects to readings through which to connect with *the feminine* Imaginary, recoverable through a process of *interpretation* in the dynamic literary exchange, and it is in these respects that these texts call for *une lecture féminine*[4] irrespectively of the gender of the reading subject. In this definition and in concurrence with Cixous's position, *the feminine* is not a biological condition but an Imaginary signifier that is equally available to men and to women (and to boys and girls) during reading. This conception of *the feminine* is not a negation of Irigaray's insistence on sexual difference but is, rather, a confirmation of it. However, as Cixous also suggests, the women's bodily functions and experiences, and her experience of exclusion from paternal signification predisposes her more readily to *the feminine* position. As it is for Cixous in her *l'écriture féminine*, and Irigaray in her *le parler femme*, so it is with *une lecture féminine* as a mirror reflection and inevitability of all that they imply. Cixous identified the significance and importance of the reading, and writing, subject to *l'écriture féminine*, and has called for a correspondingly feminine reading, when she says: "I gather words to make a great straw-yellow fire, but if you don't put in your own flame, my fire won't take, my words won't burst into pale yellow sparks. My words will remain dead words."[5] In this definition, the theory would go so far as to propose that, without the inspiration of readings in *the feminine*, the words on the page will remain masculine words.

Through *une lecture féminine* the reading subject locates the repressed history of her sexuality and experiences by attending to the gaps—repressed and marginalised in the text. From readings like these, unintended, marginalised, silenced, or distorted, meanings surface,[6] and in this space she experiences "what she is not, what she is, what she can be."[7] As with *l'écriture féminine*, so, too, *une lecture féminine* involves adopting a corresponding predisposition to openness and risk, and an opening-up of self to *other* (which is the text) in what Cixous has described as an "economy of love" comparable to the love that can take place between two human beings. "To understand the *other*, it is necessary to go in their language, to make the journey through the other's imaginary."[8]

In Transferential relations between the literary text constituted as other (as distinct from Other) through *une lecture féminine*, and through the reading subject's connecting with *the feminine* Imaginary through *l'écriture féminine*, different ways of knowing circulate, and new modes of relations:[9] non-hierarchical, plural, and open. In her recovery of *the feminine* Imaginary the reading subject, in Cixous's description, recognizes, studies, respects, doesn't take, doesn't claw "but attentively, with gentle relentlessness, contemplates and reads, caresses, bathes, makes the other gleam. Brings back to light the life that's been buried, fugitive, made too prudent. Illuminates it and sings it its name"[10] This is the site in which literary subjectivity is inscribed in *the feminine*.

This book has journeyed from Lacan's work on subject formation, without which the deconstructive work of Kristeva, Irigaray, and Cixous would not have been possible, through the work of these three critics, to an alternative critical discourse for liberating new readings of children's literature texts. Readings in *the feminine* have been proposed as an alternative mode of literary engagement. A literary subjectivity inscribed in *the feminine* is, in the words of Cixous, who shall have the last word: "the other country without boundaries . . . where the repressed survive."[11] Literary subjectivity that is the product of reading in the *the feminine* in all these senses is, then, "The Newly Born Woman": *La Jeune Née*.[12]

NOTES TO CONCLUSION

1.   David Almond, *Skellig* (London: Hodder Children's Books, 1998); Natalie Babbitt, *Tuck Everlasting*, 3rd edition (New York: Farrar, Straus and Giroux, 2000);

Tim Bowler, *River Boy*, (Oxford: Oxford University Press, 1997); Berlie Doherty, *Dear Nobody* (New York: Orchard, 1991); Katherine Paterson, *Bridge to Terabithia* (London: Victor Gollancz, 1978).

2. Cixous and Clément, *Newly Born*, 93.
3. Cixous, "Coming to Writing," 52–3.
4. The term *une lecture féminine* is used by Sissel Lie, "Pour une Lecture Féminine," *The Body and the Text: Hélène Cixous, Reading and Teaching*, ed. Helen Wilcox, et al., 196–203.
5. Cixous, "The Last Painting," 107.
6. Cixous and Clément, *Newly Born*, 147–60.
7. Ibid., 86.
8. Cixous, "Conversations," 146.
9. Cixous and Clément, *Newly Born*, 96.
10. Cixous, "Coming to Writing," 51.
11. Cixous and Clément, *Newly Born*, 98.
12. Ibid. *The Newly Born Woman* is translated from the original French title *La Jeune Née*.

Bibliography

Abraham, Nicolas and Maria Torok. "Introjection—Incorporation: *Mourning* or *Melancholia*." In *Psychoanalysis in France*, edited by S. Lebovici and D. Widlocker. New York: International University Press, 1980.

———. *The Wolf Man's Magic Word: A Cryptonymy*. Translated by Nicholas Rand. Minneapolis: University of Minnesota Press, 1986.

Ahlberg, Allan and Janet Ahlberg. *The Jolly Postman or Other People's Letters*. London: Heinemann, 1986.

Almond, David. *Skellig*. London: Hodder Children's Books, 1998.

Arnold, Matthew. "Philomela." In *Poetry and Criticism of Matthew Arnold*, ed. A. Dwight Culler. Boston: Houghton Mifflin, 1961.

Babbitt, Natalie. *Tuck Everlasting*. 3rd ed. New York: Farrar, Straus and Giroux, 2000.

Bachelard, Gaston. *L'Air et les songes*. Paris: Jose Corti, 1943.

Badcock, Christopher. *Essential Freud*. Oxford: Basil Blackwell, 1992.

Bakhtin, Mikhail. *Speech Genres and Other Late Essays*, translated by Vern W. McGee. Austin: University of Texas Press, 1986.

———. *Rabelais and His World*. Translated by Hélène Iswolky. Bloomington: Indiana University Press, 1984.

Bamman, Lorraine and Margaret Marshment, eds. *The Female Gaze*: *Women as Viewers of Popular Culture*. London: The Women's Press, 1988.

Barthes, Roland. *Mythologies*. New York: Hill and Wang, 1972.

———. "The Death of the Author." In *Image Music Text*. Translated by Stephen Heath. London: Fontana, 1977. 142–8.

———. *A Lover's Discourse*: *Fragments*. Translated by Richard Howard. Harmondsworth: Penguin Books, 1979.

———. *S/Z*. Translated by Richard Miller. London: Jonathan Cape, 1976.

————. *The Pleasure of the Text*. Translated by Richard Miller. London: Jonathan Cape, 1976.

Baudrillard, Jean. "The Evil Demon of Images and the Precession of Simulacra." In *Postmodernism: A Reader*, edited by Thomas Docherty. London: Harvester Wheatsheaf, 1993. 194–99.

————. "Simulacra and Simulations." In *Jean Baudrillard Selected Writings*, edited by Mark Poster. Stanford, California: Stanford University Press, 1988. 166–84.

————. "The Ecstasy of Communication." In *Postmodern Culture*, edited by Hal Foster. Translated by John Johnstone. London: Pluto Press, 1985. 126–133.

————. *Simulations*. Translated by Paul Patton, Paul Foss, and Philip Beitchman. New York: Semiotext(e), 1983.

Benveniste, Émile. "Subjectivity in Language." In *Problems in General Linguistics*. Translated by Elizabeth Meek. Miami: University of Miami Press, 1981. 223–30.

————. *Problems in General Linguistics*. Translated by Elizabeth Meek. Miami: University of Miami Press, 1981.

Berger, John. *Ways of Seeing*. London and Harmondsworth: The British Broadcasting Corporation, Penguin, 1972.

Bersani, Leo. *A Future for Asyntax, Character and Desire in Literature*. Boston and Toronto: Little, Brown and Co., 1976.

Bessière, Irène. *Le récit fantastique: la poétique de l'incertain*. Paris: Minuit, 1974.

Bonaparte, Marie. *The Life and Works of Edgar Allan Poe: A Psycho-Analytic Interpretation*. Translated by John Rodker. London: Imago, 1949.

Boothby, Richard. *Death and Desire: Psychoanalytic Theory in Lacan's Return to Freud*. London: Routledge, 1991.

Bowler, Tim. *River Boy*. Oxford: Oxford University Press, 1997.

Brooke-Rose, Christine. "The Dissolution of Character in the Novel." In *Reconstructing Individualism: Autonomy, Individuality and the Self*, edited by Thomas C. Heller, et al. Stanford and California: Stanford University Press, 1986. 185–221.

————. *A Rhetoric of the Unreal: Studies in Narrative and Structure Especially of the Fantastic*. Cambridge: Cambridge University Press, 1981.

Brooks, Peter. "Freud's Master Plot: Questions of Narrative." *Yale French Studies* 55–6 (1977): 280–300.

————. "The Idea of Psychoanalytic Criticism." *Critical Inquiry* 13 (Winter 1987): 334–48.

————. *Reading For the Plot*. New York: Knopf, 1984.

Burgin, Victor. *The End of Art Theory: Aestheticism and Postmodernism*. London: Macmillan, 1986.

Burke, Peter. *Popular Culture in Early Modern Europe*. London: Temple Smith, 1979.

Burke, Carolyn. "Irigaray Through the Looking Glass." *Feminist Studies* 7, no. 2 (1981): 288–306.

Butler, Judith. "The Body Politics of Julia Kristeva." *Hypatia* 3 (Winter 1989): 104–18.

Cameron, Deborah, ed. *The Feminist Critique of Language: A Reader*. London: Routledge, 1990.

Carroll, David. *The Subject in Question: The Languages of Theory and the Strategies of Fiction*. Chicago and London: University of Chicago Press, 1982.

Carter, Angela. "The Company of Wolves." In *The Bloody Chamber*. London: Vintage, 1995.

Chase, Cynthia. " 'Transference' as trope and persuasion." In *Discourse in Psychoanalysis and Literature*, edited by Shlomith Rimmon-Kenan. London: Methuen, 1987. 211–29.

———. "Desire and Identification in Lacan and Kristeva." In *Feminism and Psychoanalysis*, edited by Richard Feldstein and Judith Roof. Ithaca: Cornell University Press, 1989. 63–83.

Chodorow, Nancy. *The Reproduction of Motherhood: Psychoanalysis and the Sociology of Gender*. Berkeley: University of California Press, 1978.

Cixous, Hélène. "The Character of 'Character.' " Translated by Keith Cohen. *New Literary History* 5, no. 2 (Winter 1974): 383–402.

———. *Souffles*. Paris: des femmes, 1975.

———. "Fiction and its Phantoms: A reading of Freud's Das Unheimliche (the 'Uncanny')." *New Literary History* 7, no. 3 (Spring 1976): 525–48.

———. "The Laugh of the Medusa." Translated by Keith Cohen and Paula Cohen. *Signs: Journal of Women in Culture and Society* 1, no. 4 (1976): 875–93. Reproduced in *New French Feminisms*, edited by Elaine Marks and Isabelle de Courtivron. Brighton: Harvester, 1981. 56–67.

———. "Castration or Decapitation?" Translated by Annette Kuhn. *Signs: Journals of Women in Culture* 7, no. 1 (Autumn 1981): 41–55.

———. "Conversations," interview by Susan Sellers. In *Writing Differences: Readings from the Seminar of Hélène Cixous*, edited by Susan Sellers. Milton Keynes: Open University Press; New York: St. Martin's Press, 1988.

———. *"Coming to Writing" and Other Essays*. Translated by Sarah Cornell, et al. Cambridge, Mass.: Harvard University Press, 1991.

Cixous, Hélène and Catherine Clément. "Sorties." In *The Newly Born Woman*. Translated by Betsy Wing. Minneapolis: University of Minnesota Press, 1986. 63–132.

Copjec, Joan, ed. *Supposing the Subject*. London: Verso, 1994.

Coward, Rosalind. *Patriarchal Precedents*. London: Routledge and Kegan Paul, 1983.

Cross, Gillian. *Wolf*. London: Penguin Books, 1990.

Cross, Gillian. *Pictures in the Dark*. Oxford: Oxford University Press, 1996.

Culler, A. Dwight, ed. *Poetry and Criticism of Matthew Arnold*. Boston: Houghton Miflin, 1961.

Culler, Jonathan. "Semiotics as a Theory of Reading." In *The Pursuit of Signs: Semiotics, Literature, Deconstruction*. London: Routledge and Kegan Paul, 1981. 47–79.

———. "Textual Self Consciousness and the Textual Unconscious." *Style* 18, no. 3 (Summer 1984): 369–76.

Davis, Robert Con, ed. *The Fictional Father*. Amherst: The University of Massachusetts Press, 1981.

Deleuze, Gilles and Félix Guattari. *Anti-Oedipus: Capitalism and Schizophrenia*. Translated by Robert Hurley, et al. Minneapolis: University of Minnesota Press, 1983.

Derrida, Jacques. *Of Grammatology*. Translated by Gayatri Chakravorty Spivak. Baltimore and London: Johns Hopkins University Press, 1976.

———. "Cogito and the History of Madness." In *Writing and Difference*. Chicago: Chicago University Press, 1978. 31–63.

———. *Writing and Difference*. Chicago: Chicago University Press, 1978.

———. *Spurs: Nietzsche's Styles*. Translated by B. Harlow. Chicago: University of Chicago Press, 1979.

Doane, Janice and Devon Hodges. *From Klein to Kristeva: Psychoanalytic Feminism and the Search for the 'Good Enough' Mother*. Ann Arbor. University of Michigan Press, 1992.

Docherty, Thomas, ed. *Postmodernism: A Reader*. London: Harvester Wheatsheaf, 1993.

Doherty, Berlie. *Dear Nobody*. New York: Orchard, 1991.

Eagleton, Terry. "Enjoy." *London Review of Books* 19, no. 23 (1997): 7–9.

Feldstein, Richard and Judith Roof, eds. *Feminism and Psychoanalysis*. Ithaca: Cornell University Press, 1989.

Felman, Shoshana. "Women and Madness: The Critical Phallacy." *Diacritics* 5, no. 4 (Winter 1975): 2–10.

———. *Writing and Madness*. Translated by Martha Noel Evans and Shoshana Felman. Ithaca: Cornell University Press, 1978.

———. "Turning the Screw of Interpretation." In *Literature and Psychoanalysis: The Question of Reading Otherwise*, edited by Shoshana Felman. Baltimore: The Johns Hopkins University Press, 1982. 94–207.

———, ed. *Literature and Psychoanalysis: The Question of Reading Otherwise*. Baltimore and London: Johns Hopkins Univesity Press, 1982.

Flax, Jane. "Signifying the Father's Desire: Lacan in the Feminist Gaze." In *Criticism and Lacan: Essays and Dialogue on Language, Structure and the Unconscious*, edited by Patrick Colm Hogan and Lalita Pandit. Athens and London: The University of Georgia Press, 1990. 109–19.

———. *Thinking Fragments: Psychoanalysis, Feminism, and Postmodernism in the Contemporary West*. Berkeley and Los Angeles: University of California Press, 1990.

Fletcher, John and Andrew Benjamin, eds. *Abjection, Melancholia and Love: The Work of Julia Kristeva*. London and New York: Routledge, 1990.

Forrester, John. *The Seductions of Psychoanalysis: Freud, Lacan and Derrida*. Cambridge: Cambridge University Press, 1990.

Foster, Hal, ed. *Postmodern Culture*. London: Pluto Press, 1985.

Foster, Shirley and Simons Judy. *What Katy Read: Feminist Re-Readings of "Classic" Stories for Girls*. London: Macmillan, 1995.

Foucault, Michel. *The Order of Things: An Archaeology of Human Sciences*. New York: Pantheon, 1970.

———. *Madness and Civilisation: A History of Insanity in the Age of Reason*. Translated by Richard Howard. London: Tavistock, 1989.

Freud, Sigmund. *The Interpretation of Dreams* (1900), edited and translated by James Strachey. Vols. 4–5 of *The Standard Edition of the Complete Psychological Works of Sigmund Freud*. 24 vols. London: Hogarth Press, 1953–74. 633–87.

———. "On Dreams" (1901), edited and translated by James Strachey. In Vol. 5 of *The Standard Edition of the Complete Psychological Works of Sigmund Freud*. 24 vols. London: Hogarth Press 1953–74. 633–87.

———. "Three Essays on the Theory of Sexuality" (1905), edited and translated by James Strachey. Vol. 7 of *The Standard Edition of the Complete Psychological Works of Sigmund Freud*. 24 vols. London: Hogarth Press, 1953–74. 253–43.

———. "Family Romances" (1908), edited and translated by James Strachey. Vol.9 of *The Standard Edition of The Standard Edition of the Complete Psychological Works of Sigmund Freud*. 24 vols. London: Hogarth Press 1953–74. 237–41.

———. "An Evidential Dream" (1911–13), edited and translated by James Strachey. Vol. 12. of *The Standard Edition of the Complete Psychological Works of Sigmund Freud*. 24 vols. London: Hogarth Press 1953–74. 267–77.

———. "The Occurrence in Dreams of Material from Fairy Tales" (1913), edited and translated by James Strachey. Vol. 12 of *The Standard Edition of the Complete Psychological Works of Sigmund Freud*. 24 vols. London: Hogarth Press 1953–74. 281–7.

———. "Totem and Taboo" (1912–13), edited and translated by James Strachey. Vol. 13 of *The Standard Edition of the Complete Psychological Works of Sigmund Freud*. 24 vols. London: Hogarth Press 1953–74. 1–162.

———. "Mourning and Melancholia" (1917), edited and translated by James Strachey. Vol. 14 of *The Standard Edition of the Complete Psychological Works of Sigmund Freud*. 24 vols. London: Hogarth Press 1953–74. 243–58.

———. "The 'Uncanny,' " and "From the History of An Infantile Neurosis and Other Works" (1918), edited and translated by James Strachey. Vol. 17 of *The Standard Edition of the Complete Psychological Works of Sigmund Freud*. 24 vols. London: Hogarth Press 1953–74. 219–52.

———. "The Wolf-Man." "From the History of an Infantile Neurosis and Other Works" (1918), edited and translated by James Strachey. Vol. 17 of *The Standard Edition of the Complete Psychological Works of Sigmund Freud*. 24 vols. London: Hogarth Press 1953–74. 7–122.

———. "Beyond the Pleasure Principle" (1920), edited and translated by James Strachey. Vol. 18 of *The Standard Edition of the Complete Psychological Works of Sigmund Freud*. 24 vols. London: Hogarth Press 1953–74. 7–64.

———. "Female Sexuality" (1931), edited and translated by James Strachey. Vol. 21 of *The Standard Edition of the Complete Psychological Works of Sigmund Freud*. 24 vols. London: Hogarth Press 1953–74. 225–43.

———. "The Medusa's Head" (1940), edited and translated by James Strachey. Vol. 23 of *The Standard Edition of the Complete Psychological Works of Sigmund Freud*. 24 vols. London: Hogarth Press 1953–74. 7–137.

Fuery, Patrick. *The Theory of Absence: Subjectivity, Signification and Desire*. Westport, Conn. and London: Greenwood Press, 1995.

Fuss, Diana. *Essentially Speaking: Feminism, Nature and Difference*. London: Routledge, 1990.

Gallop, Jane. "*Quand Nos Lèvres S'écrivant*: Irigaray's Body Politic." *Romantic Review* 74, no. 1 (1983): 77–83.

———. *Reading Lacan*. Ithaca: Cornell University Press, 1985.

Gardiner, Muriel. *The Wolf-Man and Sigmund Freud*. Harmondsworth: Penguin, 1973.

Garner, Shirley Nelson, et al., eds. *The (M)other Tongue: Essays in Feminist Psychoanalytic Interpretation*. Ithaca and London: Cornell University Press 1985.

Genette, Gérard. *Narrative Discourse*. Translated by Jane E. Lewin. Oxford: Blackwell, 1980.

Gilbert, Sandra and Susan Gubar. *The Madwoman in the Attic: The Woman Writer and the Nineteenth-Century Literary Imagination*. New Haven: Yale University Press, 1979.

Ginsburg, Ruth. "The Pregnant Text. Bakhtin's Ur-Chronotope: The Womb." In *Critical Studies, Bakhtin: Carnival and Other Subjects. Selected Papers from the Fifth International Bakhtin Conference*, edited by David Shepherd. The University of Manchester 3, nos. 2–4. Amsterdam and Atlanta, GA: Rodopi, 1993.

Graves, Robert. *The White Goddess: A Historical Grammar of Poetic Myth.* (First published 1948) London: Faber, 1997.

Greene, Gayle and Coppélia Kahn, eds. *Making a Difference: Feminist Literary Criticism.* London: Routledge, 1985.

Gross, Elizabeth. "The Body of Signification." In *Abjection, Melancholia, and Love: The Work of Julia Kristeva*, edited by John Fletcher and Andrew Benjamin. London and New York: Routledge, 1990. 80–103.

———. "Love Letters in the Sand: Reflections on *Feminine Sexuality: Jacques Lacan and the École Freudienne*, Juliet Mitchell and Jacqueline Rose." *Critical Philosophy* 1, no. 2 (1984): 69–87.

Grosz Elizabeth, *New Literary History* 7, no 3 (Spring 1976): 526–48.

Grosz, Elizabeth. *Sexual Subversions: Three French Feminists.* St. Leonards, NSW: Allen and Unwin, 1989.

———. *Jacques Lacan: A Feminist Introduction.* London: Routledge, 1990.

Guerber, H. A. *The Myths of Greece and Rome: Their Stories, Signification, and Origin.* London: George G. Harrap, 1907.

Gustafson, Susan E. *Absent Mothers and Orphaned Fathers.* Detroit: Wayne State University Press, 1995.

Hanzo, Thomas A. "Paternity and the Subject in *Bleak House.*" *The Fictional Father.* Edited by Robert Con Davis. Amherst: The University of Massachusetts Press, 1981.

Harvey, David. *The Condition of Postmodernity: An Enquiry into the Origins of Cultural Change.* Oxford: Basil Blackwell, 1990.

Heller, Thomas C., et al., eds. R*econstructing Individualism: Autonomy, Individuality and the Self in Western Thought.* Stanford and California: Stanford University Press, 1986.

Hirsch, Marianne. *The Mother/Daughter Plot: Narrative, Psychoanalysis, Feminism.* Bloomington and Indianapolis: Indiana University Press, 1989.

Hogan, Patrick Colm and Lalita Pandit, eds. *Criticism and Lacan: Essays and Dialogue on Language, Structure and the Unconscious.* Athens and London: The University of Georgia Press, 1990.

Holland, Norman. "I-ing Lacan." In *Criticism and Lacan: Essays and Dialogue on Language, Structure and the Unconscious*, edited Patrick Colm Hogan, and Lalita Pandit. Athens and London: University of Georgia Press, 1990. 87–108.

Hollandale, Peter. *Signs of Childness in Children's Books.* Stroud: The Thimble Press, 1997.

Homans, Margaret. " 'Her Very Own Howl': The Ambiguities of Representation in Recent Women's Fiction." *Signs* 9, no. 2 (1986): 163–8.

———. *Bearing the Word: Language and Experience in Nineteenth-Century Women's Writing.* Chicago: University of Chicago Press, 1986.

Hunt, Peter, ed. *The Routledge International Companion Encyclopaedia of Children's Literature.* London: Routledge, 1996.

Hutcheon, Linda. *A Poetics of Postmodernism, History Theory, Fiction.* London: Routledge, 1989.

Ian, Marcia. *Remembering the Phallic Mother: Psychoanalysis, Modernism and the Fetish.* Ithaca: Cornell University Press, 1993.

Irigaray, Luce. "La Misére de la psychanalyse." *Critique* 33, no. 363 (1977): 879–903.

———. "Woman's Exile: Interview with Luce Irigaray." Translated by Couze Venn. *Ideology and Consciousness* 1 (1977): 62–76. Reprinted in *The Feminist Critique of Langauge: A Reader*, edited by Deborah Cameron. London: Routledge, 1990. 80–96.

———. "Etablir un généalogie de femmes." *Maintenant* 12 (1979): 119–21.

———. "And the One Doesn't Stir without the Other." Translated by Hélène Vivienne Wenzel. *Signs: Journal of Women in Culture* 7, no.1 (Autumn 1981): 60–7.

———. *Le Corps-à-corps avec la mère*. Montreal: Les Éditions de la Pleine Lune, 1981.

———. *L'Oubli de l'air: Chez Martin Heidegger*. Paris: Les Éditions de Minuit, 1983.

———. "Veiled Lips." *Mississippi Review* 11, no. 3 (1983): 93–131.

———. *L'Éthique de la différence Sexuelle*. Paris: Les Éditions de Minuit, 1984.

———. "The 'Mechanics' of Fluids." In *This Sex Which is Not One*. Translated by Catherine Porter, with Carolyn Burke. Ithaca: Cornell University Press, 1985. 106–18.

———. "The Looking Glass from the Other Side." In *This Sex Which Is Not One*. Translated by Catherine Porter, with Carolyn Burke. Ithaca: Cornell University Press, 1985. 9–22.

———. "Any Theory of the 'Subject' Has Always Been Appropriated by the 'Masculine.' " In *Speculum of the Other Woman*. Translated by Gillian C. Gill. Ithaca: New York: Cornell University Press, 1985. 133–46.

———. "This Sex Which Is Not One." In *This Sex Which Is Not One*. Translated by Catherine Porter, with Carolyn Burke. Ithaca: Cornell University Press. 1985. 23–33.

———. "When Our Lips Speak Together." In *This Sex Which Is Not One*. Translated by Catherine Porter, with Carolyn Burke. Ithaca: Cornell University Press, 1985. 205–18.

———. *Parler n'est jamais neuter*. Paris: Les Éditions de Minuit, 1985.

———. *This Sex Which is Not One*. Translated by Catherine Porter, with Carolyn Burke. Ithaca: Cornell University Press, 1985.

———. "Women on the Market." In *This Sex Which is Not One*. Translated by Catherine Porter, with Carolyn Burke. Ithaca: Cornell University 1985. 170–91.

———. *Speculum of the Other Woman*. Translated by. Gillian C. Gill. Ithaca: Cornell University Press, 1985.

———. *Divine Women*. Translated by Steven Muecke. Sydney Local Consumption Occasional Papers, no. 8 (1986).

———. "The Bodily Encounter With the Mother." In *The Irigaray Reader*. Edited by Margaret Whitford. Translated by David Macey. Oxford: Basil Blackwell, 1991. 34–46.

———. *Amante Marine: de Freidrich Nietzsche*. Paris: Les Éditions de Minuit, 1980. *Marine Lover of Friedrich Nietzsche*. Translated by Gillian C. Gill. New York: Columbia University Press, 1991.

———. *Passions Élémentaires*. Paris: Les Édition de Minuit, 1982. *Elemental Passions*. Translated by Joanne Collie and Judith Still. London: The Athlone Press, 1992.

Isaacs, Susan. "The Nature and Function of Phantasy." *International Journal of Psycho-Analysis* 29 (1948). Quoted in Jean Laplanche and Jean-Baptiste Pontalis, "Fantasy and the Origins of Sexuality." *The International Journal of Psycho-Analysis* 49, no. 1 (1968): 1–18.

Iser, Wolfgang. *The Act of Reading: A Theory of Aesthetic Response*. Baltimore: Johns Hopkins University Press, 1978.

Jackson, Rosemary. *Fantasy: The Literature of Subversion*. London: Methuen, 1981.

Jakobson, Roman. "The Dominant." In *Readings in Russian Poetics: Formalist and Struc-turalist Views*, edited by Ladislav Matejka and Krystyna Pomorska. Cambridge, Mass-achusetts: MIT Press, 1971. 105–10.

Jacobus, Mary. "*Dora*, and the Pregnant Madonna." In *Reading Woman: Essays in Feminist Criticism*. London: Methuen, 1986. 137–93.

Jacobus, Mary. "Judith, Holofernes, and the Phallic Woman." In *Reading Women: Essays in Feminist Criticism*. London: Methuen, 1986. 110-36.

Jameson, Fredric. "Imaginary and Symbolic in Lacan: Marxism, Psychoanalytic Criticism, and the Problem of the Subject." *Yale French Studies* 48 (1972): 338–361.

———. *The Political Unconscious: Narrative as a Socially Symbolic Act*. Ithaca: Cornell University Press, 1981.

———. "Periodizing the Sixties." In *The Sixties Without Apology*. Edited by S. Saynes, et al. Minneapolis: The University of Minnesota Press, 1984. 178–218.

———. "Postmodernism and Consumer Society." In *Postmodern Culture*, edited by Hal Foster. London: Pluto Press, 1985. 111–25.

———. *Postmodernism or The Cultural Logic of Late Capitalism*. London: Verso, 1992.

Jardine, Alice A. *Gynesis: Configurations of Woman and Modernity*. Ithaca and London: Cornell University Press, 1985.

Johnson, Barbara. *The Critical Difference: Essays in the Contemporary Rhetoric of Read-ing*. Baltimore: The Johns Hopkins University Press, 1980.

Johnson, Barbara. "The Frame of Reference: Poe, Lacan, Derrida." *Yale French Studies* 55–6 (1977): 457–505.

Jones, Ann Rosalind. "Inscribing femininity: French theories of the feminine." In *Making A Difference: Feminist Literary Criticism*, edited by Gayle Greene and Coppélia Kahn. London: Routledge, 1985. 80–112.

Jones, Ernest. *On the Nightmare*. London: Hogarth Press, 1931.

Jones, Richard, M. *The New Psychology of Dreaming*. Harmondsworth: Penguin Books, 1970.

Kaplan Ann, E. "Is the Gaze Male?" In *Desire: the Politics of Sexuality*, edited by Ann Sni-tow, et al. London: Virago, 1984. 321–338.

Kaplan, Ann, E. *Motherhood and Representation: The Mother Popular Culture and Melo-drama*. London: Routledge, 1992.

Kellner, Douglas. "Constructing Postmodern Identities." In *Modernity and Identity*, edited by Scott Lash and Jonathan Friedman. Oxford: Blackwell, 1992. 141–77

Krell, David Farrell. *Of Memory, Reminiscence, and Writing: On the Verge*. Bloomington and Indianopolis: Indiana University Press, 1990.

Kristeva, Julia. "Un nouveau type d'intellectuel: le dissident." *Tel Quel* 74 (Winter 1977): 158–64.

———. *Polylogue* Paris: Éditions du Seuil, 1981.

———. "The Novel as Polylogue." In *Desire in Language: A Semiotic Approach to Art and Literature*, edited by Leon S. Roudiez. Translated by Thomas Bora, et al. Oxford: Basil Blackwell, 1982. 159–209.

———. "From One Identity to An Other." *Desire in Language: A Semiotic Approach to Art and Literature*. Edited by Leon S. Roudiez. Translated by Thomas Gora et al. Oxford: Basil Blackwell, 1982. 124–47.

———. "Giotto's Joy." In *Desire in Language: A Semiotic Approach to Art and Literature*, edited by Leon S. Roudiez. Translated by Thomas Gora et al. Oxford: Basil Blackwell, 1982. 210–36.

———. "Motherhood According to Giovanni Bellini." In *Desire in Language: A Semiotic Approach to Art and Literature*, edited by Leon S. Roudiez. Translated by Thomas Gora, et al. Oxford: Basil Blackwell, 1982. 160–86.

———. *Desire in Language: A Semiotic Approach to Art and Literature*, edited by Leon S. Roudiez. Translated by Thomas Gora, et al. Oxford: Basil Blackwell, 1982.

———. *The Powers of Horror: An Essay in Abjection*. Translated by Leon S. Roudiez. New York: Columbia University Press, 1982.

———. *Revolution in Poetic Language*. Translated by Margaret Waller. New York: Columbia University Press, 1984. First published as *La Revolution du langage poétique*. Paris: Éditions du Seuil, 1974.

———. "About Chinese Women." In *The Kristeva Reader*, edtited by Toril Moi. Oxford: Basil Blackwell, 1986. 138–159.

———. "The System and the Speaking Subject." *The Kristeva Reader*. Edited by Toril Moi. Oxford: Basil Blackwell, 1986. 89–136.

———. "Revolution in Poetic Language." In *The Kristeva Reader*, edited by Toril Moi. Oxford: Basil Blackwell, 1986. 43–50.

———. "Stabat Mater." In *The Kristeva Reader*, edited by Toril Moi. Oxford Basil Blackwell, 1986. 160–86.

———. "The True-Real." In *The Kristeva Reader*, edited by Toril Moi. Oxford: Basil Blackwell, 1986. 197–213.

———. "Women's Time." In *The Kristeva Reader*, edited by Toril Moi. Oxford: Basil Blackwell, 1986. 187–213.

———. *Tales of Love*. Translated by Leon R Roudiez. New York: Columbia University Press, 1987.

———. *Black Sun*. Translated by Leon S. Roudiez. New York: Columbia University Press, 1989.

———. "The Adolescent Novel." In *Abjection, Melancholia and* Love, edited by John Fletcher and Andrew Benjamin. London and New York: Routledge, 1990. 8–23.

Kroker, Arthur and David Cook. *The Postmodern Scene: Excremental Culture and Hyper-Aesthetics*. Basingstoke: Macmillan, 1988.

Lacan, Jacques. "Cure psychanalytique à l'aide de la poupée fleur." Comptes rendus, réunion 18 Octobre. *Revue francaise de la psychanalyse* 4 (1949): 567.

———. *The Language of the Self: The Function of Language in Psychoanalysis*. Translated by Anthony Wilden. Baltimore: Johns Hopkins University Press, 1968.

———. "Seminar on "The Purloined Letter.' " *Yale French Studies*, 48 (1972): 38–72.

———. "Desire and the Interpretation of Desire in Hamlet." *Yale French Studies* 55–6 (1977): 11–52.

———. *Écrits: A Selection*. Translated by Alan Sheridan. London: Routledge, 1977.

———. *The Four Fundamental Concepts of Psycho-Analysis*, edited by Jacques-Alain Miller. Translated by Alan Sheridan. Harmondsworth: Penguin Books, 1979.

———. "God and Jouissance of ~~The~~ Woman." In *Feminine Sexuality: Jacques Lacan and the École Freudienne*, edited by Juliet Mitchell, and Jacqueline Rose. London: Macmillan, 1982. 137–48.

Lacan, Jacques. "Seminar of 21st January, 1975." In *Feminine Sexuality: Jacques Lacan and the École Freudienne*, edited by Juliet Mitchell and Jacqueline Rose. London: Macmillan, 1982. 162–71.

Laplanche, Jean. *New Foundations for Psychoanalysis*. Translated by David Macey. Oxford: Blackwell, 1989.

Laplanche, Jean and Serge Leclaire. "The Unconscious: A Psychoanalytic Study." *Yale French Studies* 48 (1972): 118–78.

Laplanche, Jean and Jean-Baptiste Pontalis. *The Language of Psychoanalysis*. Translated by Donald Nicholson-Smith. London: Karnac Books, 1988.

———. "Fantasy and the Origins of Sexuality." *The International Journal of Psycho-Analysis* 49, no. 1 (1968): 1–18.

Lash, Scott and Jonathan Friedman, eds. *Modernity and Identity*. Oxford: Basil Blackwell, 1992.

Lebovici, S. and D. Widlocker, eds. *Psychoanalysis in France*. New York: International University Press, 1980.

Lechte, John. "Art, Love and Melancholy in the Work of Julia Kristeva." In *Abjection, Melancholia and Love: The Work of Julia Kristeva*. Edited by John Fletcher and Andrew Benjamin. London and New York: Routledge, 1990. 24–41.

Lechte, John. *Julia Kristeva*. London: Routledge, 1990.

Lechte, John, ed. *Writing and Psychoanalysis: A Reader*. London: Edward Arnold, 1996.

Lemaire, Anika. *Jacques Lacan*. Translated by David Macey. London: Routledge, 1970.

Lesnik-Oberstein, K. "Defining Children's Literature and Childhood." In *The Routledge International Encyclopaedia of Children's Literature*, edited by Peter Hunt. London: Routledge, 1996. 17–31.

Lesnik-Oberstein, *Children's Literature: Criticism and the Fictional Child*. Oxford: Clarendon Press, 1994.

Lie, Sissel. "Pour une Lecture Féminine." In *The Body and the Text: Hélène Cixous, Reading and Teaching*, edited by Helen Wilcox, et al. Hertfordshire: Harvester Wheatsheaf, 1990. 196–203.

Lyotard, Jean-Francois. *The Postmodern Condition*. Manchester: Manchester University Press, 1985.

Lyotard, Jean-Francois. "The Dream-Work Does Not Think." *Oxford Literary Review* 6 (1983): 3–34.

MacCannell, Juliet Flower. *Figuring Lacan: Criticism and the Cultural Unconscious*. Lincoln: University of Nebraska Press, 1986.

———. "Things To Come: A Hysteric's Guide to the Future Female Subject." In *Supposing the Subject*, edited by Joan Copjec. London: Verso, 1994. 106–32.

Mahy, Margaret. *Memory*. London: Penguin Books, 1987.

———. *The Changeover*. London: Magnet Books, 1985.

———. *The Other Side of Silence*. London: Hamish Hamilton, 1995.

———. *The Tricksters*. London: Penguin Books, 1986.

———. *Dangerous Spaces*. London: Penguin Books, 1991.

Marcus, Steven. "Freud and Dora: Story, History, Case History." In *In Dora's Case: Freud—Hysteria—Feminism*, edited by Charles Bernheimer and Claire Kahane. New York, Columbia University Press, 1989. 56–91.

Marks, Elaine, and Isabelle de Courtivron, eds. *New French Feminisms*. Brighton: Harvester, 1981.

McCabe, Colin, ed. *The Talking Cure*. London: Macmillan, 1981.

McHale, Brian. *Postmodernist Fiction*. London: Routledge, 1987.

Mellard, James M. *Using Lacan, Reading Fiction*. Urbana and Chicago: University of Illinois Press, 1991.

Mitchell, Juliet, and Jacqueline Rose, eds. *Feminine Sexuality: Jacques Lacan and the École Freudienne*. London: Macmillan, 1982.

Moi, Toril. *Sexual Textual Politics*. London and New York: Methuen, 1985.

———. "Language, Femininity, Revolution." In *Psychoanalytic Criticism: A Reader*. Edited by Sue Vice. Cambridge: Polity Press, 1996. 158–64.

———, ed. *The Kristeva Reader*. Oxford: Basil Blackwell, 1986.

Mulvey, Laura. "Visual Pleasure and Narrative Cinema." *Screen* 16, no. 3 (Autumn 1975): 6–18.

Neu, Jerome. *The Cambridge Companion to Freud*. Cambridge: Cambridge University Press, 1991.

Nicholls, Peter, "Divergences: Modernism, Postmodernism, Jameson and Lyotard." *Critical Quarterly* 33, no. 3 (Autumn 1991): 1–18.

Nicholls, Peter. "The Belated Postmodern: History, Phantoms, and Toni Morrison." In *Psychoanalytic Criticism: A Reader*, edited by Sue Vice, Cambridge: Polity Press, 1996. 50–74.

Nietzche, Friedrich. *Ecce Homo: How One Becomes What One Is*. Translated by R. J. Hollingdale. Harmondsworth: Penguin, 1979.

Norris, Christopher. *Deconstruction Theory and Practice*. London: Routledge, 1990.

Oliver, Kelly. *Reading Kristeva: Unravelling the Double-bind*. Bloomington: Indiana University Press, 1993.

———, ed. *The Portable Kristeva*. New York: Columbia University Press, 1997.

Oneal, Zibby. *A Formal Feeling*. New York: Viking, 1982.

Ovid. *Metamorphoses*. Translated by Mary M. Innes. Harmondsworth: Penguin, 1955.

Paterson, Katherine. *Bridge to Terabithia*. London: Victor Gollancz Ltd., 1978.

Paul, Lissa. *Reading Otherways*. South Woodchester, Glos.: Thimble Press, 1995.

Poster, Mark, ed. *Jean Baudrillard Selected Writings*. Stanford, California: Stanford University Press, 1988.

Purkiss, Diane. *The Witch in History: Early Modern and Twentieth-Century Representations*. London: Routledge 1996.

Rabinow, Paul, ed. *The Foucault Reader*. Harmondsworth: Penguin, 1984.

Ragland-Sullivan, Ellie. *Jacques Lacan and the Philosophy of Psychoanalysis*. London: Croom Helm, 1986.

———. "The Magnetism between Reader and Text: Prolegomena to a Lacanian Poetics." *Poetics* 13 (1984): 381–406.

Reynolds, Kimberley. *Girls Only: Gender and Popular Fiction in Britain, 1880–1910*. Hemel Hempstead: Harvester Wheatsheaf, 1990.

Rice, Philip and Patricia Waugh, eds. *Modern Literary Theory: A Reader*. London: Edward Arnold, 1989.

Rich, Adrienne. *Of Woman Born: Motherhood as Experience and Institution*. London: Virago, 1977.

Richardson, William J. "Lacan and the Subject of Psychoanalysis." In *Interpreting Lacan*, edited by Joseph H. Smith and William Kerrigan. Volume 6 of *Psychiatry and Humanities*. New Haven and London: Yale University Press, 1983. 56–63.

Rimmon-Kenan, Shlomith, ed. *Discourse in Psychoanalysis and Literature*. London: Methuen, 1987.

Rose, Jacqueline. "Julia Kristeva: Take Two." In *Coming to Terms: Feminism, Theory and Politics*, edited by Elizabeth Weed. London: Routledge, 1989. 17–33.

Saler, J. "Semiotique de la nourriture dans la Bible." *Annales* (July-August 1973). Quoted in *Feminine Sexuality: Jacques Lacan and the École Freudienne*, Juliet Mitchell and Jacqueline Rose, eds. London: Macmillan, 1982.

Sayers, Janet. *Biological* Politics. London: Tavistock, 1982.

Saynes, S. et al., eds. *The Sixties Without Apology*. Minneapolis: The University of Minnesota Press, 1984.

Schor, Naomi. "Introducing Feminism." Vol. 8 of *Paragraph*. Oxford: Oxford University Press 1986. 93–101.

Segal, Naomi. "Patrilinear and Matrilinear." In *The Body and the Text: Hélène Cixous, Reading and Teaching*, edited by Helen Wilcox, et al. Hertfordshire: Harvester Wheatsheaf, 1990. 131–46.

Sellers, Susan. "Creating a Feminine Subject." In *Hélène Cixous, Authorship, Autobiography and Love*. Cambridge: Polity Press, 1996. 40–54.

———. *The Hélène Cixous Reader*. London: Routledge, 1994.

Shavit, Zohar, *Poetics of Children's Literature*. Athens, GA: University of Georgia Press, 1986.

Shepherd. David, ed. *Critical Studies, Bakhtin: Carnival and Other Subjects. Selected Papers from the Fifth International Bakhtin Conference*. The University of Manchester 3, nos. 2–4. Amsterdam and Atlanta, Ga.: Rodopi, 1993.

Showalter, Elaine. "Women's time women's space." *Tulsa Studies in Women's Literature* 3 (1984): 29–43.

———, ed. *The New Feminist Criticism*. London: Virago, 1986.

Silverman, Kaja. *The Subject of Semiotics*. New York: Oxford University Press, 1983.

Smith, Joseph H. and William Kerrigan, eds. *Interpreting Lacan*. Volume 6 of *Psychiatry and Humanities*. New Haven and London: Yale University Press, 1983.

Snitow, Ann, et al. *Desire: The Politics of Sexuality*. London: Virago, 1984.

Stallybrass, Peter and Allon White. *The Politics and Poetics of Transgression*. London: Methuen, 1986.

States, Bert O. *The Rhetoric of Dreams*. Ithaca and London: Cornell University Press, 1988.

Stevenson, Robert Louis. "Requiem" (1887). In *The Oxford Book of Victorian Verse*, edited by Arthur Quiller-Couch. Oxford: Oxford University Press, 1912. 741.

Storr, Catherine. *Marianne Dreams*. Cambridge: Lutterworth, 1989.

Suleiman, Rubin Susan. "Writing and Motherhood." In *The (M)other Tongue: Essays in Feminist Psychoanalytic Interpretation*, edited by Shirley Nelson Garner, et al. Ithaca and London: Cornell University Press, 1985. 352–381.

Todorov, Tzvetan. "The Fantastic in Fiction." Translated by Vivien Mylne. *Twentieth Century Studies* 3 (1970): 76–92.

———. *The Fantastic: A Structural Approach to a Literary Genre*. Translated by Richard Howard. Ithaca and New York: Cornell University Press, 1975.

———. "The Categories of Literary Narrative." Translated by K. Kester. *Papers on Language and Literature* 16, no. 1 (1980): 3–37.

———. "The Origin of Genres." *New Literary History* 8, no. 1 (Autumn 1978): 159–70.

Trites, Roberta Seelinger, *Waking Sleeping Beauty: Feminist Voices in Children's Novels.* Iowa City: University of Iowa Press, 1997.

Vallone, Lynn. *Disciplines of Virtue: Girls' Culture in the Eighteenth and Nineteenth Centuries.* New Haven: Yale University Press, 1995.

Vice, Sue, ed. *Psychoanalytic Criticism: A Reader.* Cambridge: Polity Press, 1996.

Wakefield, Neville. *Postmodernism: The Twilight of the Real.* Winchester: Pluto Press, 1990.

Walker, Nancy A. *Feminist Alternatives: Irony and Fantasy in the Contemporary Novel by Women.* Jackson and London: University of Mississippi, 1990.

Wall, Barbara, *The Narrator's Voice: The Dilemma of Children's Fiction..* London: Macmillan, 1991.

Wallace, Jennifer. "The Feminine Mystique." *The Times Higher* (18 September 1998): 19.

Waugh, Patricia. "Reassessing Subjectivity: Modernity Postmodernity and Feminism in Theory and Aesthetic Practice." *Bête Noir* 8–9 (1989): 64–77.

———. *Practising Postmodernism, Reading Modernism.* London: Edward Arnold, 1992.

———. "Stalemates? Feminists, Postmodernists and Unfinished Issues." In *Modern Literary Theory: A Reader*, edited by Philip Rice and Patricia Waugh. London: Edward Arnold, 1992. 341–60.

———. *Feminine Fictions, Revisiting the Postmodern.* London: Routledge, 1989.

Webster, John. *The White Devil.* In *Three Jacobean Tragedies.* Harmondsworth: Penguin, 1965.

Weed, Elizabeth, ed. *Coming to Terms: Feminism, Theory and Politics.* London: Routledge, 1989.

Whitford, Margaret, "Re-Reading Irigaray: Luce Irigaray and the Female Imaginary: Speaking as a Woman." *Radical Philosophy* 43, nos. 3–8 (1986): 3–8.

Whitford, Margaret, ed. *The Irigaray Reader.* Oxford: Basil Blackwell, 1991.

Wilcox, Helen, et al., eds. *The Body and the Text: Hélène Cixous, Reading and Teaching.* Hertfordshire: Harvester Wheatsheaf, 1990.

Wilden, Anthony. "Lacan and the Discourse of the Other." In *The Language of The Self: The Function of Language in Psychoanalysis.* Translated by Anthony Wilden. Baltimore: Johns Hopkins University Press, 1968. 159–311.

Wilkie, Christine. "The Dilemma of *Children's Literature and its Criticism.*" *File: A Literary Journal* 6, no. 3 (1995): 1–7.

———. "Intertextuality." In *The Routledge International Companion Encyclopaedia of Children's Literature*, edited by Peter Hunt. London: Routledge, 1996. 131–7.

Wilkie-Stibbs, Christine, " 'Body Language': Speaking the *féminine* in Young Adult Fiction." *Children's Literature Association Quarterly* 25, no. 2 (2000): 76–87.

Williams, Linda R. *Critical Desire: Psychoanalysis and the Literary Subject.* London: Edward Arnold, 1995.

Woolf, Virginia. "Professions for Women." In *The Death of the Moth and Other Essays.* New York: Harcourt, Brace, 1942. 236–38.

Wordsworth, William. "Lines Composed upon Westminster Bridge" (1802). In *William Wordsworth*, edited by Stephen Gill. Oxford: Oxford University Press, 1984. 285.

Wright, Patrick. "The Ghosting of the Inner City." In *On Living in an Old Country.* London: Verso, 1985. 228–9.

Wright, Elizabeth. *Psychoanalytic Criticism: Theory in Practice.* London: Routledge, 1987.

———. "Another Look at Lacan and Literary Criticism." *New Literary History* 19, no. 3 (Spring 1988): 617–27.

Xenophon. "The March to the Sea." In *The Persian Expedition*. Translated by Rex Warner. Harmondsworth: Penguin, 1949.

Zukin, Sharon. "Postmodern Urban Landscapes: Mapping Culture and Power." In *Modernity and Identity*, edited by Scott Lash and Jonathan Friedman. Oxford: Basil Blackwell, 1992. 212–45.

Index

abjection, 71–3, 85–6, 94–7
Abraham, Nicolas, 153 (n49)
adolescence, 47
alienation, 8, 166–8
    see also loss
Almond, David, 23, 175
alterity, 24, 33 n60
anorexia, 65, 101, 117 n103
Ariadne, 58
art, 83–4
Athena, 56
Atwood, Margaret, 57, 139 n35
Austen, Jane, 65

Babbitt, Natalie, 23, 175
Bachelard, Gaston, 78–9 n85
Badcock, Christopher, 173 n72
Bakhtin, Mikhail, 49, 52, 54, 69
Barthes, Roland, x, 14, 18, 49, 57, 120
    (n6), 173 n51
Bataille, George, 24
Baudrillard, Jean, 121, 128, 130, 131, 135
Benveniste, Émile, 11, 13, 14, 15
Bersani, Leo, 24–5
body language, 37, 71–2, 84, 98–9, 106–7,
    176

Bowler, Tim, 23, 175
boys, 2, 10
Bridge to Terabithia, 175
Brooke-Rose, Christine, 23 (n105), 122
Brooks, Peter, 14, 15–16, 22, 147, 156,
    172 n34
Burgin, Victor, 120
Burke, Carolyn, 89 (n47), 90 (n49)
Burke, Peter, 52 (n60)

carnivalesque, 52–3, 54, 55
Carroll, David, 34 n69, 143–4
Carroll, Lewis, 59
Carter, Angela, 57, 139 n35, 161
Chambers, Aidan, 119
The Changeover, xi
    agents of transformation, xi
    family, xi
    fantasy, 23
    the feminine Imaginary and the witch,
        108, 109–11
    looking glass from the other side,
        107–9
    mother/child relations, 111–13
    le parler femme, 111–13
    transformational space, xi, 25, 26

character, 26–7
Chase, Cynthia, 143 (n16)
child/mother relations, *see* mother/child
    relations
children's literature, ix, xi, xii, 5, 43, 119,
    123
Cixous, Hélène
    on artistic identity, 49
    on character, 26–7
    on *l'écriture féminine*, 37–9, 43–4, 45,
        62–3, 124, 176–7
    on *the feminine*, 1–2, 14, 42–3, 47, 176
    on *the feminine* Imaginary, 37, 38, 39,
        176, 177
    feminist criticism, 1, 3–4, 19, 161, 162
    on hysterics, 66, 67, 69–70
    on language, 84, 99
    on the mother, 98–9, 105
    on the pre-Symbolic, 26, 84–5
    on sexual difference, 115 n53
communication, 128, 130, 131
the conscious, 6, 11–12
Cook, David, 128–9, 130
Cormier, Robert, 119
Cross, Gillian, ix
    see also Pictures in the Dark; *Wolf*
Culler, Jonathan, 21

Dahl, Roald, 86
Dangerous Spaces, xi
    agents of transformation, xi
    dreaming, 26, 150, 156–7, 164, 165, 170
    dual ontology, 165–6
    family, xi
    fantasy, 23
    mother/child relations, 25, 106–7, 168
    le parler femme, 106–7
    revenant, 168–70
    speaking the body, 106–7
    textual unconscious, 145–6, 147
    Transference, 145–6, 168
    transformational space, xi, 25

the *vel* of alienation, 166–8
Dear Nobody, 175
death-drive, 9, 22, 168
deconstruction, 3, 41, 74–5 n6
deferral (*Nachträglichkeit*), 142, 152–3
Deleuze, Gilles, 92, 159 (n63)
Derrida, Jacques, 3, 4, 20, 38, 41, 66, 74–5
    n6
desire
    and loss, 12, 22, 81, 166–7
    of the mother, 6
    reciprocal, 22
    violence in, 24–5
    in writing, 48–50
diegetic levels, 63–4, 79 n97
différance, 38, 41, 74–5 n6
Disney World, 136
Doherty, Berlie, 119, 175
dreaming, 141–3, 145–6, 147, 149
    Dangerous Spaces, 26, 150, 156–7, 164,
        165, 170
    Wolf, 26, 157–61, 162–3, 164
dual ontology, 25, 165–6

Eagleton, Terry, 8
l'écriture féminine
    Cixous on, 37–9, 43–4, 45, 62–3, 124,
        176–7
    The Other Side of Silence, 73–4
    The Tricksters, 44, 47, 48, 62–3
ego (*moi*), 6, 8, 17, 147
    see also ideal ego; *moi* and *je*
the elemental *feminine*, 57, 60–1
Eliot, T.S., 59
essentialism, 3, 30 n12, 41

fairy tales, 26, 68–9, 87, 110, 158
    see also "Little Red Riding Hood"
family, xi, 44, 47, 63, 91, 105
fantasy, 23–7
    agents of transformation, 25–6
    and *the feminine*, 23, 24, 25, 26

and postmodernism, 25
psychoanalytic dimension, 26–7
transformational space, 25
transgressive energies, 24–5
The Tricksters, 23, 50–1
the uncanny, 23, 53, 165
see also hyperreality
father, 9–10, 13, 34 n69, 67–8, 81, 91–2
see also The-Name-of-the-Father
Felman, Shoshana, 14, 19–20, 66 (n109),
146
the feminine, ix, x–xi, xiv n1, 1–3, 108,
175–7
the elemental *feminine*, 57, 60–1
see also Cixous, Hélène; Irigaray, Luce;
Kristeva, Julia
the feminine Imaginary, 37, 38, 39–40, 42,
145, 176, 177
The Changeover, 108, 109–11
the feminine postmodern, 119, 123–5
landscapes, 127–32, 133–4
femininity, 103–4
feminist criticism, 1, 10, 29 n3, 92, 123–4,
125, 144
see also Cixous, Hélène; Irigaray, Luce;
Kristeva, Julia
fetishism, 89, 114–15 n40, 117 n94
fictional selves, 64, 68–70
fictional time, 156–7
Flax, Jane, 75 n12, 123, 125
A Formal Feeling, 175
Forrester, John, 148
Foster, Shirley, ix
Foucault, Michel, 66, 122–3
Freud, Sigmund
on the death-drive, 9, 22, 168
on dreaming, 141–2, 148, 150, 158, 165,
170 n4, 171 n29, 172 n41
Familienroman, 91
on fetishism, 114 n40
on the gaze, 56
on the phallic mother, 88

talking cure, 79 n98
on the uncanny, 53, 165, 174 n78
on the womb, 54
see also Wolf-Man
Fuery, Patrick, 69, 71

Gallop, Jane, 14
Gardiner, Muriel, 157 (n58)
Garner, Alan, 119
the gaze, 18–19, 41, 55–7, 103–4
Gee, Maggie, 139 n35
gender, 2, 10, 30 n12, 48, 63
see also sexual difference
Genette, Gérard, 79 n97, 122–3
Gilbert, Sandra, 49, 50, 56, 65
Ginsburg, Ruth, 54
girls, 2, 10
Graves, Robert, 51, 110
Gross, Elizabeth, 71, 73 (n133), 73 (n134),
74 (n135), 96 (n80)
Grosz, Elizabeth, 20 (n93), 53 (n67), 57
(n76), 58, 61, 82–3, 87, 101 (n102),
107 (n117), 117 n103, 150 (n46)
Guattari, Félix, 92, 159 (n63)
Gubar, Susan, 49, 50, 56, 65
Gustafson, Susan E., 103 (n107)

Hanzo, Thomas A., 170 (n93)
Harvey, David, 134, 148
heterotopias, 123, 138–9 n22
history, 121, 122, 128
Homans, Margaret, 92
Homer, 58
Hutcheon, Linda, 121
hyperreality, 121, 128, 135–7
hysteria, 66, 67, 68, 69–70, 117 n103

"I" and "you", 12–14, 15, 19, 88
see also moi and *je*
Ian, Marcia, 88–9 (n39)
ideal ego, 6, 8, 103
identity, 83–4

artistic, 49
"becoming", 47
female, 108
names and naming, 70–1
post-structuralism, 119
postmodern, 153–4, 173 n51
transhistorical, 51
see also abjection
the Imaginary, 5, 6, 7, 8, 22, 42, 163–4
see also the feminine Imaginary
incest taboo, 53–5, 105
interpolation, 25
intertextual space, 57–60, 120, 137–8 n3
Irigaray, Luce
on Athena, 56
on *the feminine*, 1, 14, 42, 47, 108
on *the feminine* Imaginary, 39–42
feminist criticism, 1, 3–4, 19, 30–1 n12, 41
on heterosexual relations, 112–13
on language, 79 n102, 82, 87, 89, 101, 102
on marriage, 105
on the maternal-*feminine*, 104
on the maternal role, 87–8, 90–1, 102, 103–4
on *le parler femme*, 89–90, 100, 106, 107
on the pre-Symbolic, 26
on primal elements, 57, 60
on the "proper", 87
on sexual difference, 90, 109
on subjectivity, 92, 110

Jackson, Rosemary, 23–4, 25
Jacobus, Mary, 88 (n38), 104 (n111)
Jakobson, Roman, 12
Jameson, Fredric, 3, 70, 121–2, 130, 131, 132, 133, 134, 135
Jardine, Alice A., 33 n60
Johnson, Barbara, 171 n22
Jones, Ann Rosalind, 90 (n48)

Jones, Ernest, 169 (n92)
Jones, Richard, 170 n4
"Jorinda and Joringel", 69, 70

Keats, John, 60
Kellner, Douglas, 173 n51
Kristeva, Julia
on abjection, 71, 72, 73, 85–6, 94–6
on adolescence, 47
on alterity, 24, 33 n60
on art, 83–4
on color, 97
on *l'écriture féminine*, 74 (n136)
on *the feminine*, 1, 14, 42, 83, 86, 114 n28
feminist criticism, 1, 3–4, 80 n127, 86
on language, 72, 82, 84
on love, 18
on motherhood, 86–7, 89
on narrative, 91
on the "Semiotic", 38, 82–3, 84, 98
on subjectivity, 86
on the Symbolic, 26, 81, 82, 83, 85
on the Thetic, 95, 116 n73, 141
on women's time, 84, 97–8
Kroker, Arthur, 128–9, 130

Lacan, Jacques
on the death-drive, 22
on desire, 166
on dreams, 143, 147
on fantasy, 26
on the incest taboo, 53–4
influence of, 31 n14
on interpretation, 147–8
on language and speech, 11, 12–14, 81, 127, 132, 143, 147
on literary subjectivity, 5, 143–4
on memory, 150–1
on metonymy, 167
objet petit a, 8, 32 n35, 85, 144
on the Real, 7

on subject formation, 4–12, 84, 86, 92
on 'The Purloined Letter', 143, 144, 171 n22
on Transference, 146 (n28), 148
on the unconscious, 3, 10, 158–9, 170 n4, 173 n64
on the *vel* of alienation, 166–7
lalangue, 12–13
language
  and abjection, 72, 85
  acquisition, 72
  as body function, 37
  disorder, 131–2
  and dreams, 143, 147
  literary discourse, x, 21
  masculinist linearity, 9–12, 82
  maternal, 84, 98–100
  naming function, 70
  and postmodernism, 127
  and silence, 65–8, 69–70, 71, 73–4, 82, 92, 99–103
  and speech, 12–14, 81, 84–5
  in subject formation, 4
  and time, 81, 84, 132
  see also body language; *l'écriture fémi-nine*; *le parler femme*; the Semiotic; Symbolic Order
langue, 12
Laplanche, Jean, 142 (n15), 151 (n48), 165 (n79)
laughter, 54
Law, *see* The-Name-of-the-Father
Lear, Edward, 59
Lechte, John, 18, 82, 98
Leclaire, Serge, 7–8, 151 (n48)
une lecteur féminine, 176–7, 178 n4
Lemaire, Anika, 7 (n25), 54, 146 (n27), 151 (n47), 173 n64
Lévi-Strauss, Claude, 10
Lie, Sissel, 178 n4
literary subjectivity, 3, 14–15, 16
  the feminine, 38, 113, 176, 177

Lacan on, 5, 143–4
and postmodernism, 120, 124
literary Transference, 3, 16–20, 22, 47, 61, 145, 146–8
  see also Transference
"Little Red Riding Hood", 26, 137, 158, 160–2
  see also fairy tales
loss, 8, 12, 22, 39, 81, 144, 166–7
love, 18
Lyotard, Jean-François, 121, 148, 171 n29

MacCannell, Juliet Flower, 22, 101 (n98)
madness, 24, 49, 65–8, 98
Magritte, René, 131
Mahy, Margaret, ix, 27, 109, 156
  see also The Changeover; Dangerous Spaces; Memory; The Other Side of Silence; The Tricksters
Marianne Dreams, 175
masquerade, 55
material bodily principle, 54
the maternal-*feminine*, 104–5
McHale, Brian, 16, 23, 25, 51, 120, 122, 125, 137–8 n3, 165
Medusa, 99–100, 105, 115 n53, 117 n94
Mellard, James M., 3, 5, 7, 17 (n76), 20, 148 (n39), 167 (n86), 168 (n87), 172 n34
memory, 145, 149, 150–3, 156–7
Memory, xi
  agents of transformation, xi, 26
  family, xi
  fantasy, 23
  fictional time, 156–7
  memory, 149, 150–3, 156–7
  metaphor, 151, 152
  narrative, 127–8, 129, 156
  postmodern landscapes, 127–32
  sexual subjectivity, 153–5
  the Symbolic, 26

textual unconscious, 145, 147
topography, 128, 129
transformational space, xi
men, 2
    see also father; gender
metafictional textuality, 44–8, 63, 64
metaphor, 12, 18, 22, 143, 151, 152
metonymy, 12, 22, 143, 167–8
Miller, Jacques-Alain, 33 n62
Milton, John, 58
Minerva, 56, 58
Mirror Phase, 5–6
mirrors, 60, 107–9, 163
misattribution, 25–6
Moi, Toril, 56 (n75), 80 n127, 89 (n41)
moi and *je*, 17, 19, 64, 100, 153
    see also ego (*moi*)
mother
    desire of, 6
    the maternal-*feminine*, 104–5
    as mediator of Symbolic Law, 72–3
    monstrous mothers, 89, 99–104
    from Other to (M)other, 161–3
    phallic mother, 88–9, 99–100, 115 n53,
        117 n94
    representations of, 86–7
    role, 87–8, 90–1, 102, 103–4
    subjectivity, 86, 92
mother/child relations, 2, 6, 25, 82, 87–8,
        90–1
    The Changeover, 111–13
    Dangerous Spaces, 25, 106–7, 168
    The Other Side of Silence, 72–3, 100–3
    Wolf, 162, 163
    see also Oedipal relations
Munch, Edvard, 135

Nachträglichkeit (deferral), 142, 152–3
The-Name-of-the-Father, 9–10, 34 n69, 53,
        67–8, 70–1, 72, 81, 108, 162
narcissism, 6, 9, 18–19, 103
narrative, xii, 91

Memory, 127–8, 129, 156
The Other Side of Silence, 63–5, 73, 79
    n97
Pictures in the Dark, 92, 93–4
postmodernist, 122
The Tricksters, 79 n97
Wolf, 156
Neu, Jerome, 115 n40, 117 n94
Nicholson, Linda, 123
Nietzsche, Friedrich, 46, 79 n86
nostalgia, 132, 134–5

objet petit a, 8, 32 n35, 85, 144
Oedipal relations, 5, 9–10, 22, 91, 92, 93,
        144
    The Other Side of Silence, 73
    The Tricksters, 55, 105
    Wolf, 133, 158–9, 161
Oneal, Zibby, 175
the Other, 10, 11, 13, 18, 161–3
The Other Side of Silence, xi
    agents of transformation, xi
    l'écriture féminine, 73–4
    family, xi, 63
    fantasy, 23
    the feminine and abjection, 71–3
    fictional selves/self as fiction, 64, 68–70
    language and silence, 65–8, 69,
        71, 73–4
    madness, 65–8
    metafictional textuality, 63, 64
    monstrous motherhood, 100–4
    mother/child relations, 25, 72–3, 100–3
    The-Name-of-The-Father, 70–1
    narration, 63–5, 73, 79 n97
    Oedipal relations, 73
    le parler femme, 67
    Symbolism, 26
    Transference, 64
    transformational space, xi
    "true life" and "real life", 63, 64–5, 66
Ovid, 59–60, 69

le parler femme, 39, 40–1, 42, 89–90, 91, 100
  The Changeover, 111–13
  Dangerous Spaces, 106–7
  The Other Side of Silence, 67
  Pictures in the Dark, 99
  The Tricksters, 44
parole, 12
paternal metaphor, 9
Paterson, Katherine, 175
Paul, Lissa, ix
phallocentrism, 4, 5, 9–10, 14, 33 n60, 38, 89
  see also mother: phallic mother
phalogocentrism, 4, 41
Philomel, 69, 70
Pictures in the Dark, xi
  abjection, 94–7
  agents of transformation, xi
  body language, 98–9
  family, xi
  fantasy, 23, 26
  narrative, 92, 93–4
  le parler femme, 99
  return, 94
  semiotizing the Symbolic, 98
  transformational space, xi
  women's time, 97–8
Pontalis, Jean-Baptiste, 165 (n79)
postmodernism, 14, 25, 119–25, 127, 128, 130, 131, 134
  see also the feminine postmodern
preconscious, 141, 170 n4
primal elements, 39, 57–8, 60, 61, 97, 98, 99
the "proper", 87
psyche as text, 17, 20
Purkiss, Diane, 110 (n127), 111

"R/r", 7
Ragland-Sullivan, Ellie, 6, 7, 12, 16, 17, 19, 20, 65, 147, 148

reader-response model, 3, 16
readers
  model of readership, x, 64
  reading subject, 14–15, 47, 57, 64–5, 120, 148
  and writers, 16–17, 21
  see also text/reader relations
reading, the act of, x–xi, 3, 15–16, 21–2, 146, 148
  see also literary Transference;
    text/reader relations
the Real, 5, 7–8
reconciliation, 94, 99
repetition compulsion, 142, 143, 144–5
repression, 11, 12, 21, 39, 42, 150–1
revenant, 94, 168–70
Reynolds, Kimberley, ix
Richardson, William J., 13 (n57)
River Boy, 23, 175
Rose, Jacqueline, 9, 13, 42

S/s, 11–12
Saussure, Ferdinand de, 11, 12
schizophrenia, 121
self as fiction, 64, 68–70
self-mutilation, 102
  see also anorexia
the Semiotic, 5, 38, 82–3, 84, 98
sexual difference, 2, 10, 30–1 n12, 37–8, 41, 90, 109, 115 n53
  see also gender
sexual subjectivity, 153–5
Shakespeare, William, 57, 58–9
Showalter, Elaine, 82
signification, 146, 147–8
signifier and signified, 11–12, 13, 16, 121, 131, 143–4
silence, 65–8, 69–70, 71, 73–4, 82, 92, 99, 100–3
Silverman, Kaja, 15, 20 (n89), 33 n62
Simons, Judy, ix

Skellig, 23, 175

Smith, Stevie, 59

sorceresses, *see* witches

space

    intertextual, 57–60, 120, 137–8 n3

    transformational, xi, 25, 26

speech, 12–14, 71, 81, 84–5

    see also le parler femme

States, Bert O., 147 (n33)

Stevenson, Robert Louis, 58

Storr, Catherine, 175

Strindberg, August, 58

subject

    child, 119

    cognitive registers, 5–6

    the feminine postmodern, 123

    formation, 4–12, 86, 88, 92

    in language, 5

    literary, 121

    postmodern, 120

    reading, 14–15, 47, 57, 64–5, 120,
      148

    speaking, 12–14, 71

    textualization of, 5

subjectivity, x

    as alienation and loss, 8, 12

    corporeality, 71–2, 113

    fragmented, 133–4

    in language, 170

    model of, 11–12

    of the mother, 86, 92, 110

    post-structuralism, 119

    sexual, 153–5

    voice, 69, 71, 84–5

    see also literary subjectivity

superimposition, 25

"suture", 15, 33 n62

Swindells, Robert, 119

the Symbolic, 22, 26, 38, 81, 82, 83, 85,
    98, 121, 163–4

Symbolic Order, 2, 5, 6, 7, 8–10, 66, 81,
    120

talking cures, 64, 79 n98

text, 14–15, 120, 147, 172 n34

    as psyche, 17, 20

text continuum, 16

text/reader relations, 14–16, 64, 146–8,
    176–7

textual unconscious, 3, 11, 20–2, 145–9,
    159, 164

textuality, 55, 57, 82–3

    metafictional textuality, 44–8, 63, 64

the Thetic, 95, 116 n73, 141

time

    fictional, 156–7

    historical amnesia, 121

    and language, 81, 84, 132

    women's time, 84, 97–8, 110

Todorov, Tzvetan, 23, 24, 26, 51

Torok, Maria, 153 (n49)

Transference, 3, 15, 21

    Dangerous Spaces, 145–6, 168

    Lacan on, 147, 148

    The Other Side of Silence, 64

    Wolf, 145–6, 160, 164

    see also literary Transference

transformation, xi, 25–6

transgressive energies, 24–5

The Tricksters, xi

    agents of transformation, xi

    carnivalesque, 52–3, 54, 55

    desire in writing, 48–50

    dual ontology, 25

    l'écriture féminine, 44, 47, 48, 62–3

    the elemental *feminine*, 57, 60–1

    family, xi, 44, 47

    fantasy, 23, 50–1

    the gaze, 55–7

    identity, 47, 49, 51

    the incest taboo, 53–5, 105

    intertextual space, 57–60

    the maternal-*feminine*, 104–5

    metafictional mode, 44–8

    monstrous motherhood, 100, 103

mother/child relations, 25
narration, 79 n97
le parler femme, 44
textuality, 55, 57
transformational space, xi, 25, 26
Trites, Roberta Seelinger, ix
the Truth, 7
Tuck Everlasting, 23, 175

the uncanny, 23, 53, 165, 174 n78
the unconscious
  and ego, 6
  the feminine Imaginary, 38
  Lacan on, 10, 11–12, 170 n4, 173 n64
  naming, 70
  and Transference, 19
  see also dreaming; textual unconscious

Vallone, Lynne, ix
the *vel* of alienation, 166–8
Vice, Sue, 31 n14
voice, 17, 19, 69, 71, 84–5

Wakefield, Neville, 127, 132
Waller, Margaret, 113 n8
water, 57–8, 60, 97, 98, 99
Waugh, Patricia, 121–2, 123, 124, 139
  n35, 144
Webster, John, 59
Weldon, Fay, 139 n35
Whitford, Margaret, 30–1 n12, 78–9 n85,
  102 (n106)
Wilden, Anthony, 7
Williams, Linda R., 143 (n19), 168 (n88),
  168 (n90)
Winterson, Jeanette, 139 n35
witches, 86, 87
  The Changeover, 109–11
  The Other Side of Silence, 67, 68, 69,
    102
  Pictures in the Dark, 97

Wolf, xi
  agents of transformation, xi, 26
  cultural nostalgia, 134–5
  dreaming the wolf, 26, 157–61, 162–3,
    164
  family, xi
  fantasy, 23
  fragmented subjectivity, 133–4
  hyperreality, 135–7
  imaginary pleasure/symbolic law, 163–4
  monstrous motherhood, 100
  narrative, 156
  from Other to (M)other, 161–3
  postmodern landscapes, 128, 133–4
  textual unconscious, 145–6, 147, 159,
    164
  Transference, 145–6, 160, 164
  transformational space, xi
"The Wolf and the Seven Little Goats",
  158
Wolf-Man, 142, 151–2, 157–8
women
  "the Angel in the House", 50
  female body, 40, 42, 54, 111
  as the Other, 9, 10, 18
  roles, 2
  "woman", 30 n12
  writers, 49–50
women's time, 84, 97–8, 110
Wordsworth, William, 59
Wright, Elizabeth, 7, 16–17, 22
Wright, Patrick, 134
Wrightson, Patricia, 175
writers and writing, 16–17, 21, 37, 49–50
  see also l'*écriture féminine*

Xenophon, 59

Zindell, Paul, 119
"zones", 19, 125
Zukin, Sharon, 134, 135–6